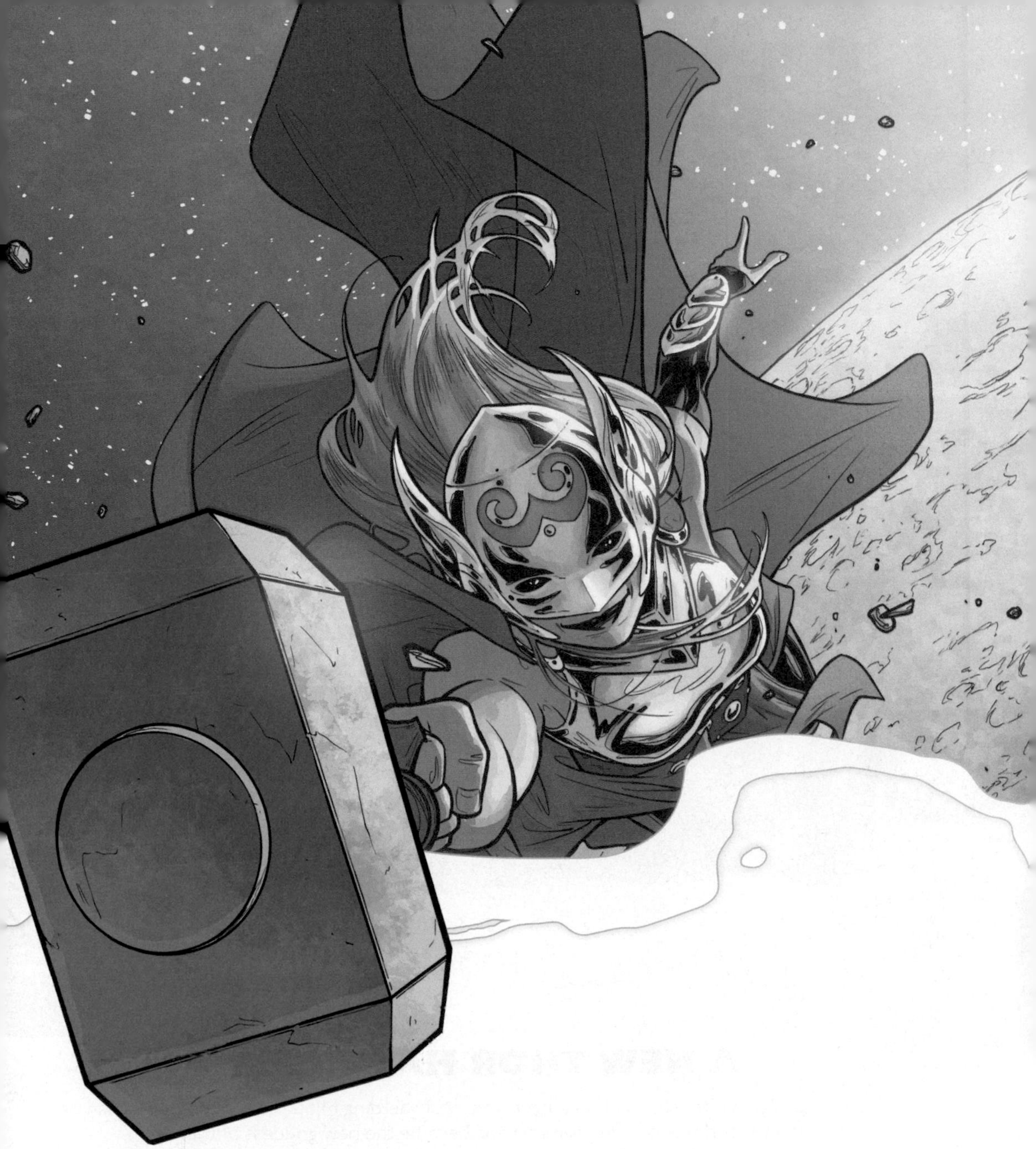

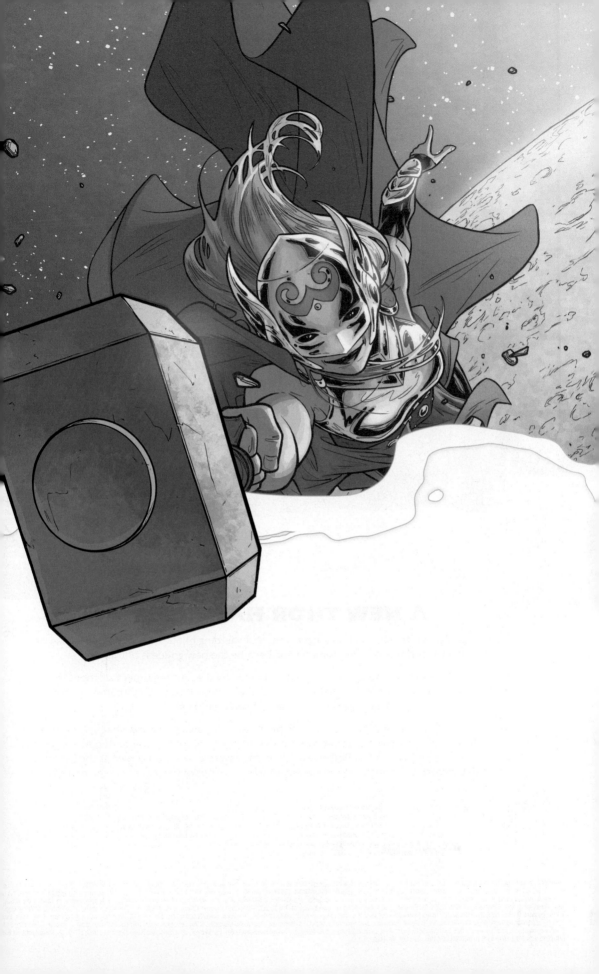

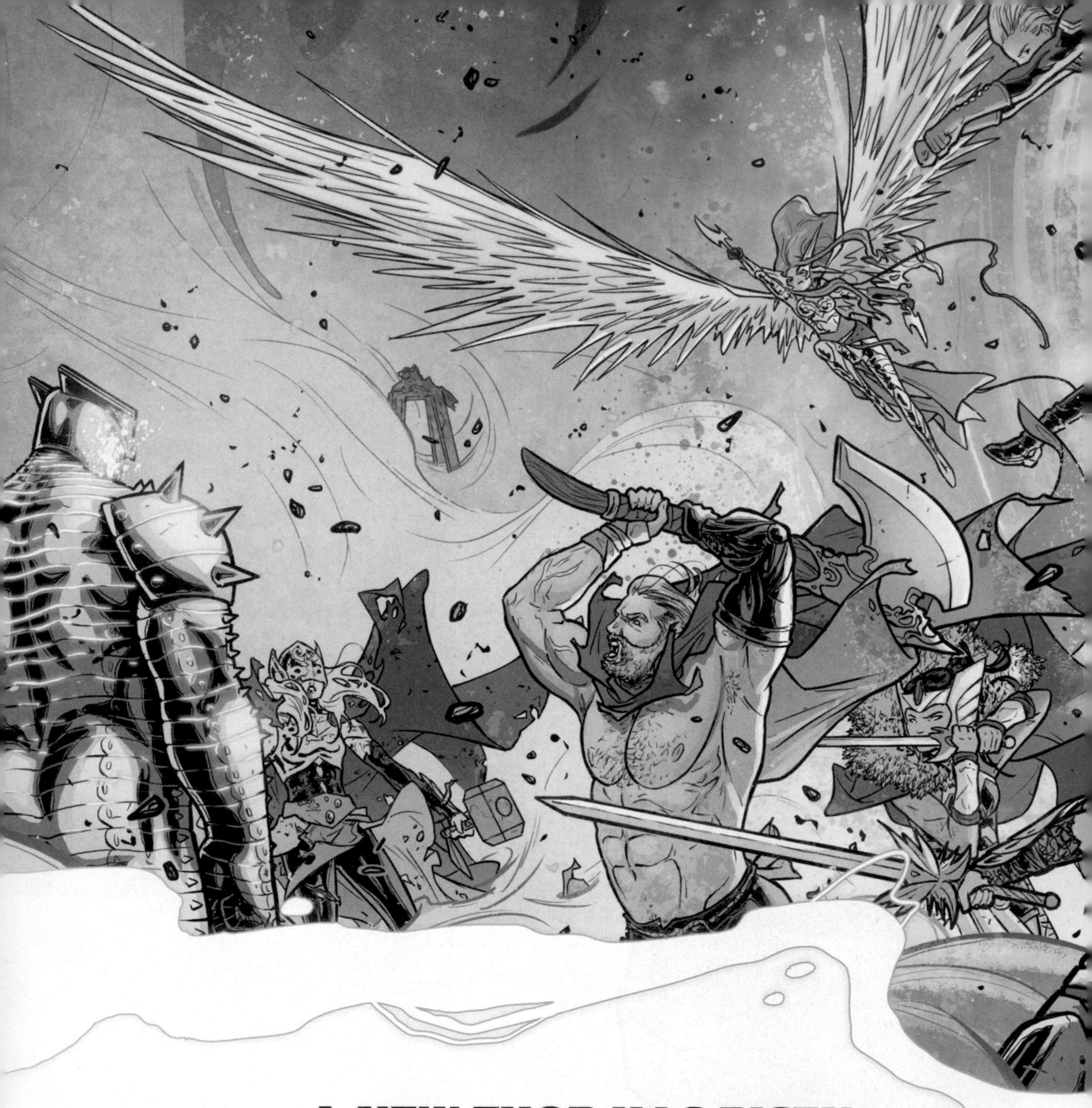

A NEW THOR HAS RISEN.

After Thor Odinson found himself no longer worthy of wielding Mjolnir, a mysterious woman was able to lift the enchanted hammer and became the new goddess of thunder!

So far she has taken down evils great and small, bolstered by the new legitimacy of Thor Odinson officially passing the name of Thor onto her — evils like villainous Roxxon CEO/part-time Minotaur Dario Agger and the dark elf sorcerer Malekith.

While Odinson may have given Thor his name, he hasn't given up on discovering what her *true* name is, and Odin the All-Father hasn't either. Offended at this affront to his omnipotence, the All-Father has called into service his brother Cul Borson as well as the Asgardian weapon known as the Destroyer. He is determined to either learn the identity of this new Thor or destroy her in the process.

COLLECTION EDITOR: **JENNIFER GRÜNWALD**
ASSISTANT EDITOR: **SARAH BRUNSTAD**
ASSOCIATE MANAGING EDITOR: **ALEX STARBUCK**
EDITOR, SPECIAL PROJECTS: **MARK D. BEAZLEY**
SENIOR EDITOR, SPECIAL PROJECTS: **JEFF YOUNGQUIST**
SVP PRINT, SALES & MARKETING: **DAVID GABRIEL**

EDITOR IN CHIEF: **AXEL ALONSO**
CHIEF CREATIVE OFFICER: **JOE QUESADA**
PUBLISHER: **DAN BUCKLEY**
EXECUTIVE PRODUCER: **ALAN FINE**

THOR VOL. 2: WHO HOLDS THE HAMMER? Contains material originally published in magazine form as THOR #6-8 and ANNUAL #1, and WHAT IF? #10. First printing 2015. ISBN# 978-0-7851-9784-3. Publish MARVEL WORLDWIDE, INC., a subsidiary of MARVEL ENTERTAINMENT, LLC. OFFICE OF PUBLICATION: 135 West 50th Street, New York, NY 10020. Copyright © 2015 MARVEL No similarity between any of the n characters, persons, and/or institutions in this magazine with those of any living or dead person or institution is intended, and any such similarity which may exist is purely coincidental. **Printed in the U.S.A.** FINE, President, Marvel Entertainment; DAN BUCKLEY, President, TV, Publishing and Brand Management; JOE QUESADA, Chief Creative Officer; TOM BREVOORT, SVP of Publishing; DAVID BOGART, SVP of Oper & Procurement, Publishing; C.B. CEBULSKI, VP of International Development & Brand Management; DAVID GABRIEL, SVP Print, Sales & Marketing; JIM O'KEEFE, VP of Operations & Logistics; DAN CARR, Exe Director of Publishing Technology; SUSAN CRESPI, Editorial Operations Manager; ALEX MORALES, Publishing Operations Manager; STAN LEE, Chairman Emeritus. For information regarding advertising in M Comics or on Marvel.com, please contact Jonathan Rheingold, VP of Custom Solutions & Ad Sales, at jrheingold@marvel.com. For Marvel subscription inquiries, please call 800-217-9158. **Manufactured bet 5/8/2015 and 6/22/2015 by R.R. DONNELLEY, INC., SALEM, VA, USA.**

10 9 8 7 6 5 4 3 2 1

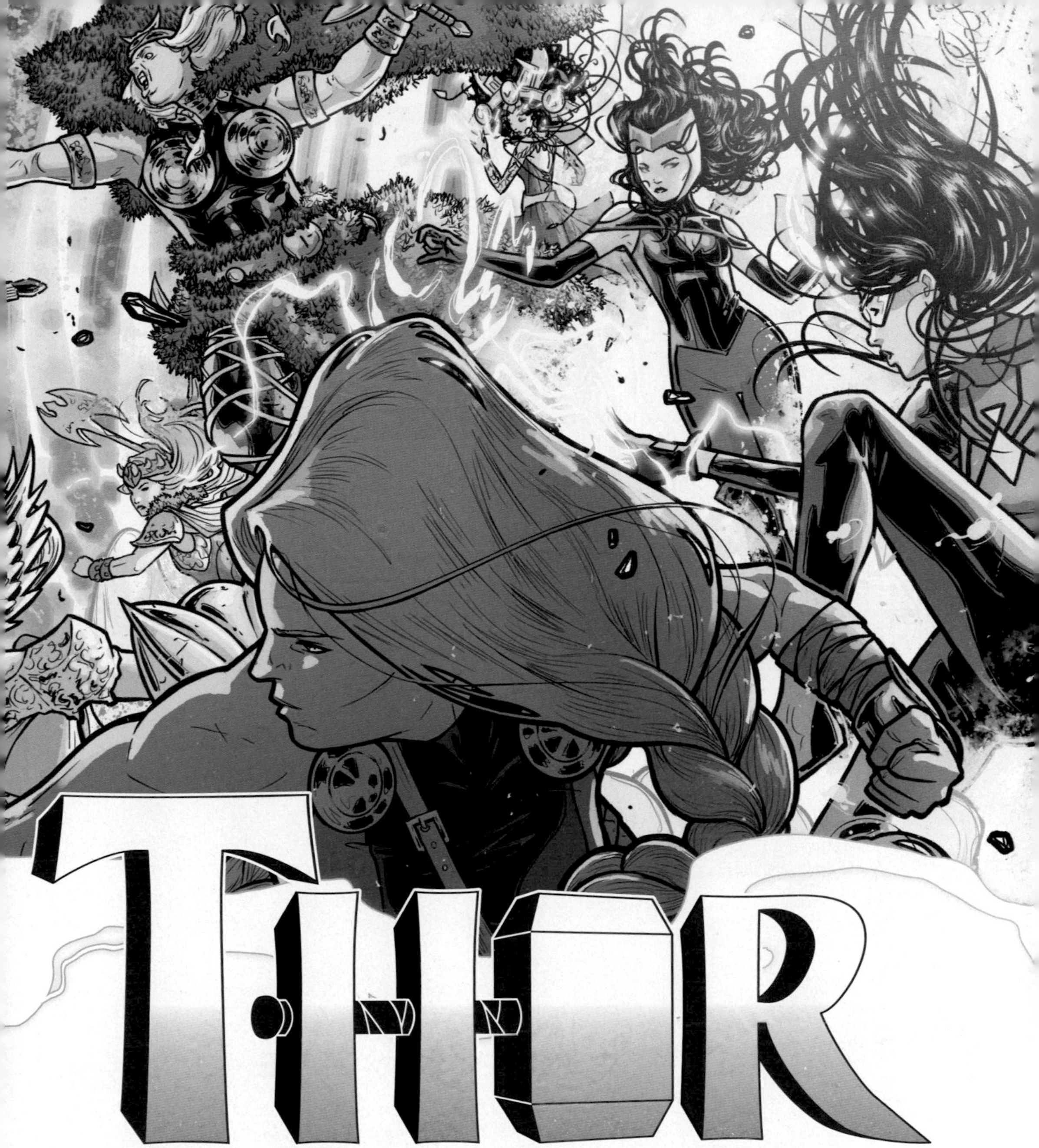

THOR

WHO HOLDS THE HAMMER?

WRITER
JASON AARON

ARTIST
RUSSELL DAUTERMAN

COLOR ARTIST
MATTHEW WILSON

COVER ART
RUSSELL DAUTERMAN & MATTHEW WILSON

ANNUAL #1

WRITERS
JASON AARON, OELLE STEVENSON & CM PUNK

ARTISTS
TIMOTHY TRUMAN, MARGUERITE SAUVAGE & ROB GUILLORY

COLOR ARTISTS
FRANK MARTIN, MARGUERITE SAUVAGE & ROB GUILLORY

COVER ART **RAFAEL ALBUQUERQUE**

LETTERER
VC'S JOE SABINO

ASSISTANT EDITOR
JON MOISAN

EDITOR
WIL MOSS

THOR CREATED BY STAN LEE, LARRY LIEBER & JACK KIRBY

6

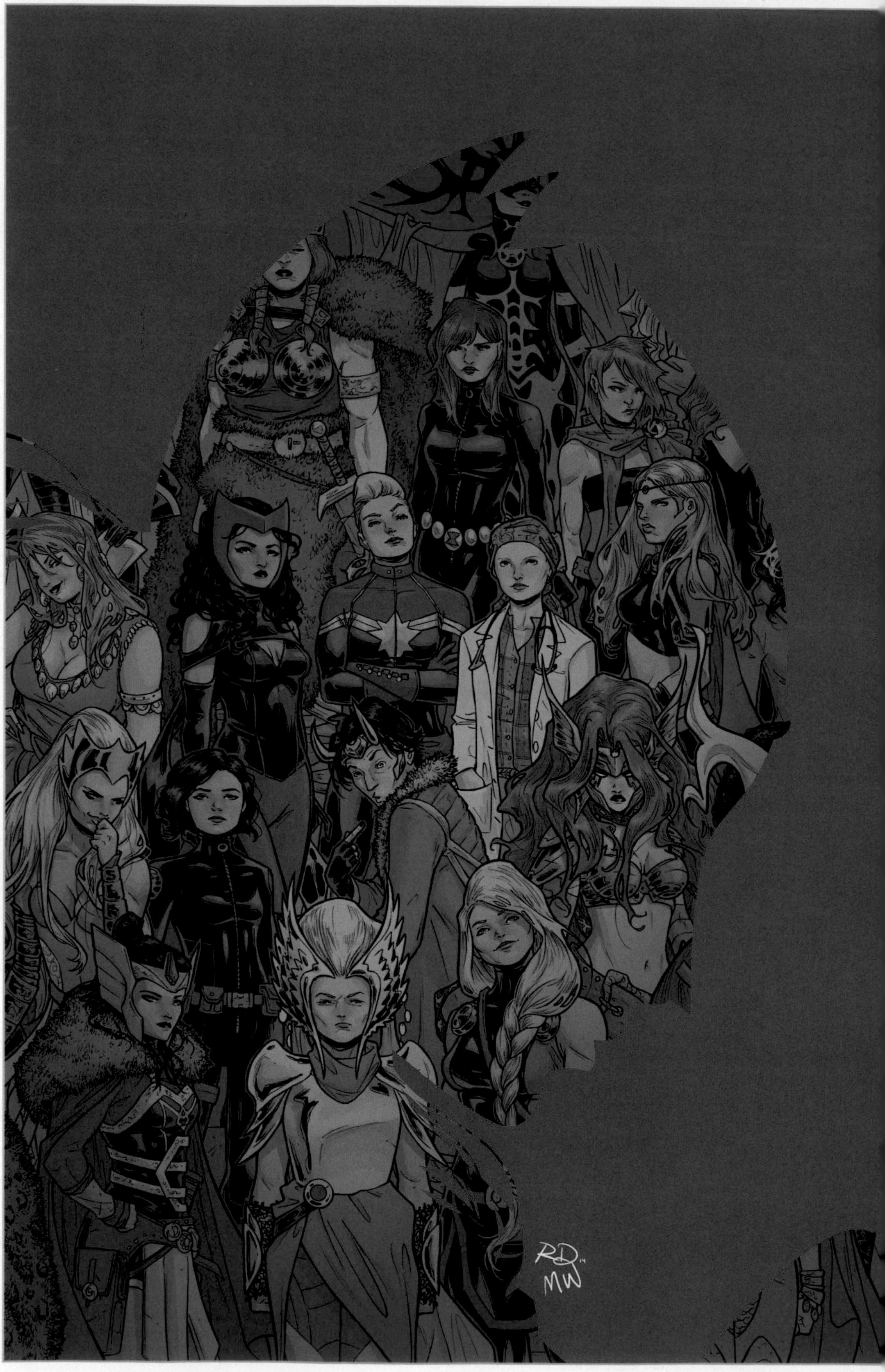
RD '14
MW

WHO HOLDS THE HAMMER?

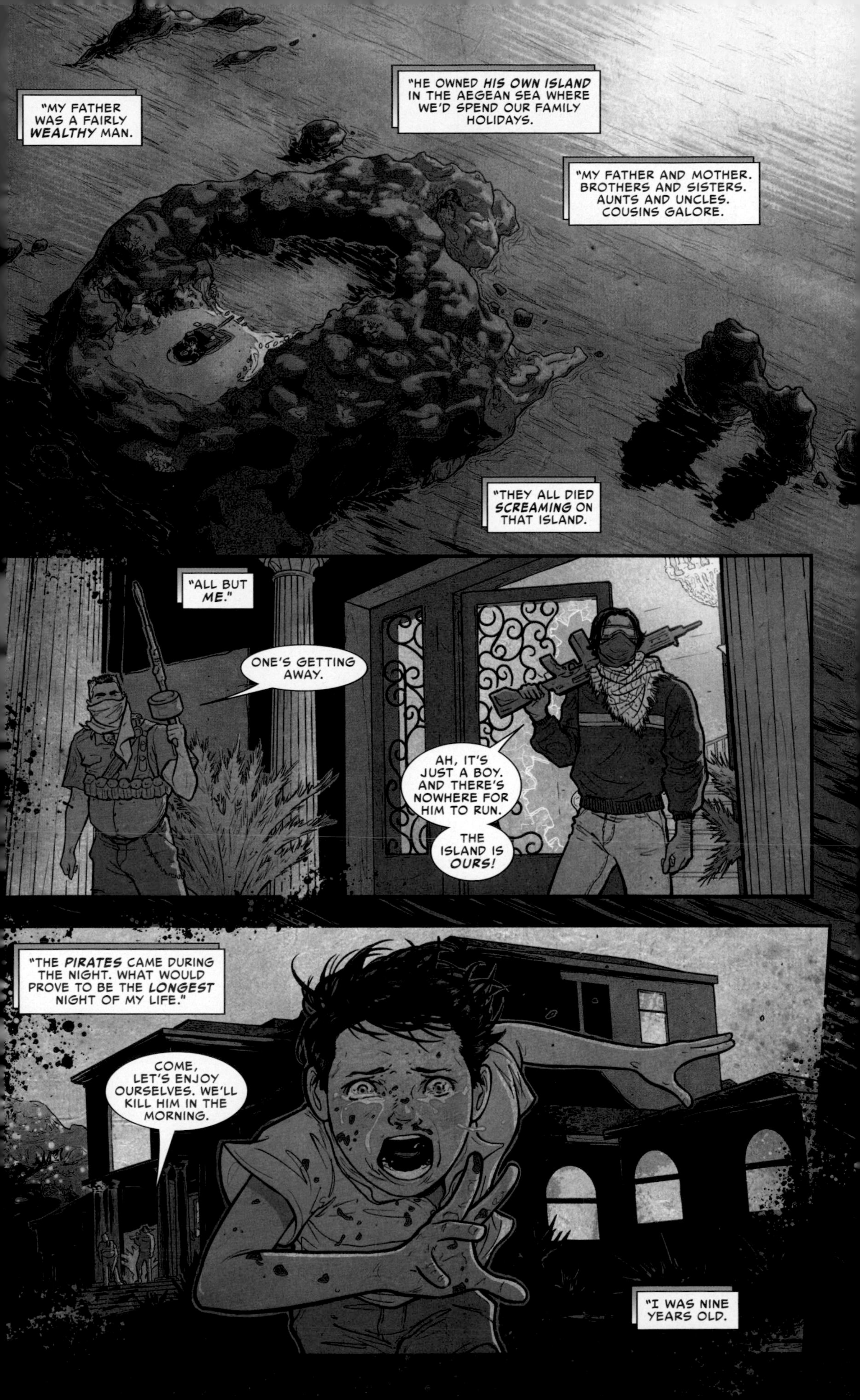
"MY FATHER WAS A FAIRLY WEALTHY MAN.
"HE OWNED HIS OWN ISLAND IN THE AEGEAN SEA WHERE WE'D SPEND OUR FAMILY HOLIDAYS.
"MY FATHER AND MOTHER. BROTHERS AND SISTERS. AUNTS AND UNCLES. COUSINS GALORE.
"THEY ALL DIED SCREAMING ON THAT ISLAND.
"ALL BUT ME."
ONE'S GETTING AWAY.
AH, IT'S JUST A BOY. AND THERE'S NOWHERE FOR HIM TO RUN.
THE ISLAND IS OURS!
"THE PIRATES CAME DURING THE NIGHT. WHAT WOULD PROVE TO BE THE LONGEST NIGHT OF MY LIFE."
COME, LET'S ENJOY OURSELVES. WE'LL KILL HIM IN THE MORNING.
"I WAS NINE YEARS OLD.

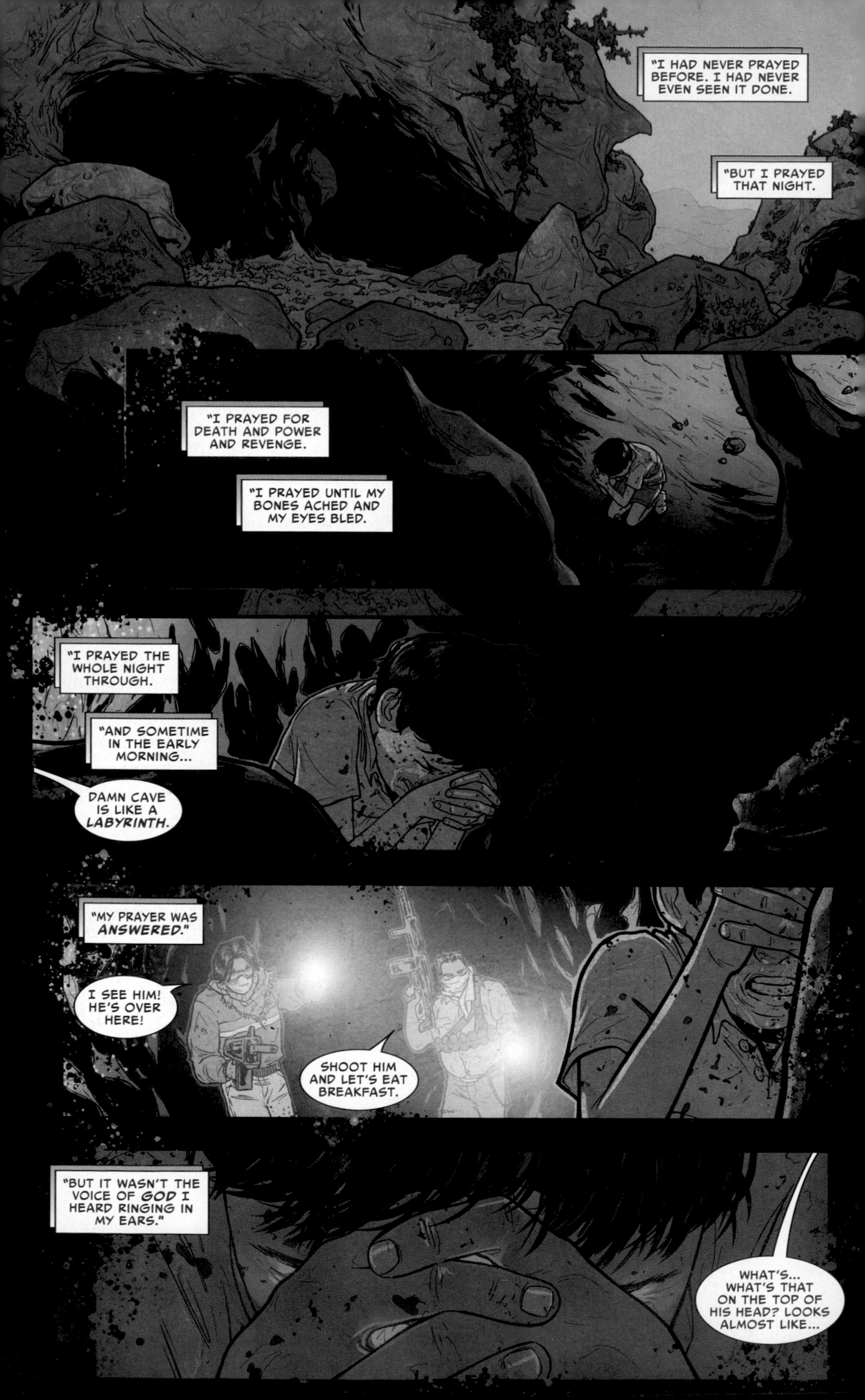
"I HAD NEVER PRAYED BEFORE. I HAD NEVER EVEN SEEN IT DONE.
"BUT I PRAYED THAT NIGHT.
"I PRAYED FOR DEATH AND POWER AND REVENGE.
"I PRAYED UNTIL MY BONES ACHED AND MY EYES BLED.
"I PRAYED THE WHOLE NIGHT THROUGH.
"AND SOMETIME IN THE EARLY MORNING...
DAMN CAVE IS LIKE A LABYRINTH.
"MY PRAYER WAS ANSWERED."
I SEE HIM! HE'S OVER HERE!
SHOOT HIM AND LET'S EAT BREAKFAST.
"BUT IT WASN'T THE VOICE OF GOD I HEARD RINGING IN MY EARS."
WHAT'S... WHAT'S THAT ON THE TOP OF HIS HEAD? LOOKS ALMOST LIKE...

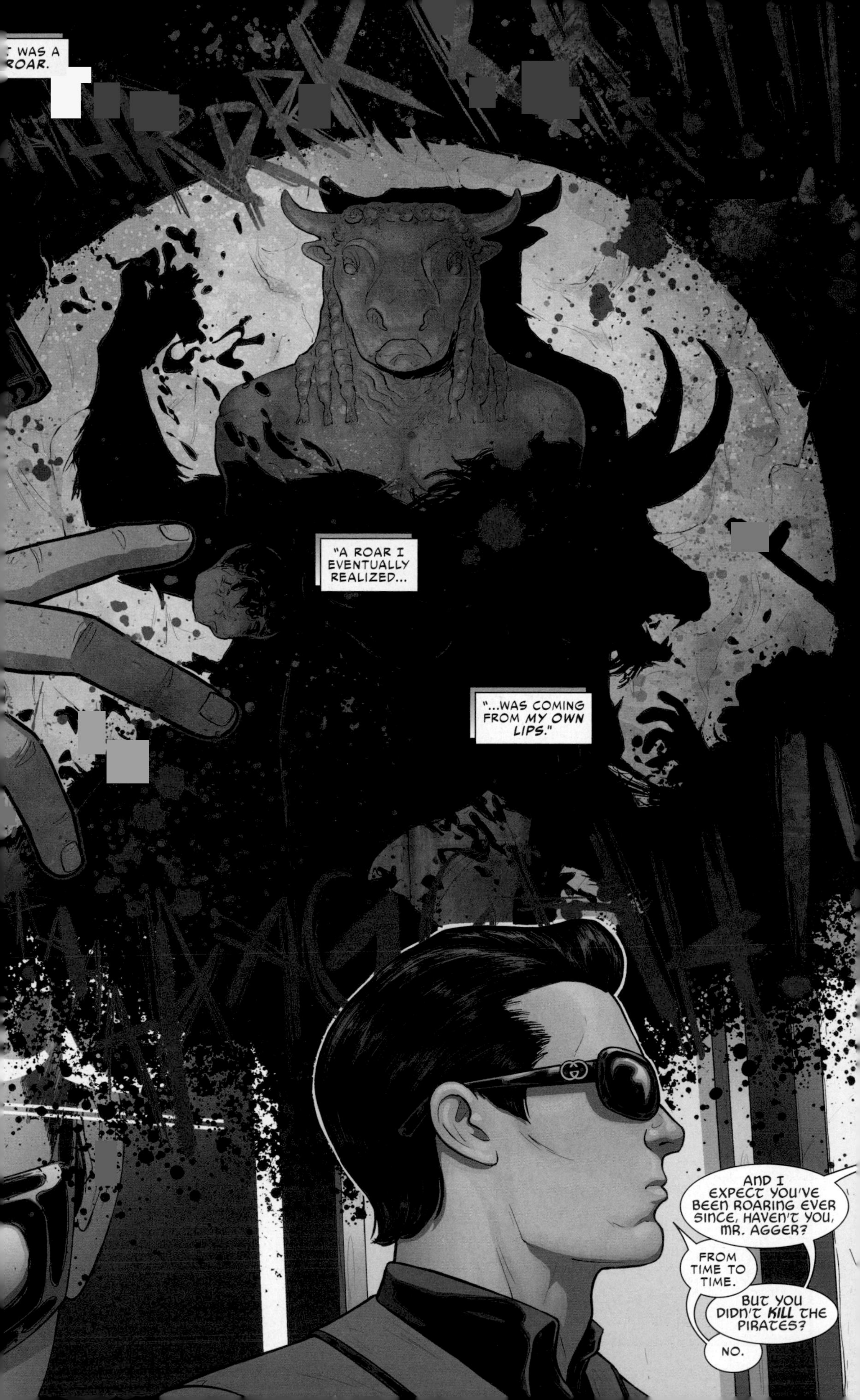
T WAS A ROAR.
"A ROAR I EVENTUALLY REALIZED...
"...WAS COMING FROM MY OWN LIPS."
AND I EXPECT YOU'VE BEEN ROARING EVER SINCE, HAVEN'T YOU, MR. AGGER?
FROM TIME TO TIME.
BUT YOU DIDN'T KILL THE PIRATES?
NO.

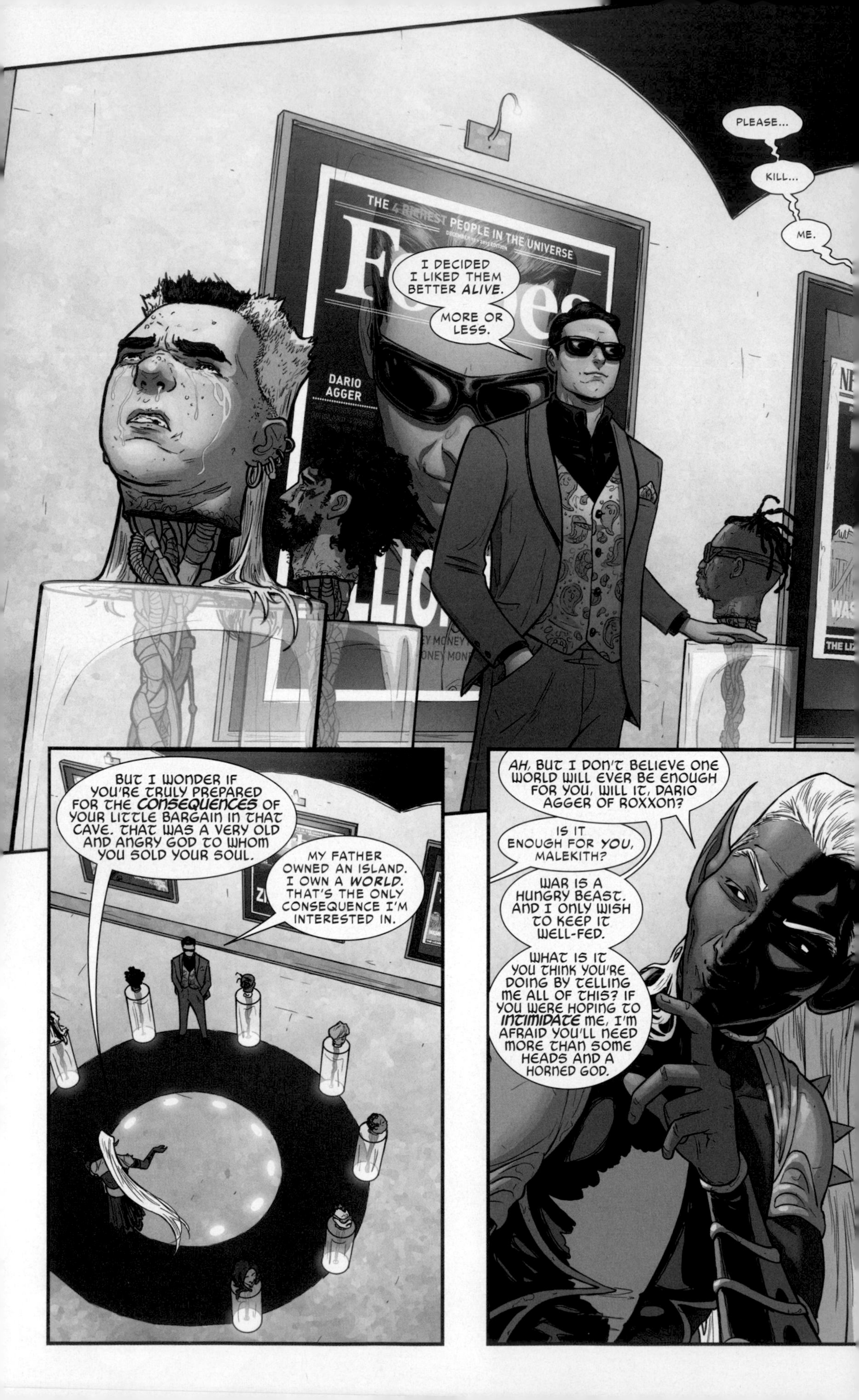

PLEASE...
KILL...
ME.
THE 4 RICHEST PEOPLE IN THE UNIVERSE
DARIO AGGER
I DECIDED I LIKED THEM BETTER *ALIVE*.
MORE OR LESS.
BUT I WONDER IF YOU'RE TRULY PREPARED FOR THE *CONSEQUENCES* OF YOUR LITTLE BARGAIN IN THAT CAVE. THAT WAS A VERY OLD AND ANGRY GOD TO WHOM YOU SOLD YOUR SOUL.
MY FATHER OWNED AN ISLAND. I OWN A *WORLD*. THAT'S THE ONLY CONSEQUENCE I'M INTERESTED IN.
AH, BUT I DON'T BELIEVE ONE WORLD WILL EVER BE ENOUGH FOR YOU, WILL IT, DARIO AGGER OF ROXXON?
IS IT ENOUGH FOR *YOU*, MALEKITH?
WAR IS A HUNGRY BEAST. AND I ONLY WISH TO KEEP IT WELL-FED.
WHAT IS IT YOU THINK YOU'RE DOING BY TELLING ME ALL OF THIS? IF YOU WERE HOPING TO *INTIMIDATE* ME, I'M AFRAID YOU'LL NEED MORE THAN SOME HEADS AND A HORNED GOD.

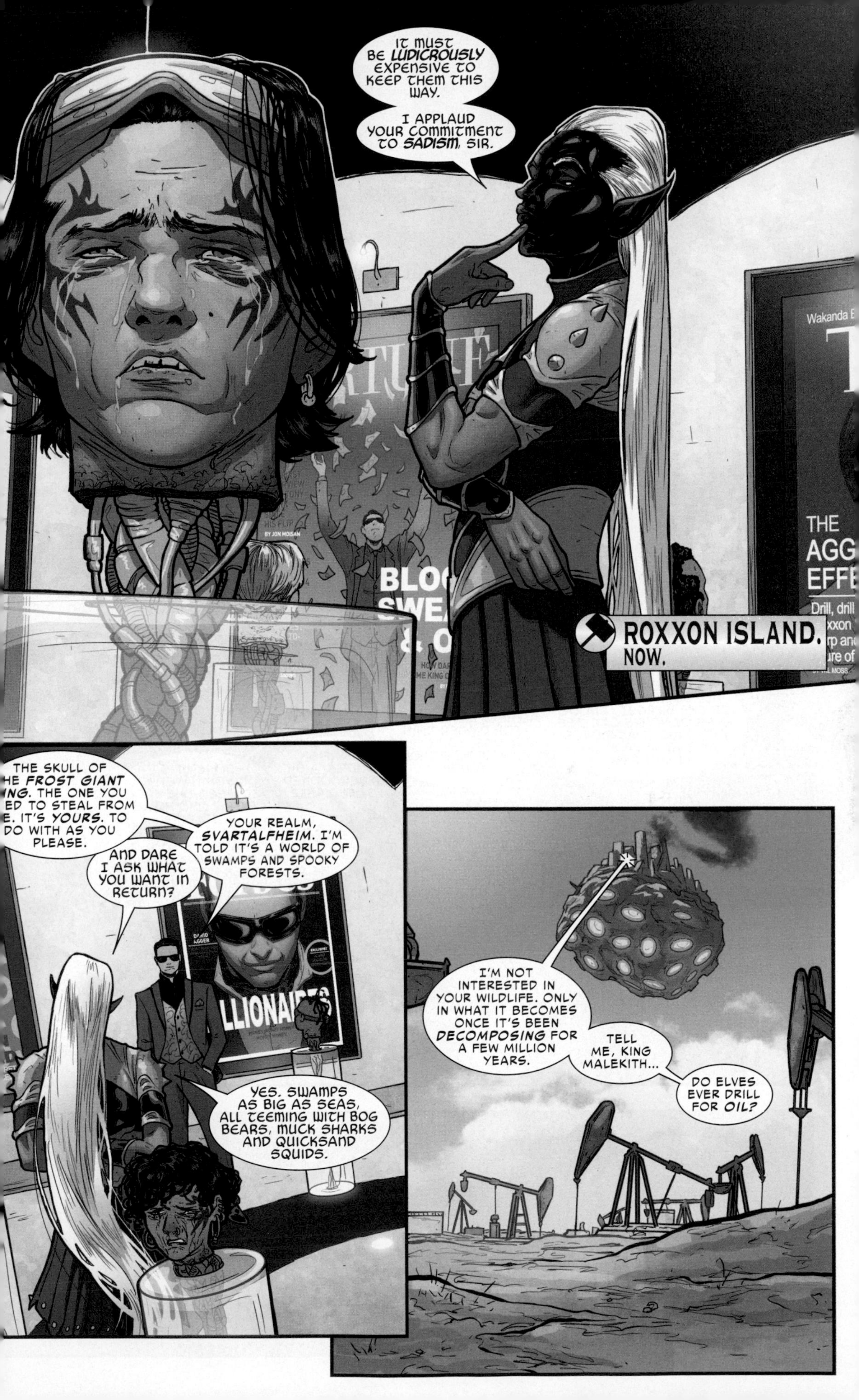
IT MUST BE LUDICROUSLY EXPENSIVE TO KEEP THEM THIS WAY.
I APPLAUD YOUR COMMITMENT TO SADISM, SIR.
Wakanda
THE AGG EFFE
Drill, drill
BLOO SWEA & O
ROXXON ISLAND. NOW.
THE SKULL OF HE FROST GIANT ING. THE ONE YOU ED TO STEAL FROM E. IT'S YOURS. TO DO WITH AS YOU PLEASE.
AND DARE I ASK WHAT YOU WANT IN RETURN?
YOUR REALM, SVARTALFHEIM. I'M TOLD IT'S A WORLD OF SWAMPS AND SPOOKY FORESTS.
YES. SWAMPS AS BIG AS SEAS, ALL TEEMING WITH BOG BEARS, MUCK SHARKS AND QUICKSAND SQUIDS.
LLIONAIRES
I'M NOT INTERESTED IN YOUR WILDLIFE. ONLY IN WHAT IT BECOMES ONCE IT'S BEEN DECOMPOSING FOR A FEW MILLION YEARS.
TELL ME, KING MALEKITH...
DO ELVES EVER DRILL FOR OIL?

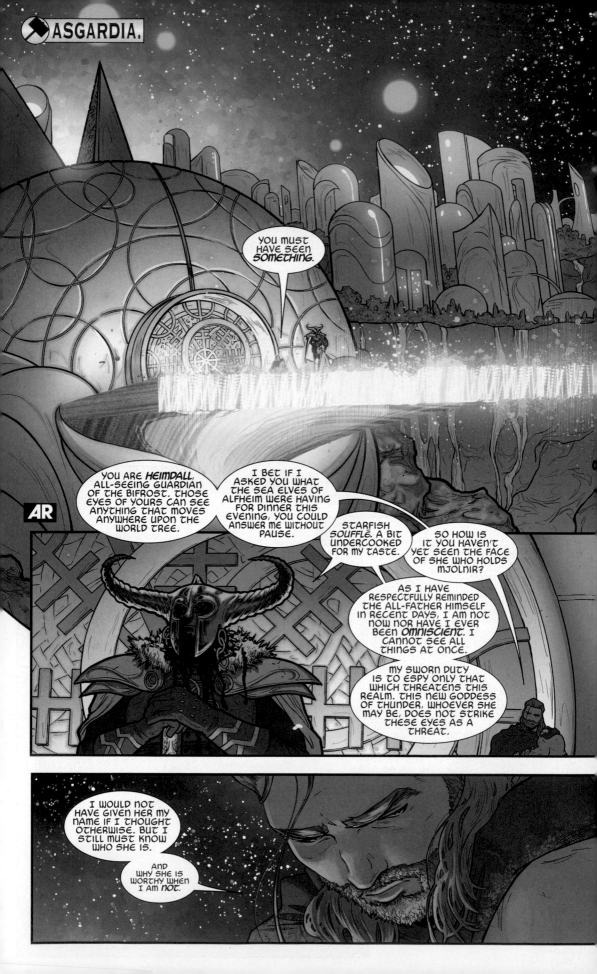

YOU MUST HAVE SEEN *SOMETHING*.

YOU ARE *HEIMDALL*, ALL-SEEING GUARDIAN OF THE BIFROST. THOSE EYES OF YOURS CAN SEE ANYTHING THAT MOVES ANYWHERE UPON THE WORLD TREE.

I BET IF I ASKED YOU WHAT THE SEA ELVES OF ALFHEIM WERE HAVING FOR DINNER THIS EVENING, YOU COULD ANSWER ME WITHOUT PAUSE.

STARFISH SOUFFLÉ. A BIT UNDERCOOKED FOR MY TASTE.

SO HOW IS IT YOU HAVEN'T YET SEEN THE FACE OF SHE WHO HOLDS MJOLNIR?

AS I HAVE RESPECTFULLY REMINDED THE ALL-FATHER HIMSELF IN RECENT DAYS, I AM NOT NOW NOR HAVE I EVER BEEN *OMNISCIENT.* I CANNOT SEE ALL THINGS AT ONCE.

MY SWORN DUTY IS TO ESPY ONLY THAT WHICH THREATENS THIS REALM. THIS NEW GODDESS OF THUNDER, WHOEVER SHE MAY BE, DOES NOT STRIKE THESE EYES AS A THREAT.

I WOULD NOT HAVE GIVEN HER MY NAME IF I THOUGHT OTHERWISE. BUT I STILL MUST KNOW WHO SHE IS.

AND WHY SHE IS WORTHY WHEN I AM *NOT.*

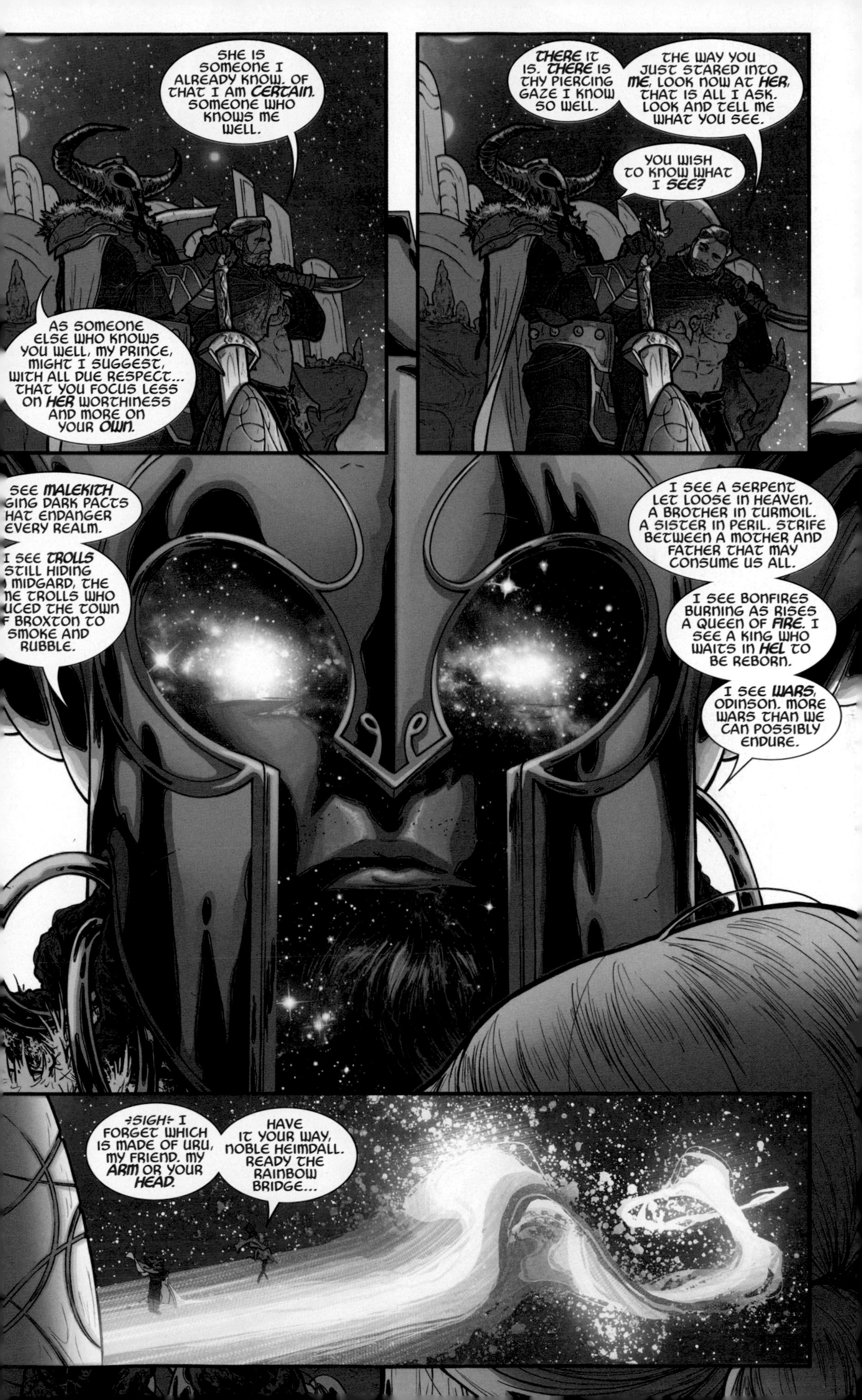

SHE IS SOMEONE I ALREADY KNOW. OF THAT I AM CERTAIN. SOMEONE WHO KNOWS ME WELL.
AS SOMEONE ELSE WHO KNOWS YOU WELL, MY PRINCE, MIGHT I SUGGEST, WITH ALL DUE RESPECT... THAT YOU FOCUS LESS ON HER WORTHINESS AND MORE ON YOUR OWN.
THERE IT IS. THERE IS THY PIERCING GAZE I KNOW SO WELL.
THE WAY YOU JUST STARED INTO ME, LOOK NOW AT HER, THAT IS ALL I ASK. LOOK AND TELL ME WHAT YOU SEE.
YOU WISH TO KNOW WHAT I SEE?
SEE MALEKITH GING DARK PACTS HAT ENDANGER EVERY REALM.
I SEE TROLLS STILL HIDING MIDGARD, THE NE TROLLS WHO UCED THE TOWN F BROXTON TO SMOKE AND RUBBLE.
I SEE A SERPENT LET LOOSE IN HEAVEN. A BROTHER IN TURMOIL. A SISTER IN PERIL. STRIFE BETWEEN A MOTHER AND FATHER THAT MAY CONSUME US ALL.
I SEE BONFIRES BURNING AS RISES A QUEEN OF FIRE. I SEE A KING WHO WAITS IN HEL TO BE REBORN.
I SEE WARS, ODINSON. MORE WARS THAN WE CAN POSSIBLY ENDURE.
÷SIGH÷ I FORGET WHICH IS MADE OF URU, MY FRIEND. MY ARM OR YOUR HEAD.
HAVE IT YOUR WAY, NOBLE HEIMDALL. READY THE RAINBOW BRIDGE...

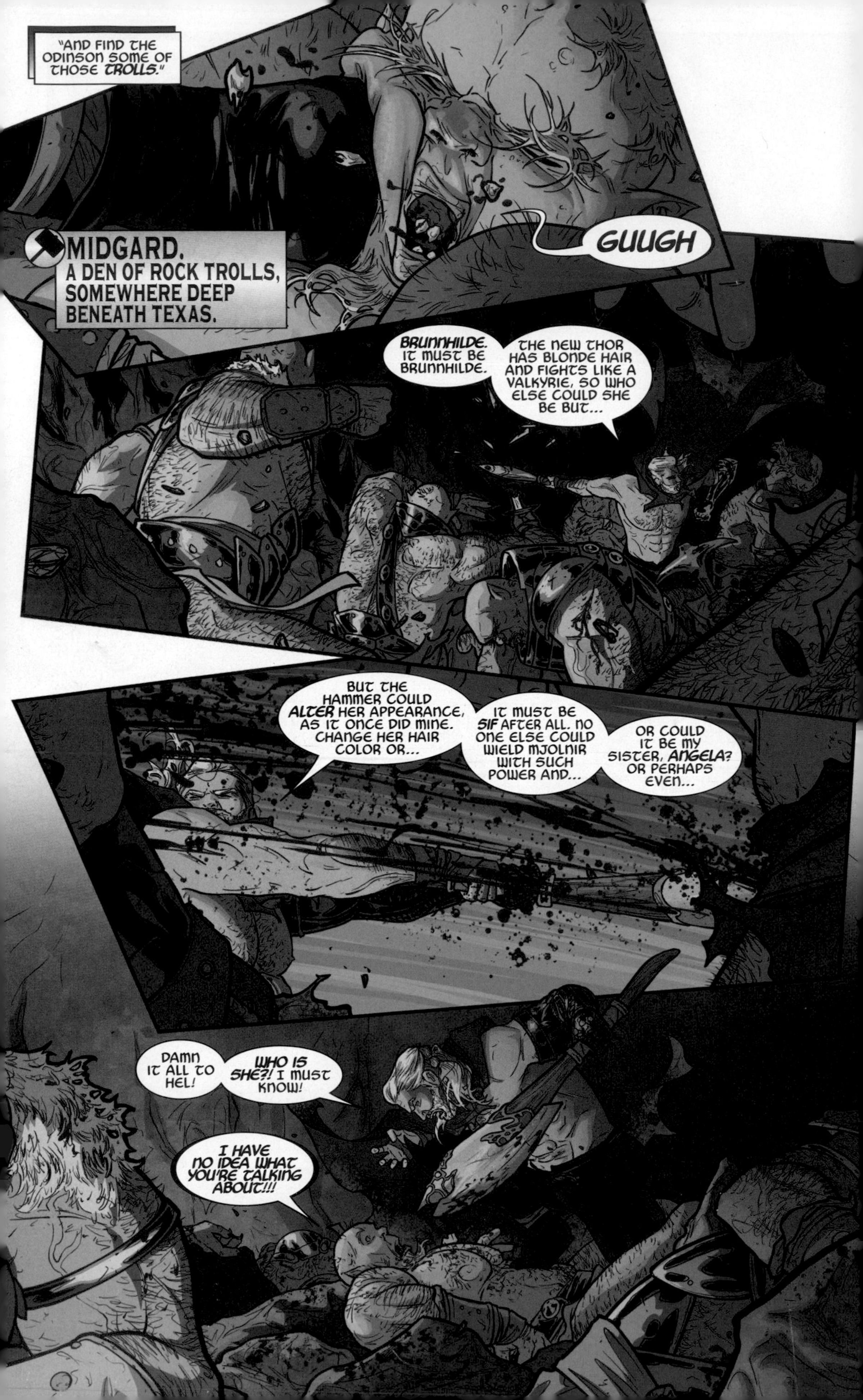
"AND FIND THE ODINSON SOME OF THOSE TROLLS."
GUUGH
MIDGARD. A DEN OF ROCK TROLLS, SOMEWHERE DEEP BENEATH TEXAS.
BRUNNHILDE. IT MUST BE BRUNNHILDE.
THE NEW THOR HAS BLONDE HAIR AND FIGHTS LIKE A VALKYRIE, SO WHO ELSE COULD SHE BE BUT...
BUT THE HAMMER COULD ALTER HER APPEARANCE, AS IT ONCE DID MINE. CHANGE HER HAIR COLOR OR...
IT MUST BE SIF AFTER ALL. NO ONE ELSE COULD WIELD MJOLNIR WITH SUCH POWER AND...
OR COULD IT BE MY SISTER, ANGELA? OR PERHAPS EVEN...
DAMN IT ALL TO HEL!
WHO IS SHE?! I MUST KNOW!
I HAVE NO IDEA WHAT YOU'RE TALKING ABOUT!!!

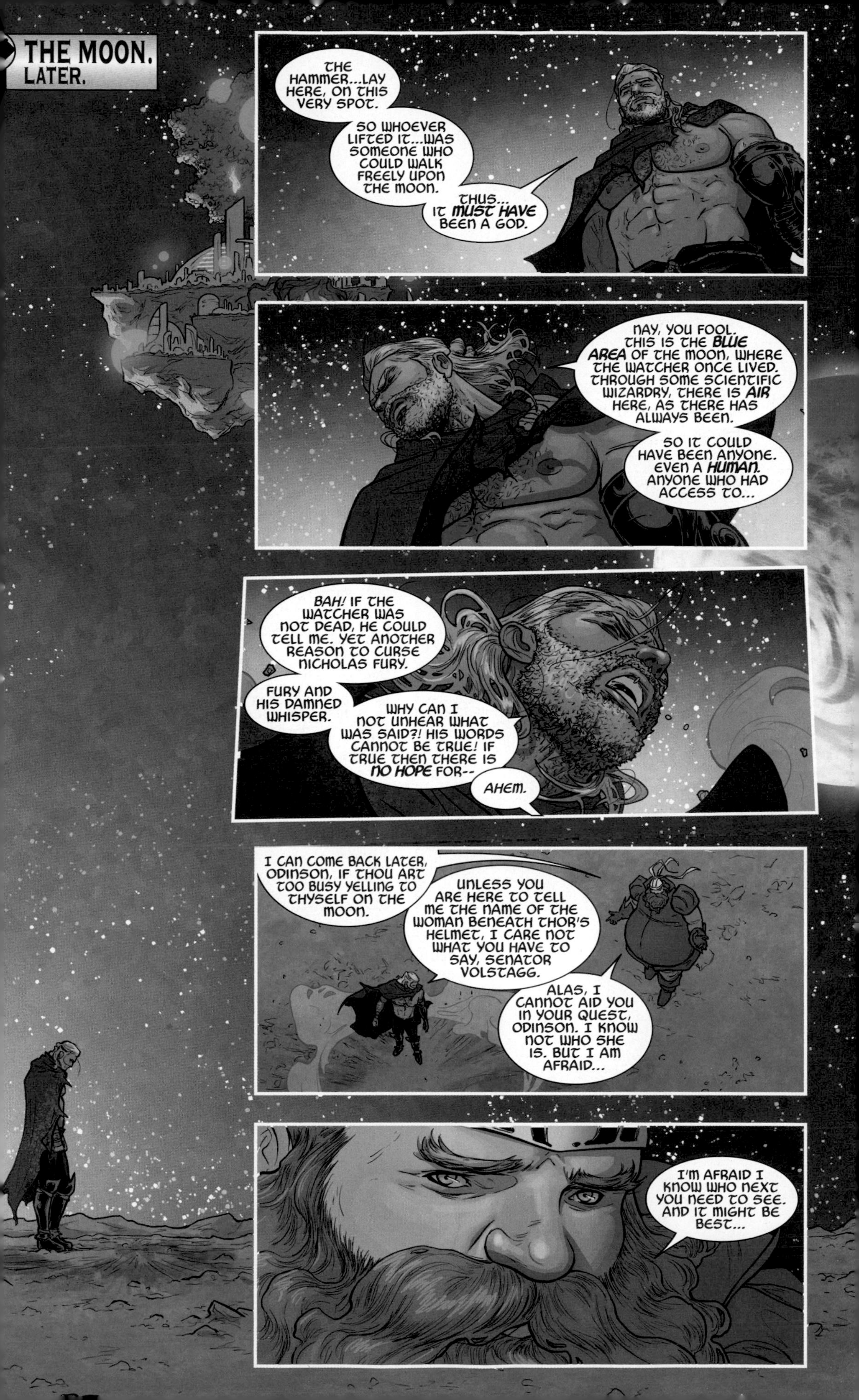
THE MOON. LATER.
THE HAMMER...LAY HERE, ON THIS VERY SPOT.
SO WHOEVER LIFTED IT...WAS SOMEONE WHO COULD WALK FREELY UPON THE MOON.
THUS... IT MUST HAVE BEEN A GOD.
NAY, YOU FOOL. THIS IS THE BLUE AREA OF THE MOON, WHERE THE WATCHER ONCE LIVED. THROUGH SOME SCIENTIFIC WIZARDRY, THERE IS AIR HERE, AS THERE HAS ALWAYS BEEN.
SO IT COULD HAVE BEEN ANYONE. EVEN A HUMAN. ANYONE WHO HAD ACCESS TO...
BAH! IF THE WATCHER WAS NOT DEAD, HE COULD TELL ME. YET ANOTHER REASON TO CURSE NICHOLAS FURY.
FURY AND HIS DAMNED WHISPER.
WHY CAN I NOT UNHEAR WHAT WAS SAID?! HIS WORDS CANNOT BE TRUE! IF TRUE THEN THERE IS NO HOPE FOR--
AHEM.
I CAN COME BACK LATER, ODINSON, IF THOU ART TOO BUSY YELLING TO THYSELF ON THE MOON.
UNLESS YOU ARE HERE TO TELL ME THE NAME OF THE WOMAN BENEATH THOR'S HELMET, I CARE NOT WHAT YOU HAVE TO SAY, SENATOR VOLSTAGG.
ALAS, I CANNOT AID YOU IN YOUR QUEST, ODINSON. I KNOW NOT WHO SHE IS. BUT I AM AFRAID...
I'M AFRAID I KNOW WHO NEXT YOU NEED TO SEE. AND IT MIGHT BE BEST...

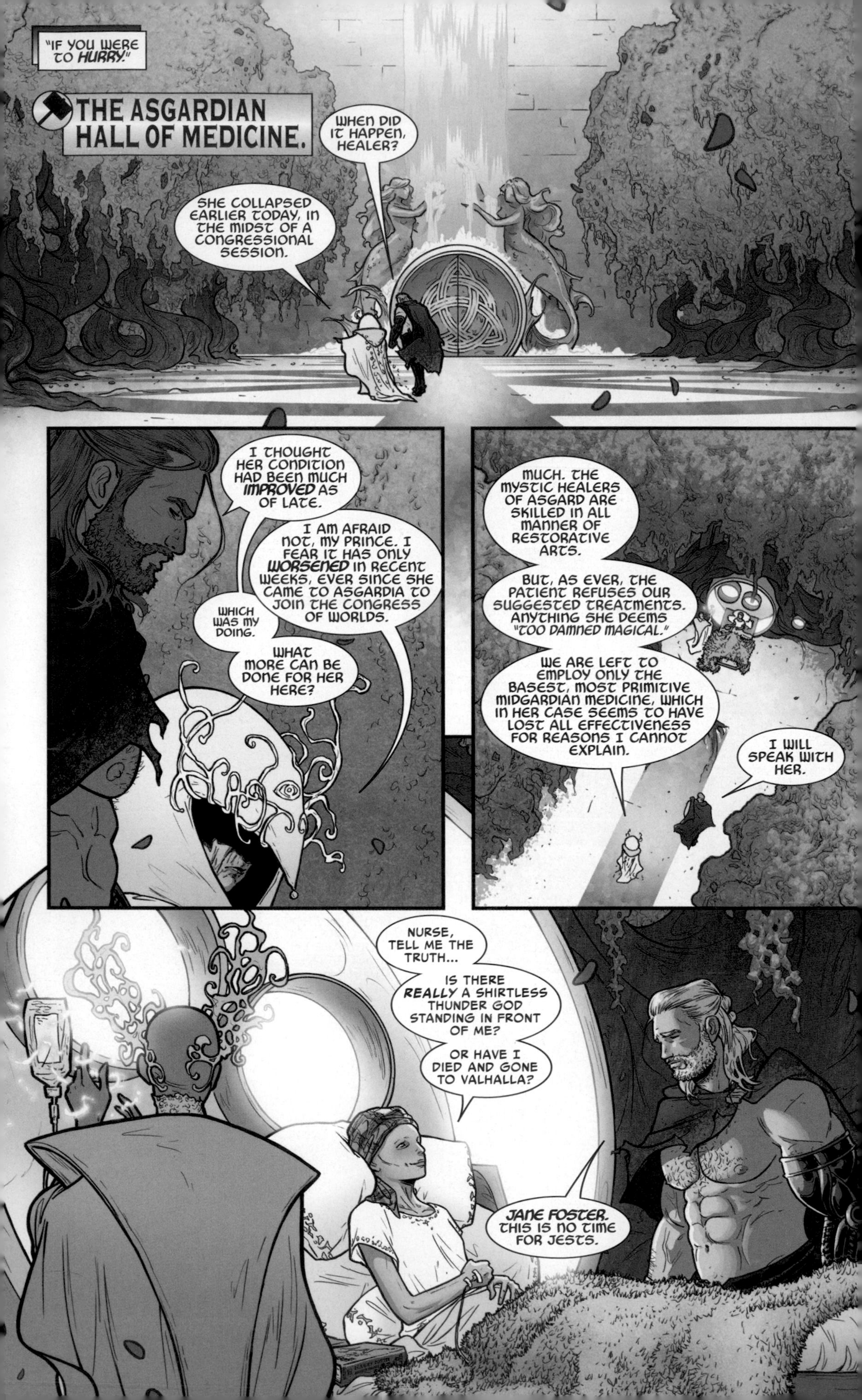
"IF YOU WERE TO HURRY."
THE ASGARDIAN HALL OF MEDICINE.
WHEN DID IT HAPPEN, HEALER?
SHE COLLAPSED EARLIER TODAY, IN THE MIDST OF A CONGRESSIONAL SESSION.
I THOUGHT HER CONDITION HAD BEEN MUCH IMPROVED AS OF LATE.
I AM AFRAID NOT, MY PRINCE. I FEAR IT HAS ONLY WORSENED IN RECENT WEEKS, EVER SINCE SHE CAME TO ASGARDIA TO JOIN THE CONGRESS OF WORLDS.
WHICH WAS MY DOING.
WHAT MORE CAN BE DONE FOR HER HERE?
MUCH. THE MYSTIC HEALERS OF ASGARD ARE SKILLED IN ALL MANNER OF RESTORATIVE ARTS.
BUT, AS EVER, THE PATIENT REFUSES OUR SUGGESTED TREATMENTS. ANYTHING SHE DEEMS "TOO DAMNED MAGICAL."
WE ARE LEFT TO EMPLOY ONLY THE BASEST, MOST PRIMITIVE MIDGARDIAN MEDICINE, WHICH IN HER CASE SEEMS TO HAVE LOST ALL EFFECTIVENESS FOR REASONS I CANNOT EXPLAIN.
I WILL SPEAK WITH HER.
NURSE, TELL ME THE TRUTH...
IS THERE REALLY A SHIRTLESS THUNDER GOD STANDING IN FRONT OF ME?
OR HAVE I DIED AND GONE TO VALHALLA?
JANE FOSTER. THIS IS NO TIME FOR JESTS.

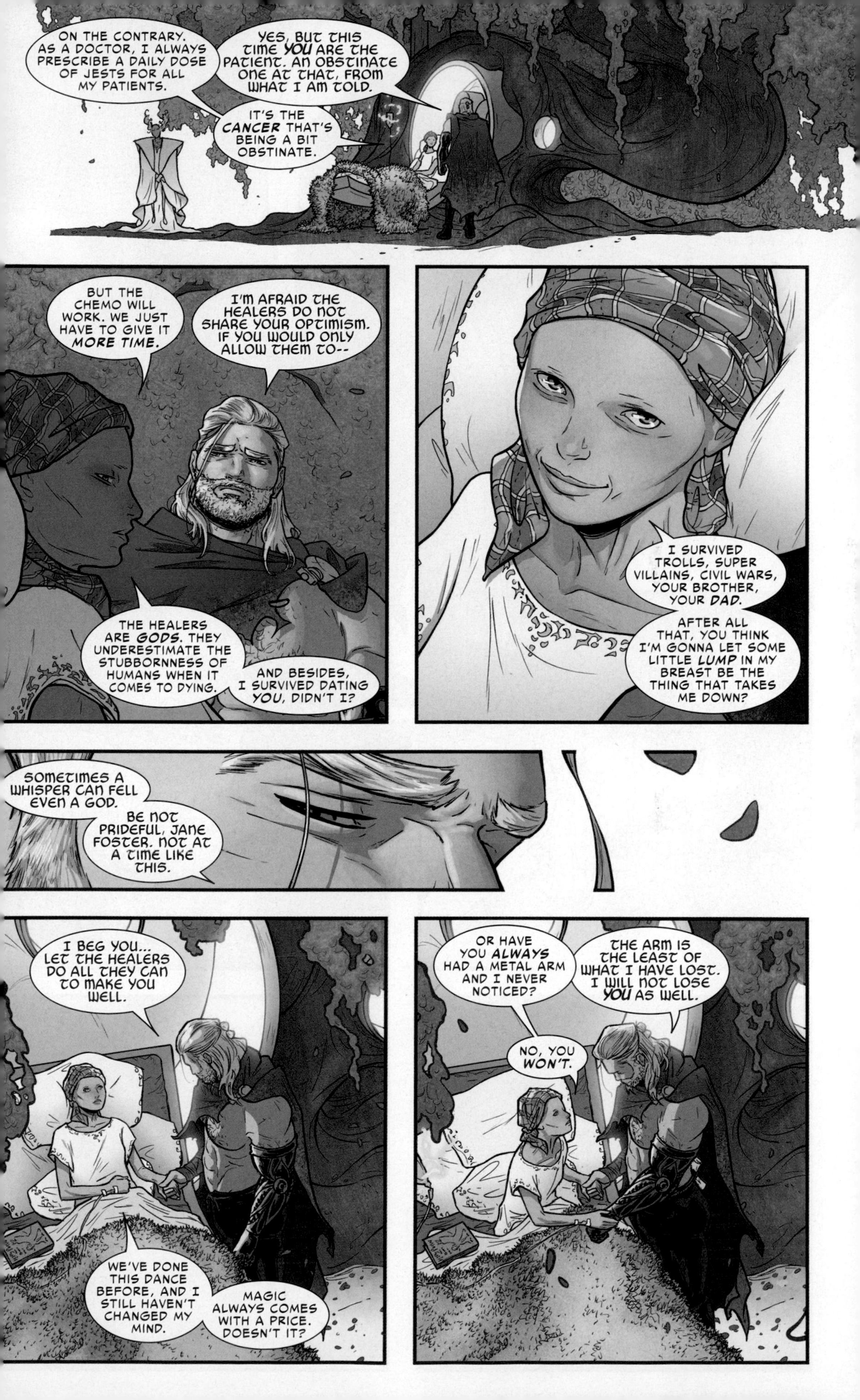

ON THE CONTRARY. AS A DOCTOR, I ALWAYS PRESCRIBE A DAILY DOSE OF JESTS FOR ALL MY PATIENTS.
YES, BUT THIS TIME YOU ARE THE PATIENT. AN OBSTINATE ONE AT THAT, FROM WHAT I AM TOLD.
IT'S THE CANCER THAT'S BEING A BIT OBSTINATE.
BUT THE CHEMO WILL WORK. WE JUST HAVE TO GIVE IT MORE TIME.
I'M AFRAID THE HEALERS DO NOT SHARE YOUR OPTIMISM. IF YOU WOULD ONLY ALLOW THEM TO--
THE HEALERS ARE GODS. THEY UNDERESTIMATE THE STUBBORNNESS OF HUMANS WHEN IT COMES TO DYING.
AND BESIDES, I SURVIVED DATING YOU, DIDN'T I?
I SURVIVED TROLLS, SUPER VILLAINS, CIVIL WARS, YOUR BROTHER, YOUR DAD.
AFTER ALL THAT, YOU THINK I'M GONNA LET SOME LITTLE LUMP IN MY BREAST BE THE THING THAT TAKES ME DOWN?
SOMETIMES A WHISPER CAN FELL EVEN A GOD.
BE NOT PRIDEFUL, JANE FOSTER. NOT AT A TIME LIKE THIS.
I BEG YOU... LET THE HEALERS DO ALL THEY CAN TO MAKE YOU WELL.
WE'VE DONE THIS DANCE BEFORE, AND I STILL HAVEN'T CHANGED MY MIND.
MAGIC ALWAYS COMES WITH A PRICE. DOESN'T IT?
OR HAVE YOU ALWAYS HAD A METAL ARM AND I NEVER NOTICED?
THE ARM IS THE LEAST OF WHAT I HAVE LOST. I WILL NOT LOSE YOU AS WELL.
NO, YOU WON'T.

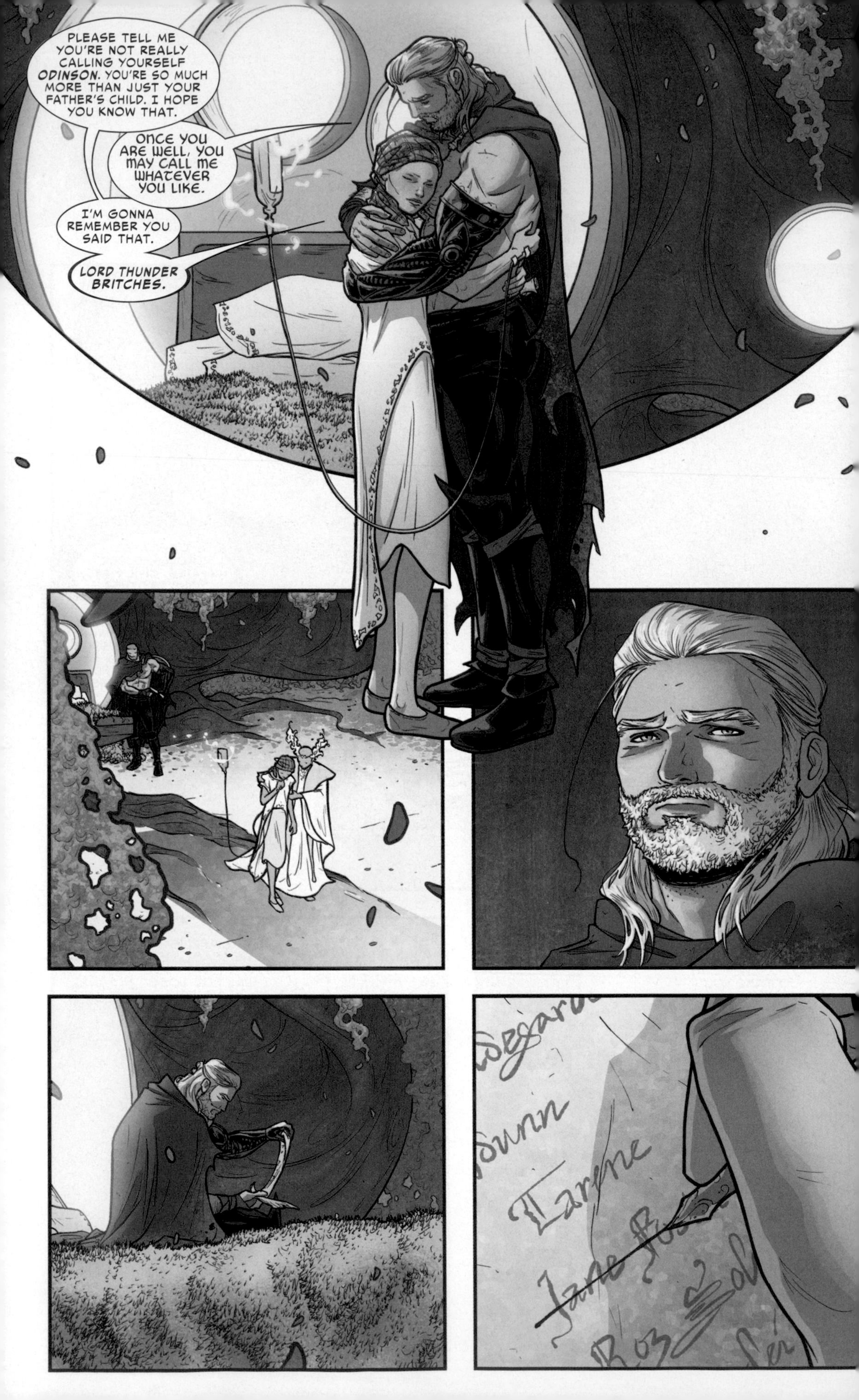
PLEASE TELL ME YOU'RE NOT REALLY CALLING YOURSELF ODINSON. YOU'RE SO MUCH MORE THAN JUST YOUR FATHER'S CHILD. I HOPE YOU KNOW THAT.
ONCE YOU ARE WELL, YOU MAY CALL ME WHATEVER YOU LIKE.
I'M GONNA REMEMBER YOU SAID THAT.
LORD THUNDER BRITCHES.

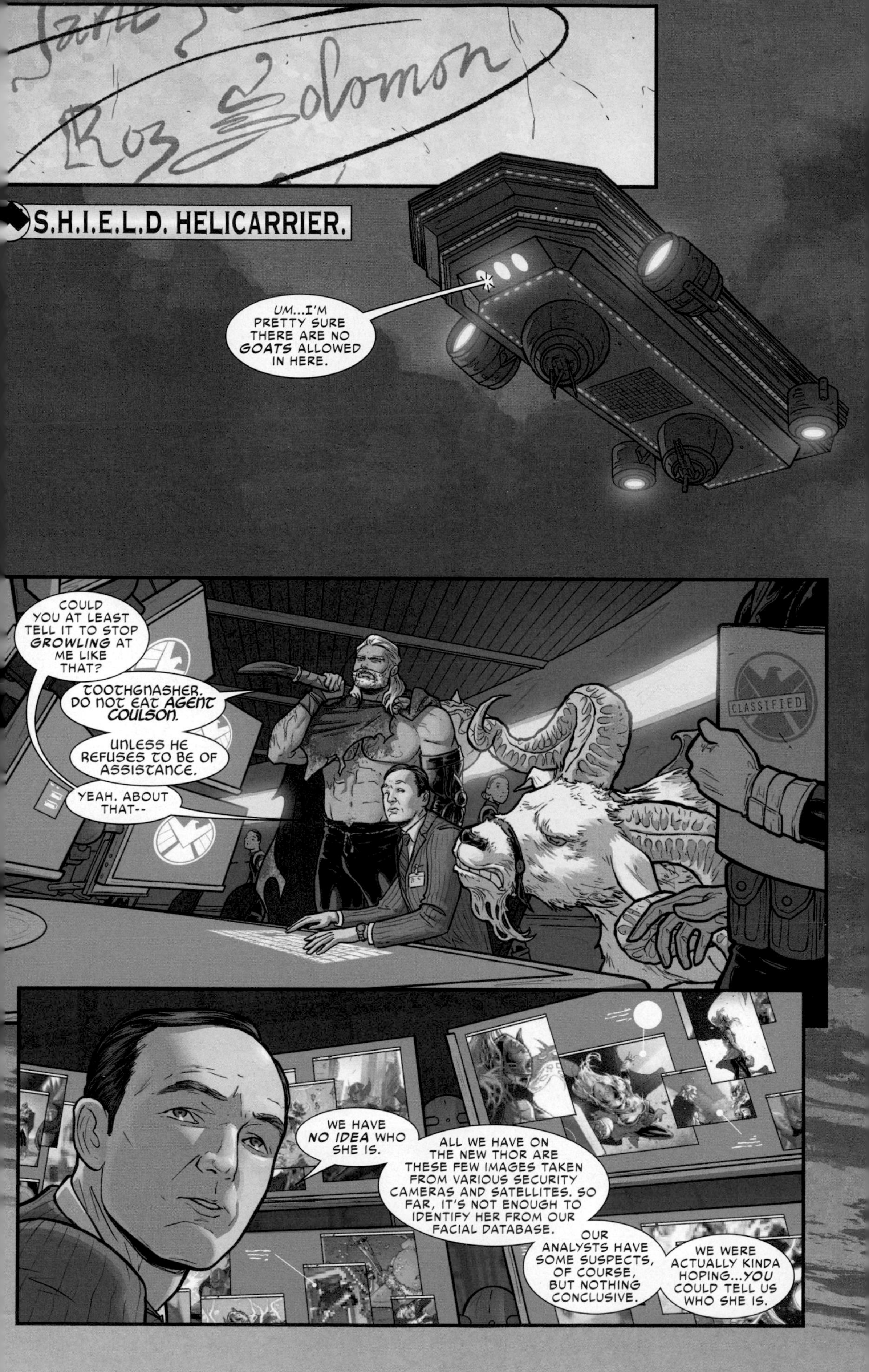
Roz Solomon
S.H.I.E.L.D. HELICARRIER.
UM...I'M PRETTY SURE THERE ARE NO GOATS ALLOWED IN HERE.
COULD YOU AT LEAST TELL IT TO STOP GROWLING AT ME LIKE THAT?
TOOTHGNASHER. DO NOT EAT AGENT COULSON.
UNLESS HE REFUSES TO BE OF ASSISTANCE.
YEAH. ABOUT THAT--
CLASSIFIED
WE HAVE NO IDEA WHO SHE IS.
ALL WE HAVE ON THE NEW THOR ARE THESE FEW IMAGES TAKEN FROM VARIOUS SECURITY CAMERAS AND SATELLITES. SO FAR, IT'S NOT ENOUGH TO IDENTIFY HER FROM OUR FACIAL DATABASE.
OUR ANALYSTS HAVE SOME SUSPECTS, OF COURSE, BUT NOTHING CONCLUSIVE.
WE WERE ACTUALLY KINDA HOPING...YOU COULD TELL US WHO SHE IS.

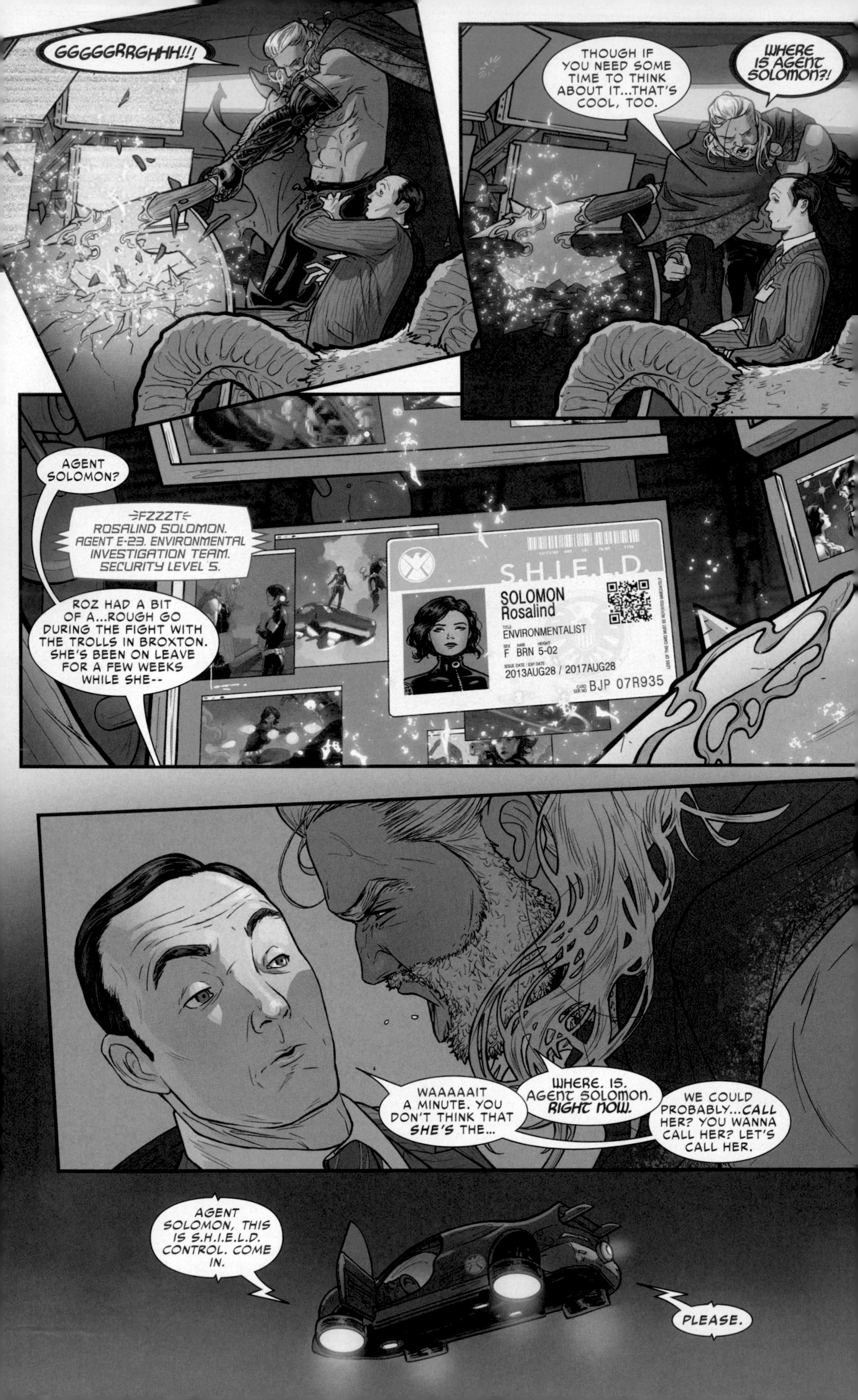
GGGGGRRGHHH!!!
THOUGH IF YOU NEED SOME TIME TO THINK ABOUT IT...THAT'S COOL, TOO.
WHERE IS AGENT SOLOMON?!
AGENT SOLOMON?
FZZZT ROSALIND SOLOMON. AGENT E-23. ENVIRONMENTAL INVESTIGATION TEAM. SECURITY LEVEL 5.
S.H.I.E.L.D.
SOLOMON
Rosalind
TITLE
ENVIRONMENTALIST
SEX HAIR HEIGHT
F BRN 5-02
ISSUE DATE / EXP DATE
2013AUG28 / 2017AUG28
CARD SER NO BJP 07R935
ROZ HAD A BIT OF A...ROUGH GO DURING THE FIGHT WITH THE TROLLS IN BROXTON. SHE'S BEEN ON LEAVE FOR A FEW WEEKS WHILE SHE--
WAAAAAIT A MINUTE. YOU DON'T THINK THAT *SHE'S* THE...
WHERE. IS. AGENT SOLOMON. ***RIGHT NOW.***
WE COULD PROBABLY...*CALL* HER? YOU WANNA CALL HER? LET'S CALL HER.
AGENT SOLOMON, THIS IS S.H.I.E.L.D. CONTROL. COME IN.
PLEASE.

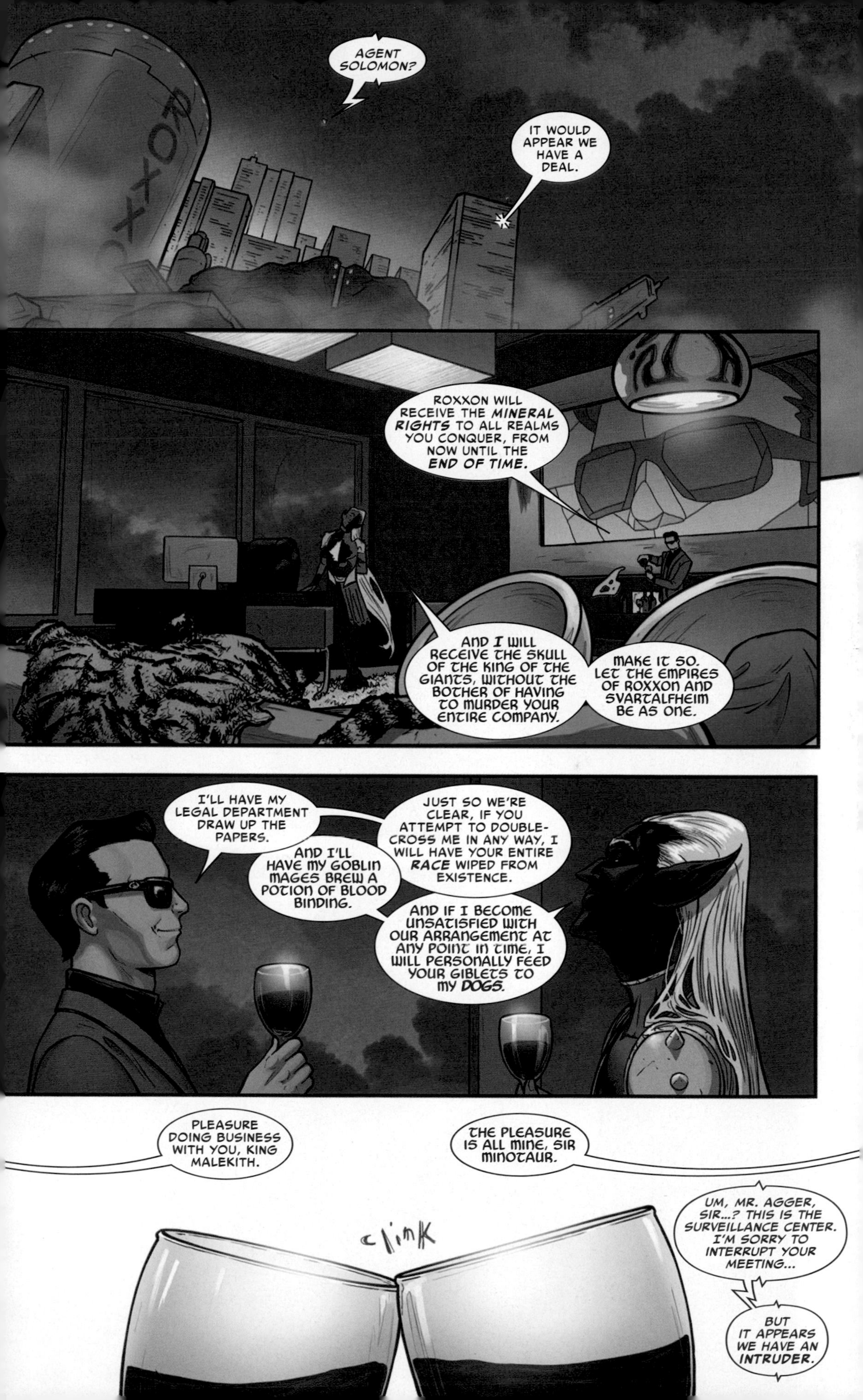
AGENT SOLOMON?
IT WOULD APPEAR WE HAVE A DEAL.
ROXXON
ROXXON WILL RECEIVE THE MINERAL RIGHTS TO ALL REALMS YOU CONQUER, FROM NOW UNTIL THE END OF TIME.
AND I WILL RECEIVE THE SKULL OF THE KING OF THE GIANTS, WITHOUT THE BOTHER OF HAVING TO MURDER YOUR ENTIRE COMPANY.
MAKE IT SO. LET THE EMPIRES OF ROXXON AND SVARTALFHEIM BE AS ONE.
I'LL HAVE MY LEGAL DEPARTMENT DRAW UP THE PAPERS.
AND I'LL HAVE MY GOBLIN MAGES BREW A POTION OF BLOOD BINDING.
JUST SO WE'RE CLEAR, IF YOU ATTEMPT TO DOUBLE-CROSS ME IN ANY WAY, I WILL HAVE YOUR ENTIRE RACE WIPED FROM EXISTENCE.
AND IF I BECOME UNSATISFIED WITH OUR ARRANGEMENT AT ANY POINT IN TIME, I WILL PERSONALLY FEED YOUR GIBLETS TO MY DOGS.
PLEASURE DOING BUSINESS WITH YOU, KING MALEKITH.
THE PLEASURE IS ALL MINE, SIR MINOTAUR.
CLINK
UM, MR. AGGER, SIR...? THIS IS THE SURVEILLANCE CENTER. I'M SORRY TO INTERRUPT YOUR MEETING...
BUT IT APPEARS WE HAVE AN INTRUDER.

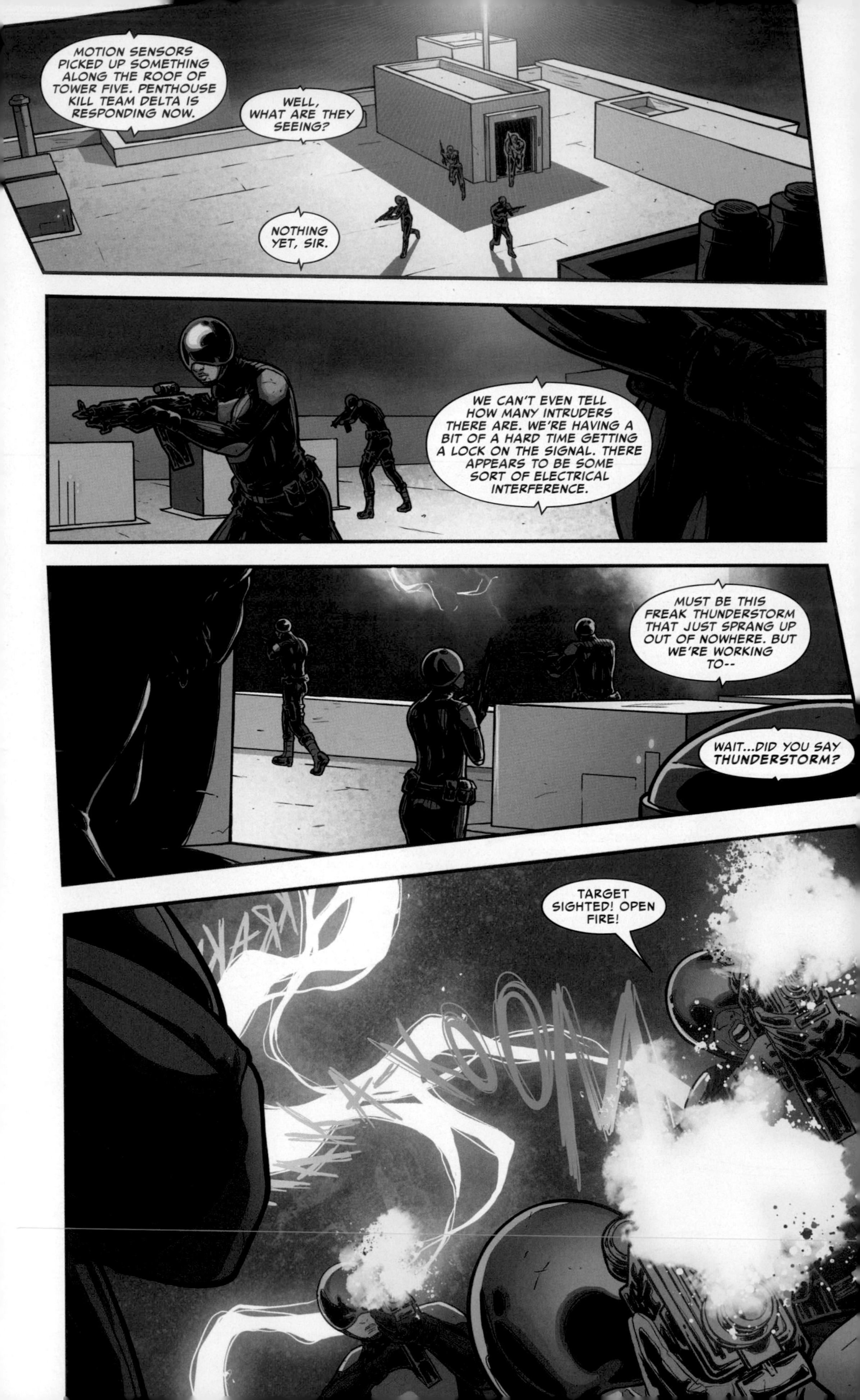
MOTION SENSORS PICKED UP SOMETHING ALONG THE ROOF OF TOWER FIVE. PENTHOUSE KILL TEAM DELTA IS RESPONDING NOW.
WELL, WHAT ARE THEY SEEING?
NOTHING YET, SIR.
WE CAN'T EVEN TELL HOW MANY INTRUDERS THERE ARE. WE'RE HAVING A BIT OF A HARD TIME GETTING A LOCK ON THE SIGNAL. THERE APPEARS TO BE SOME SORT OF ELECTRICAL INTERFERENCE.
MUST BE THIS FREAK THUNDERSTORM THAT JUST SPRANG UP OUT OF NOWHERE. BUT WE'RE WORKING TO--
WAIT...DID YOU SAY THUNDERSTORM?
TARGET SIGHTED! OPEN FIRE!

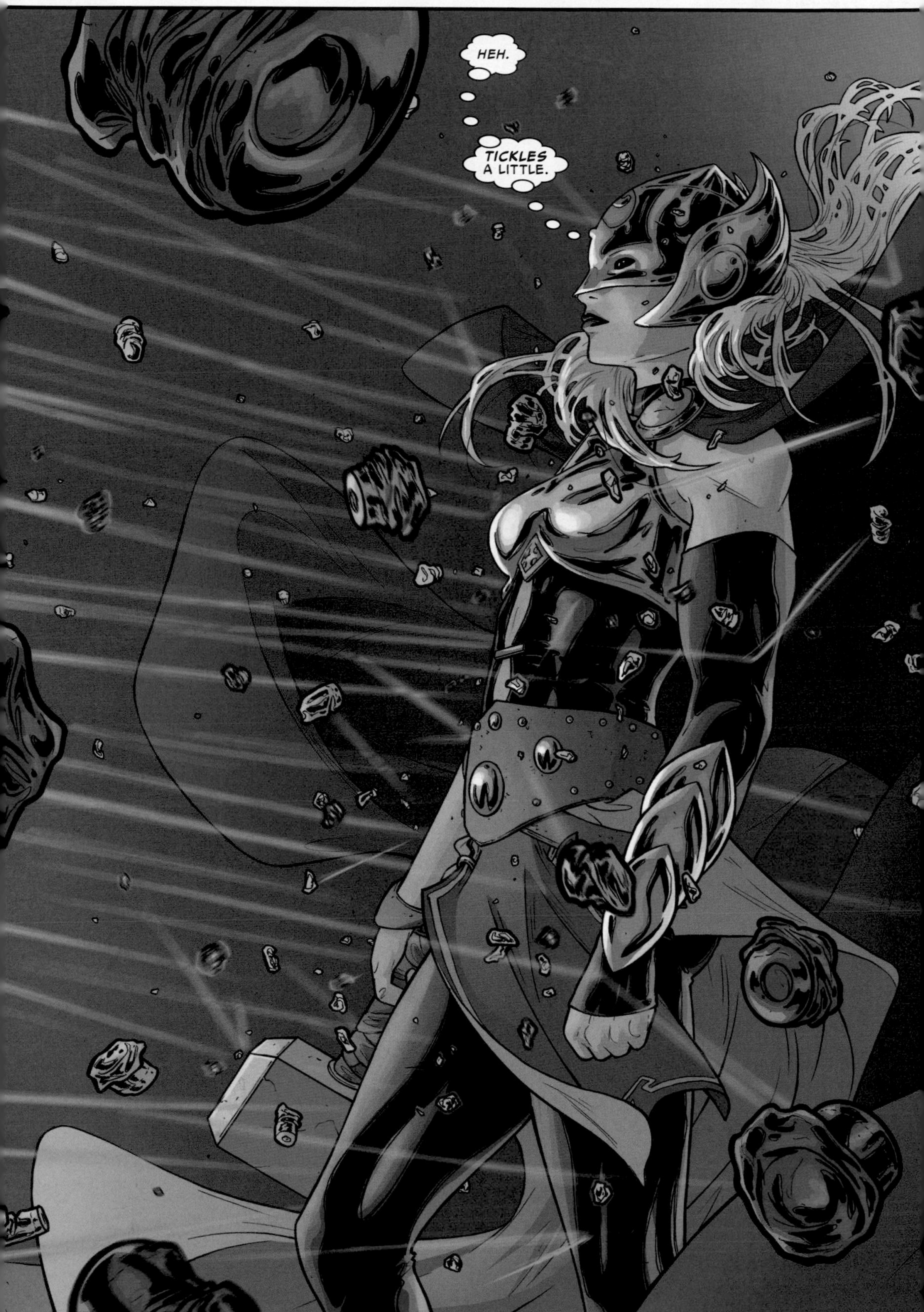
HEH.
TICKLES A LITTLE.

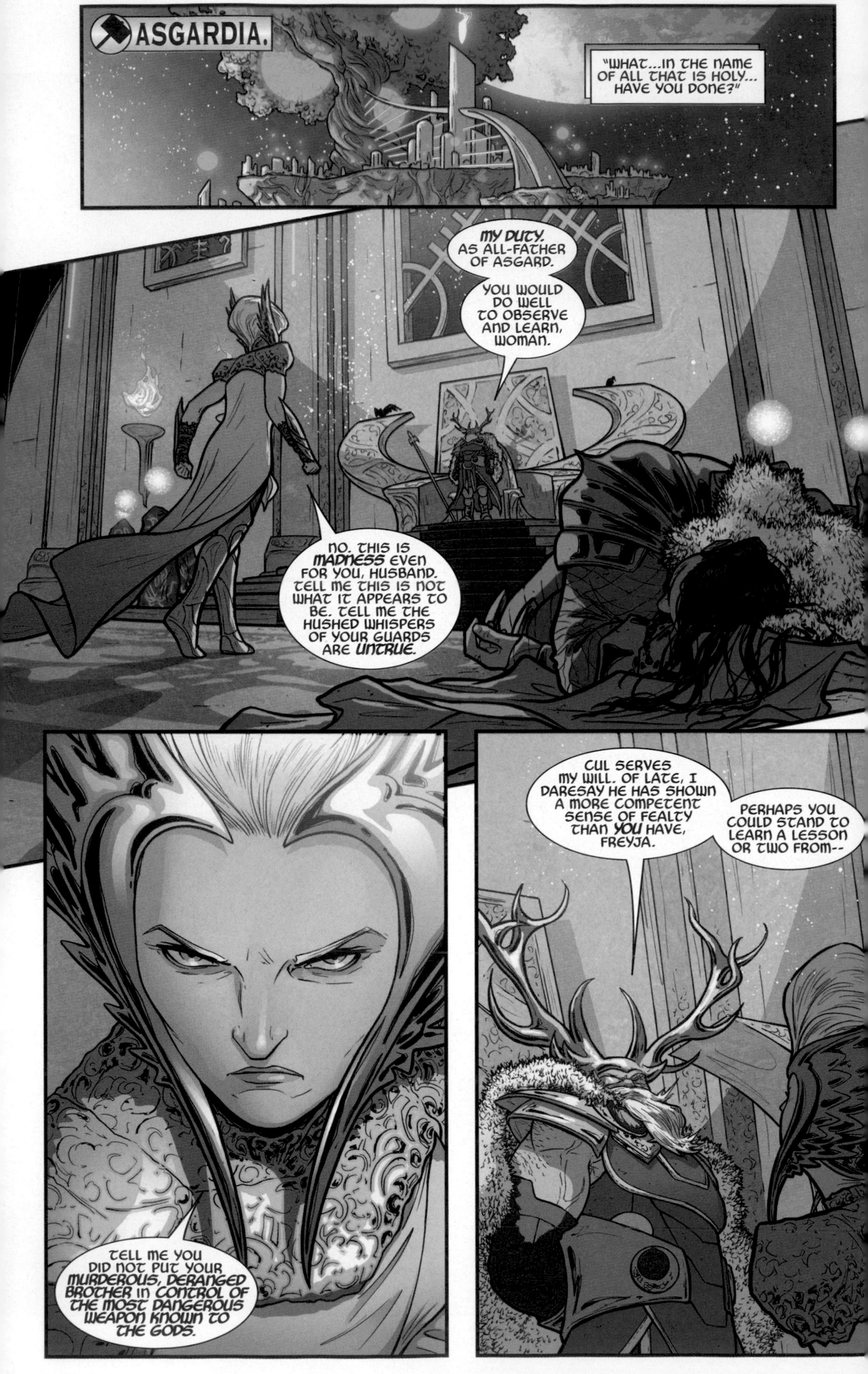
ASGARDIA.
"WHAT...IN THE NAME OF ALL THAT IS HOLY... HAVE YOU DONE?"
MY DUTY. AS ALL-FATHER OF ASGARD.
YOU WOULD DO WELL TO OBSERVE AND LEARN, WOMAN.
NO. THIS IS MADNESS EVEN FOR YOU, HUSBAND. TELL ME THIS IS NOT WHAT IT APPEARS TO BE. TELL ME THE HUSHED WHISPERS OF YOUR GUARDS ARE UNTRUE.
TELL ME YOU DID NOT PUT YOUR MURDEROUS, DERANGED BROTHER IN CONTROL OF THE MOST DANGEROUS WEAPON KNOWN TO THE GODS.
CUL SERVES MY WILL. OF LATE, I DARESAY HE HAS SHOWN A MORE COMPETENT SENSE OF FEALTY THAN YOU HAVE, FREYJA.
PERHAPS YOU COULD STAND TO LEARN A LESSON OR TWO FROM--

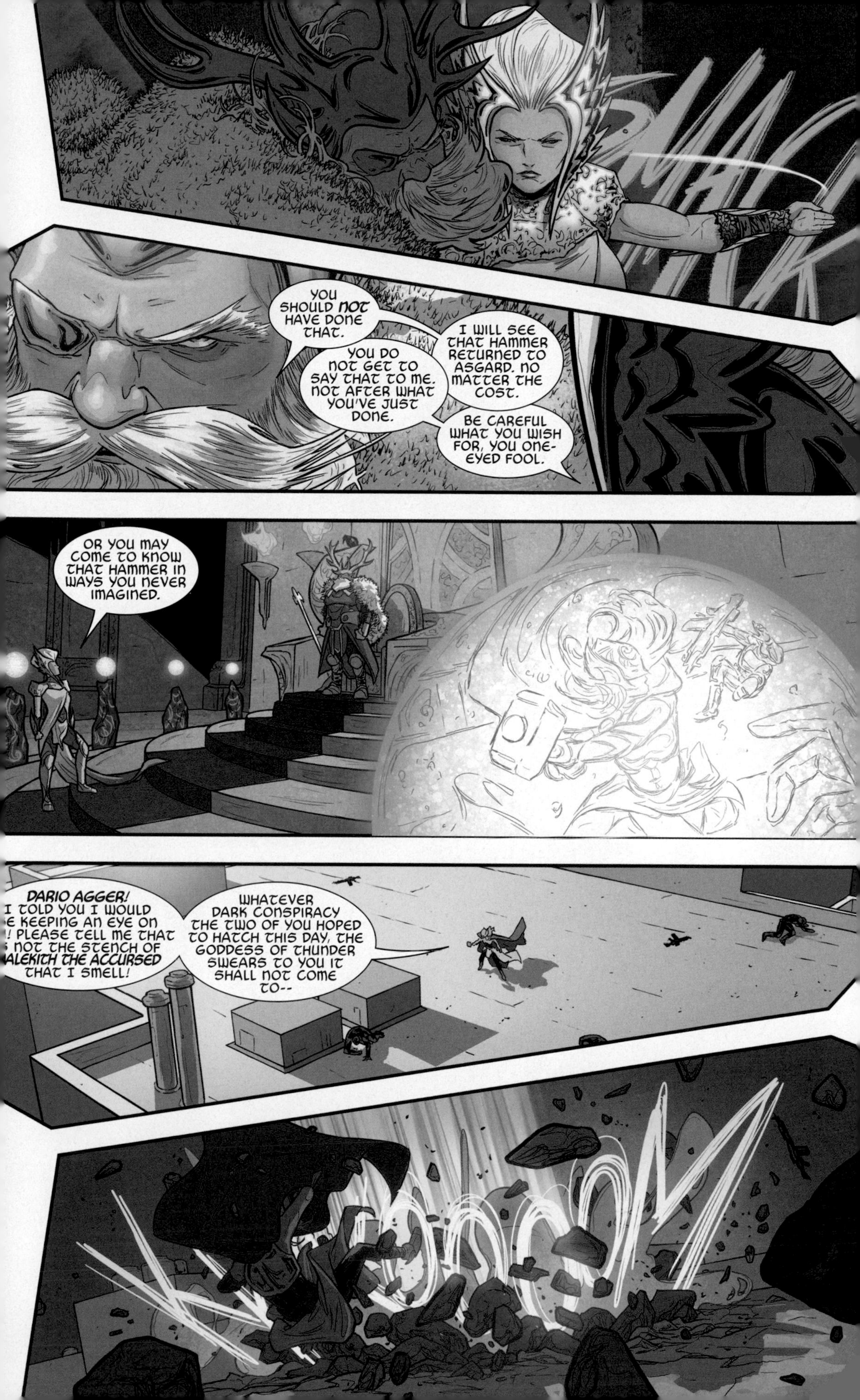

YOU SHOULD *NOT* HAVE DONE THAT.
YOU DO NOT GET TO SAY THAT TO ME. NOT AFTER WHAT YOU'VE JUST DONE.
I WILL SEE THAT HAMMER RETURNED TO ASGARD. NO MATTER THE COST.
BE CAREFUL WHAT YOU WISH FOR, YOU ONE-EYED FOOL.
OR YOU MAY COME TO KNOW THAT HAMMER IN WAYS YOU NEVER IMAGINED.
DARIO AGGER! I TOLD YOU I WOULD E KEEPING AN EYE ON ! PLEASE TELL ME THAT S NOT THE STENCH OF ***ALEKITH THE ACCURSED*** THAT I SMELL!
WHATEVER DARK CONSPIRACY THE TWO OF YOU HOPED TO HATCH THIS DAY, THE GODDESS OF THUNDER SWEARS TO YOU IT SHALL NOT COME TO--

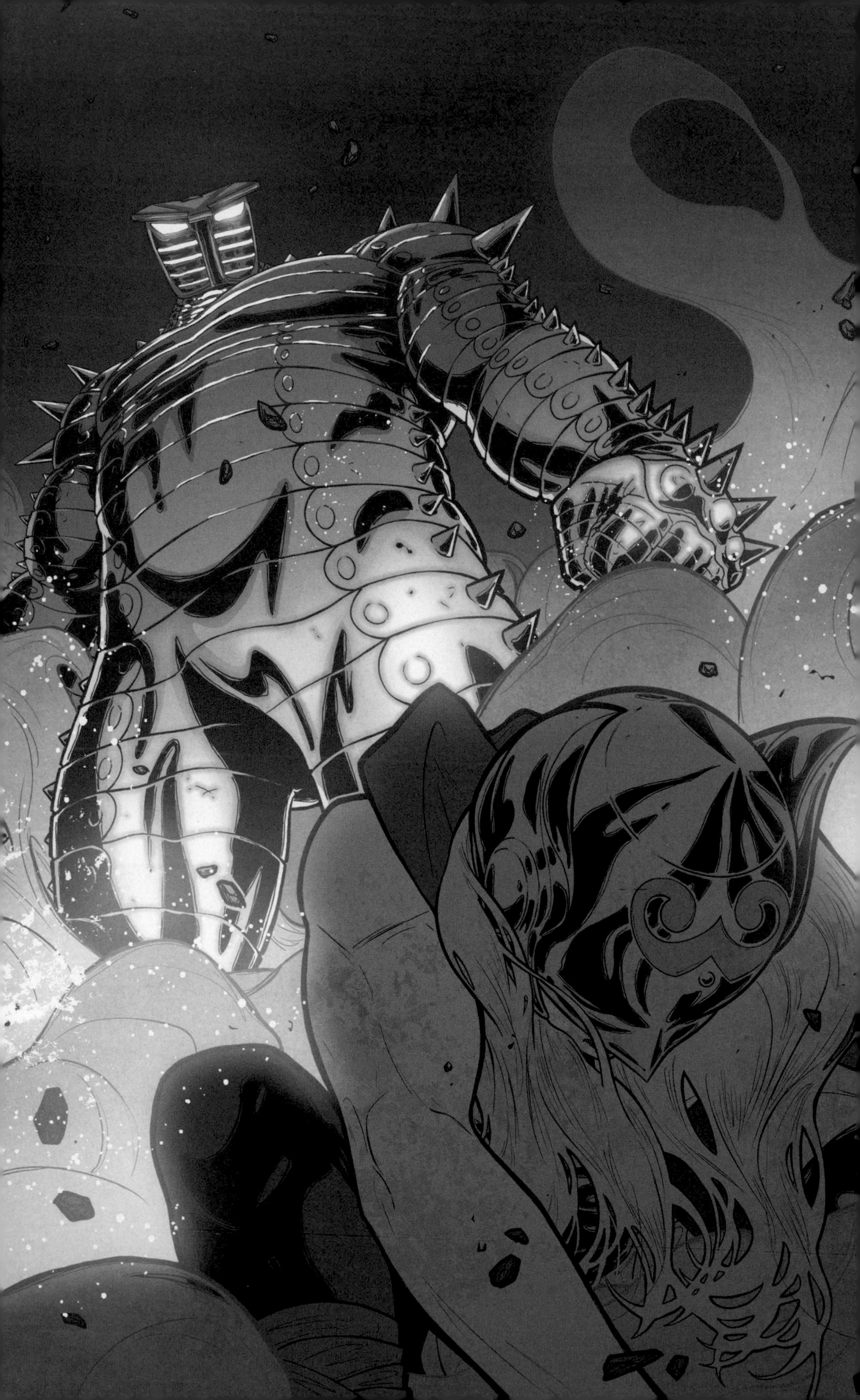

— 7 —

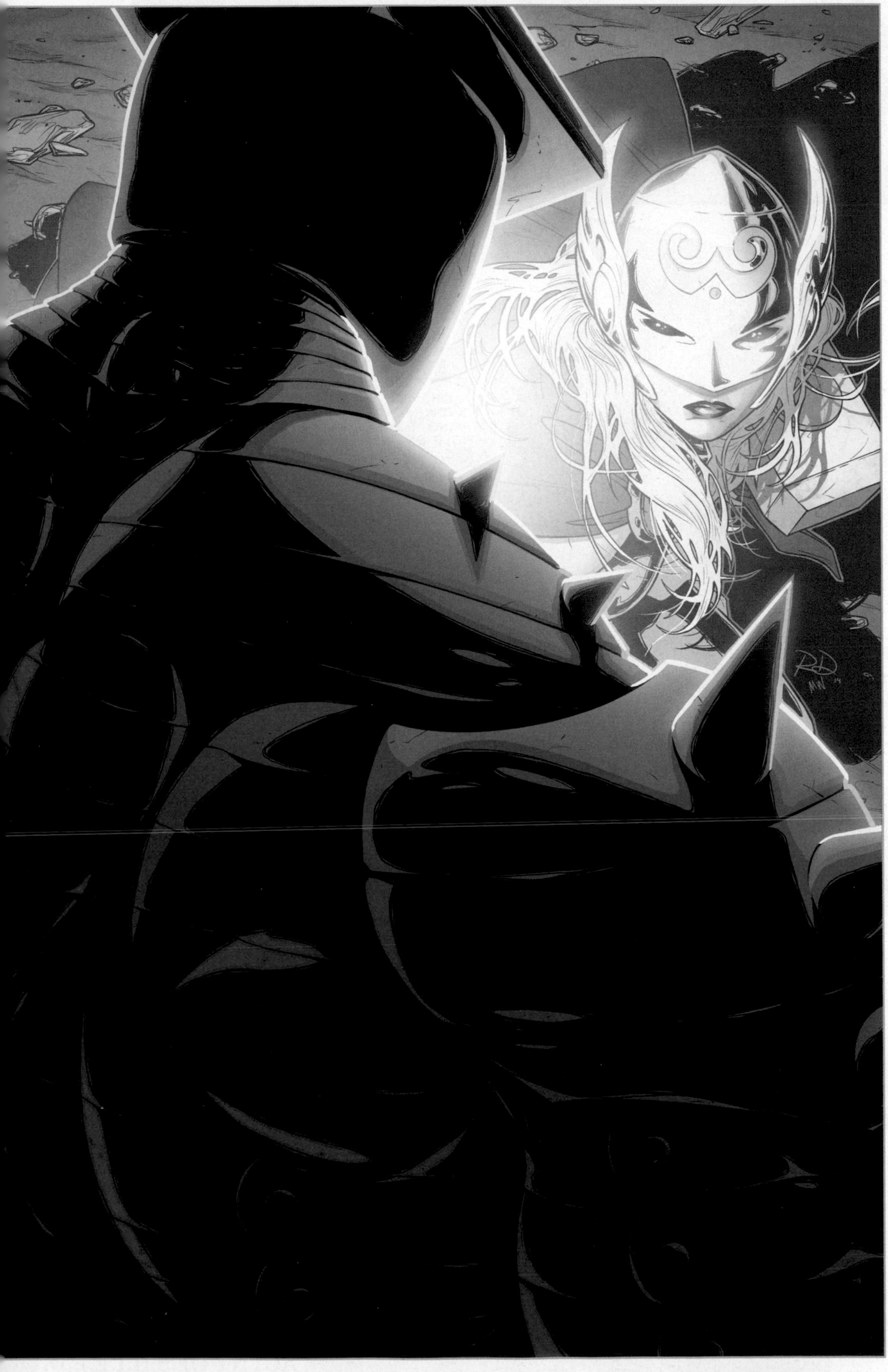

THE BATTLE FOR THE HAMMER

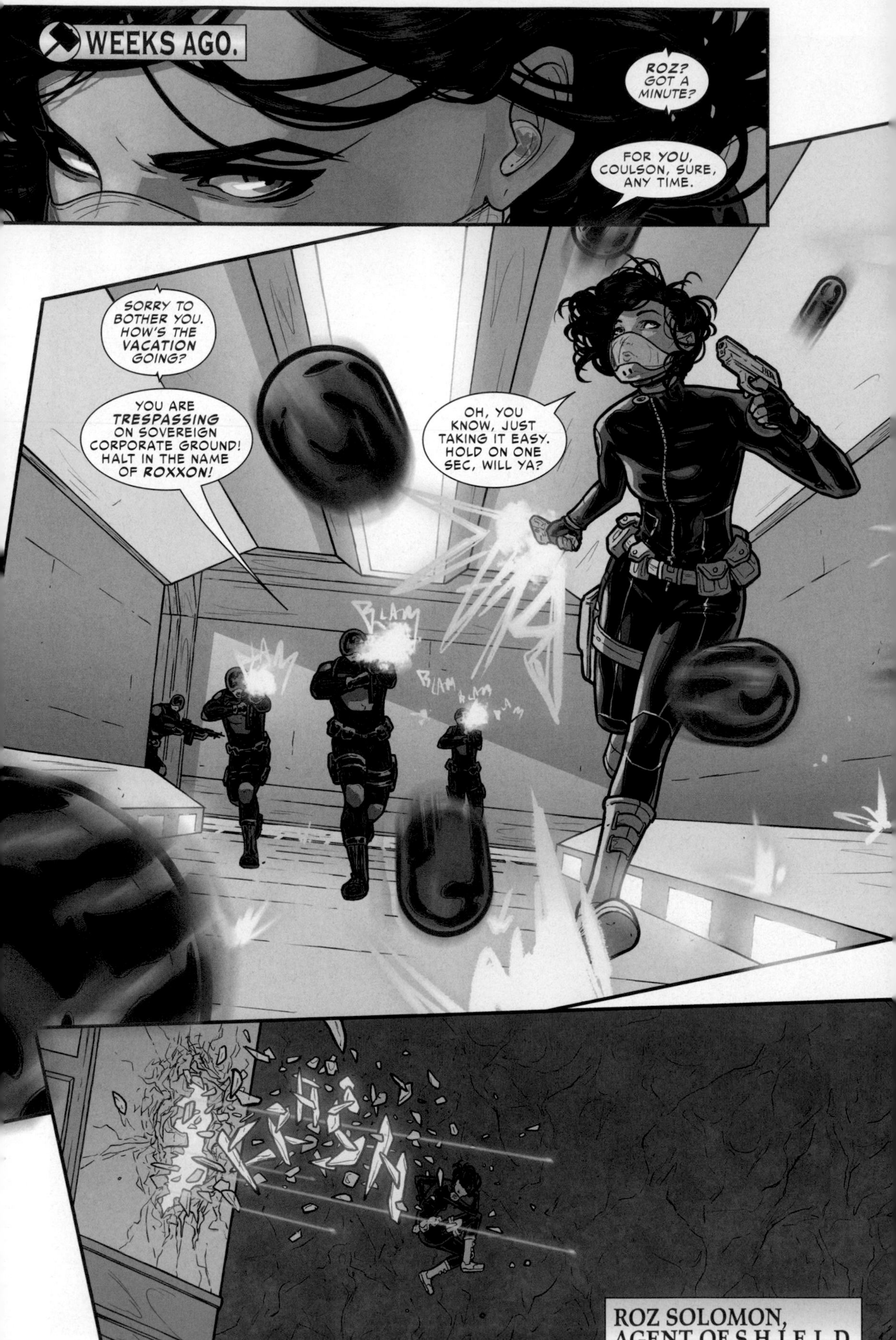

WEEKS AGO.
ROZ? GOT A MINUTE?
FOR YOU, COULSON, SURE, ANY TIME.
SORRY TO BOTHER YOU. HOW'S THE VACATION GOING?
YOU ARE TRESPASSING ON SOVEREIGN CORPORATE GROUND! HALT IN THE NAME OF ROXXON!
OH, YOU KNOW, JUST TAKING IT EASY. HOLD ON ONE SEC, WILL YA?
BLAM
BLAM
BLAM
BLAM
ROZ SOLOMON, AGENT OF S.H.I.E.L.D.
ENVIRONMENTALIST WITH A GUN.

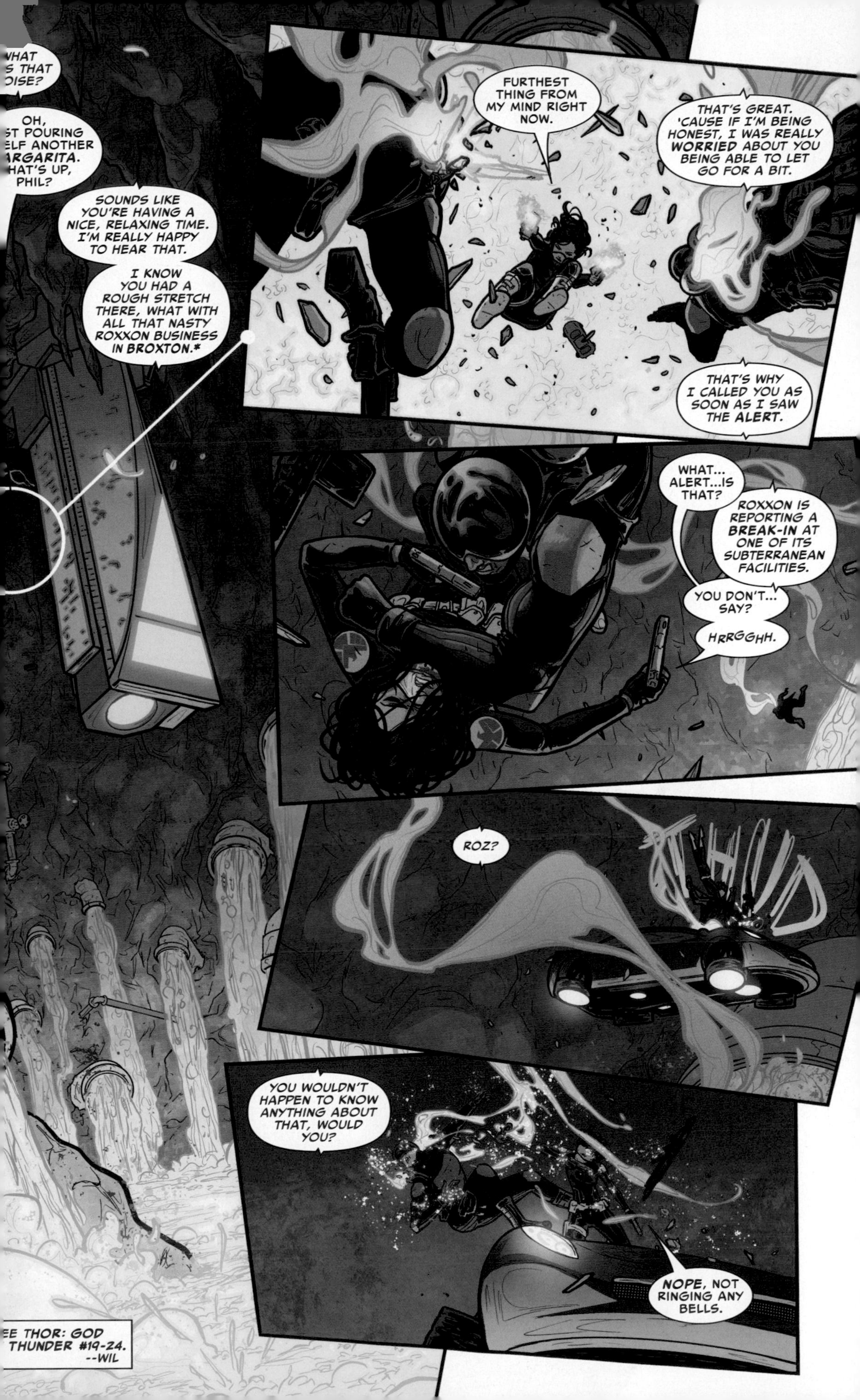
WHAT S THAT OISE?
OH, ST POURING ELF ANOTHER ARGARITA. HAT'S UP, PHIL?
SOUNDS LIKE YOU'RE HAVING A NICE, RELAXING TIME. I'M REALLY HAPPY TO HEAR THAT.
I KNOW YOU HAD A ROUGH STRETCH THERE, WHAT WITH ALL THAT NASTY ROXXON BUSINESS IN BROXTON.*
FURTHEST THING FROM MY MIND RIGHT NOW.
THAT'S GREAT. 'CAUSE IF I'M BEING HONEST, I WAS REALLY WORRIED ABOUT YOU BEING ABLE TO LET GO FOR A BIT.
THAT'S WHY I CALLED YOU AS SOON AS I SAW THE ALERT.
WHAT... ALERT...IS THAT?
ROXXON IS REPORTING A BREAK-IN AT ONE OF ITS SUBTERRANEAN FACILITIES.
YOU DON'T... SAY?
HRRGGHH.
ROZ?
THUD
YOU WOULDN'T HAPPEN TO KNOW ANYTHING ABOUT THAT, WOULD YOU?
NOPE, NOT RINGING ANY BELLS.
EE THOR: GOD THUNDER #19-24. --WIL

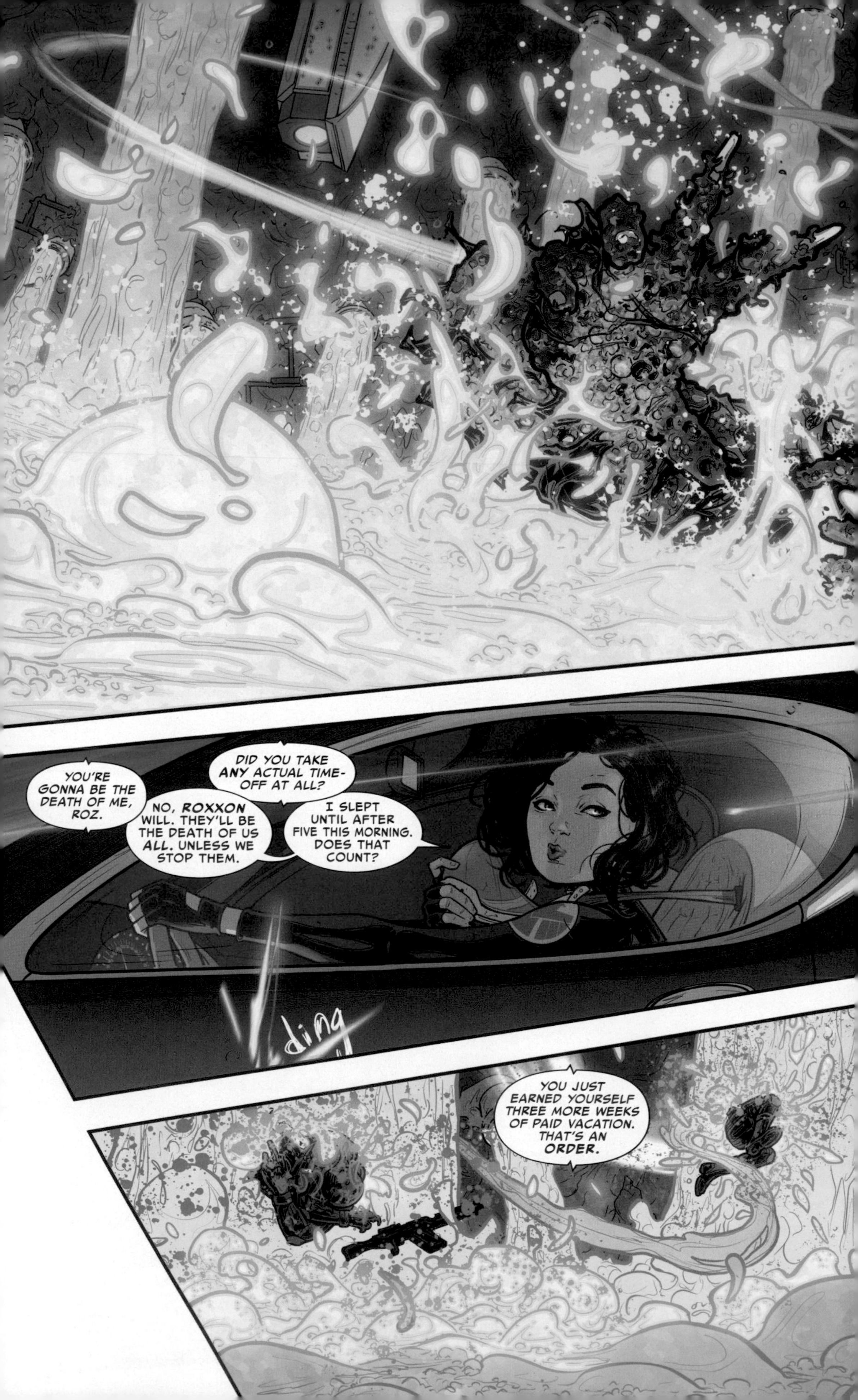
YOU'RE GONNA BE THE DEATH OF ME, ROZ.
NO, ROXXON WILL. THEY'LL BE THE DEATH OF US ALL. UNLESS WE STOP THEM.
DID YOU TAKE ANY ACTUAL TIME-OFF AT ALL?
I SLEPT UNTIL AFTER FIVE THIS MORNING. DOES THAT COUNT?
ding
YOU JUST EARNED YOURSELF THREE MORE WEEKS OF PAID VACATION. THAT'S AN ORDER.

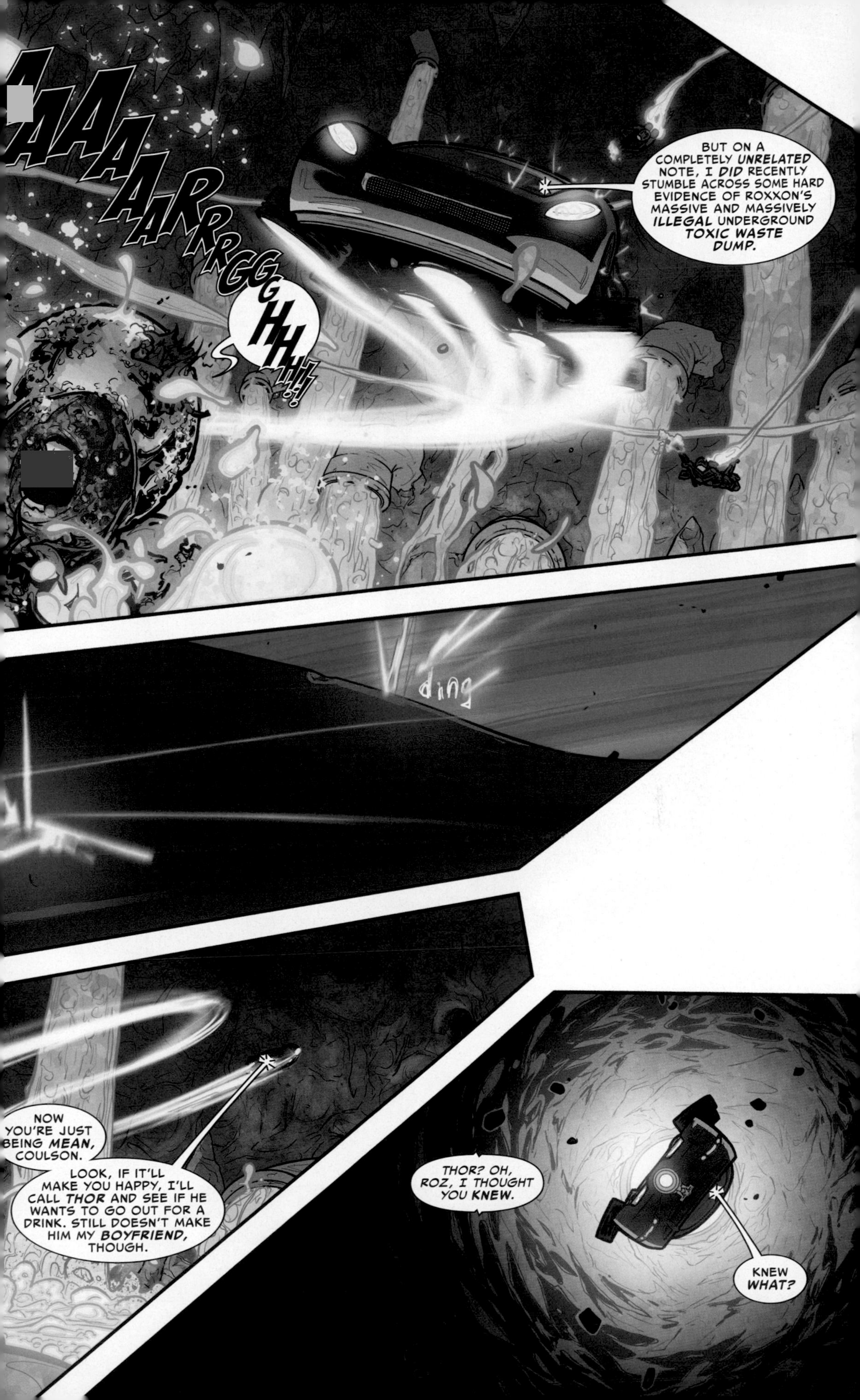
AAAAAARRRGGHHH!!
BUT ON A COMPLETELY UNRELATED NOTE, I DID RECENTLY STUMBLE ACROSS SOME HARD EVIDENCE OF ROXXON'S MASSIVE AND MASSIVELY ILLEGAL UNDERGROUND TOXIC WASTE DUMP.
ding
NOW YOU'RE JUST BEING MEAN, COULSON.
LOOK, IF IT'LL MAKE YOU HAPPY, I'LL CALL THOR AND SEE IF HE WANTS TO GO OUT FOR A DRINK. STILL DOESN'T MAKE HIM MY BOYFRIEND, THOUGH.
THOR? OH, ROZ, I THOUGHT YOU KNEW.
KNEW WHAT?

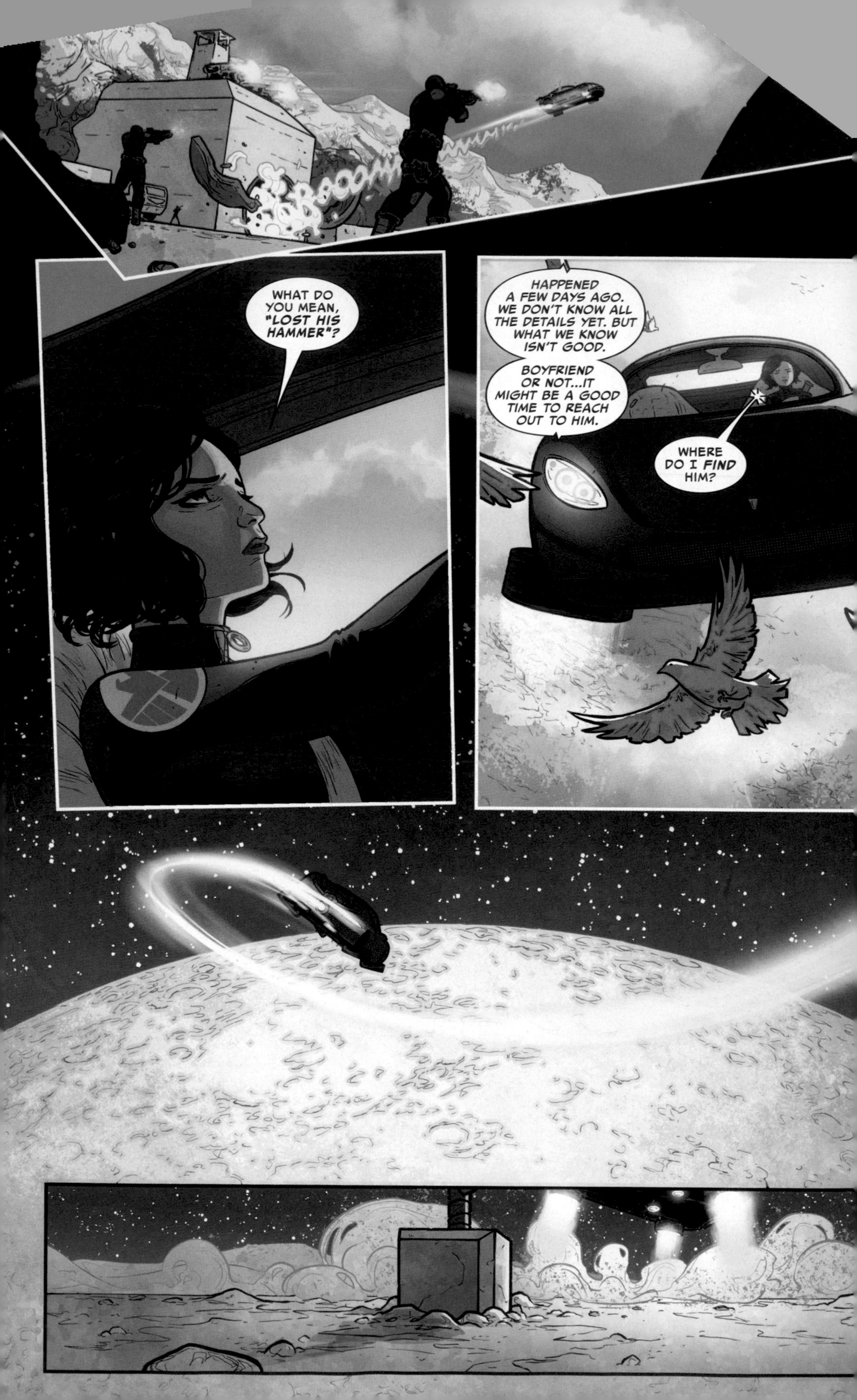

WHAT DO YOU MEAN, "LOST HIS HAMMER"?
HAPPENED A FEW DAYS AGO. WE DON'T KNOW ALL THE DETAILS YET. BUT WHAT WE KNOW ISN'T GOOD.
BOYFRIEND OR NOT...IT MIGHT BE A GOOD TIME TO REACH OUT TO HIM.
WHERE DO I FIND HIM?

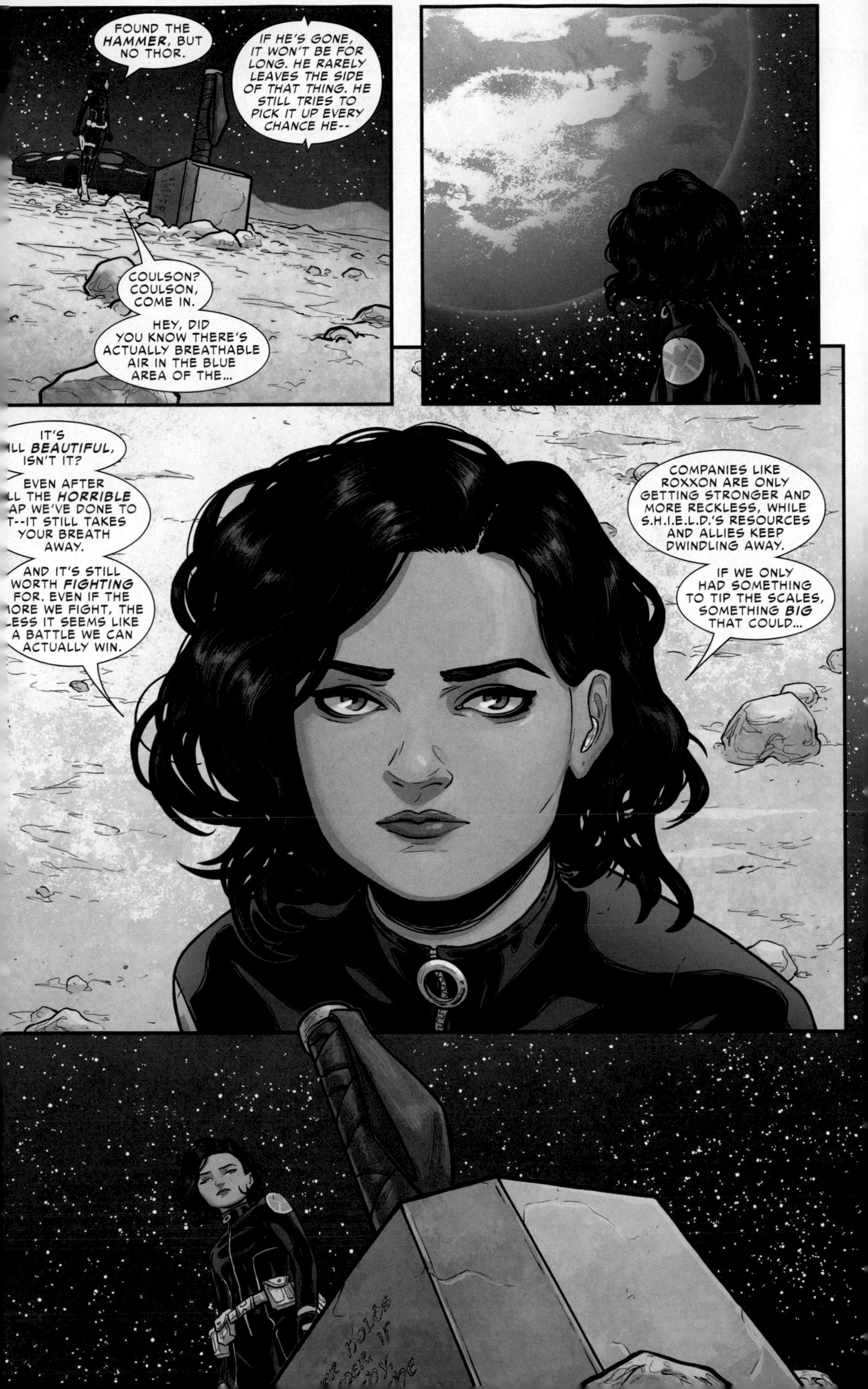

FOUND THE *HAMMER*, BUT NO THOR.
IF HE'S GONE, IT WON'T BE FOR LONG. HE RARELY LEAVES THE SIDE OF THAT THING. HE STILL TRIES TO PICK IT UP EVERY CHANCE HE--
COULSON? COULSON, COME IN.
HEY, DID YOU KNOW THERE'S ACTUALLY BREATHABLE AIR IN THE BLUE AREA OF THE...
IT'S ...LL *BEAUTIFUL*, ISN'T IT?
EVEN AFTER ...LL THE *HORRIBLE* ...AP WE'VE DONE TO ...T--IT STILL TAKES YOUR BREATH AWAY.
AND IT'S STILL WORTH *FIGHTING* FOR. EVEN IF THE ...ORE WE FIGHT, THE ...ESS IT SEEMS LIKE A BATTLE WE CAN ACTUALLY WIN.
COMPANIES LIKE ROXXON ARE ONLY GETTING STRONGER AND MORE RECKLESS, WHILE S.H.I.E.L.D.'S RESOURCES AND ALLIES KEEP DWINDLING AWAY.
IF WE ONLY HAD SOMETHING TO TIP THE SCALES, SOMETHING *BIG* THAT COULD...

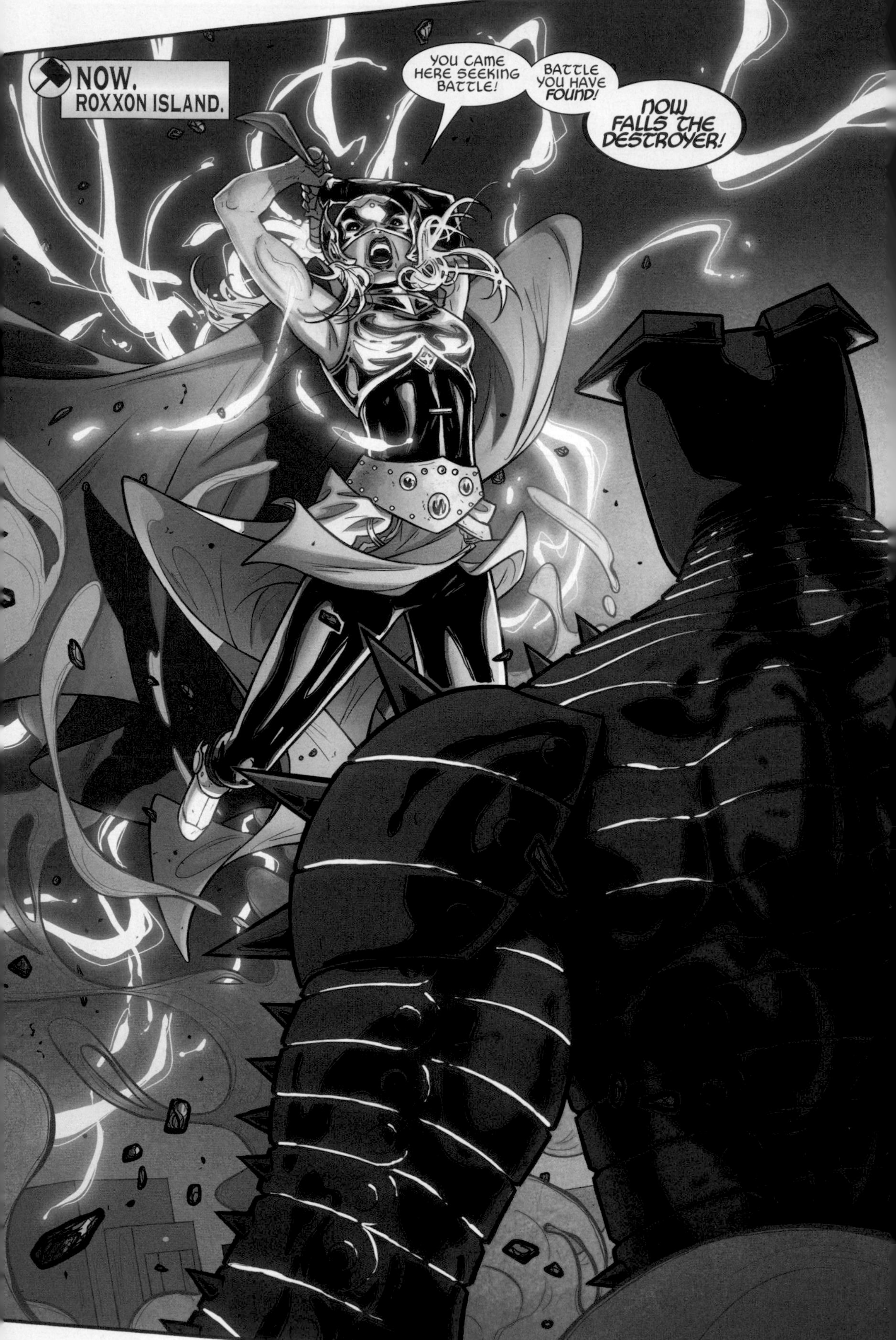
NOW.
ROXXON ISLAND.
YOU CAME HERE SEEKING BATTLE!
BATTLE YOU HAVE FOUND!
NOW FALLS THE DESTROYER!

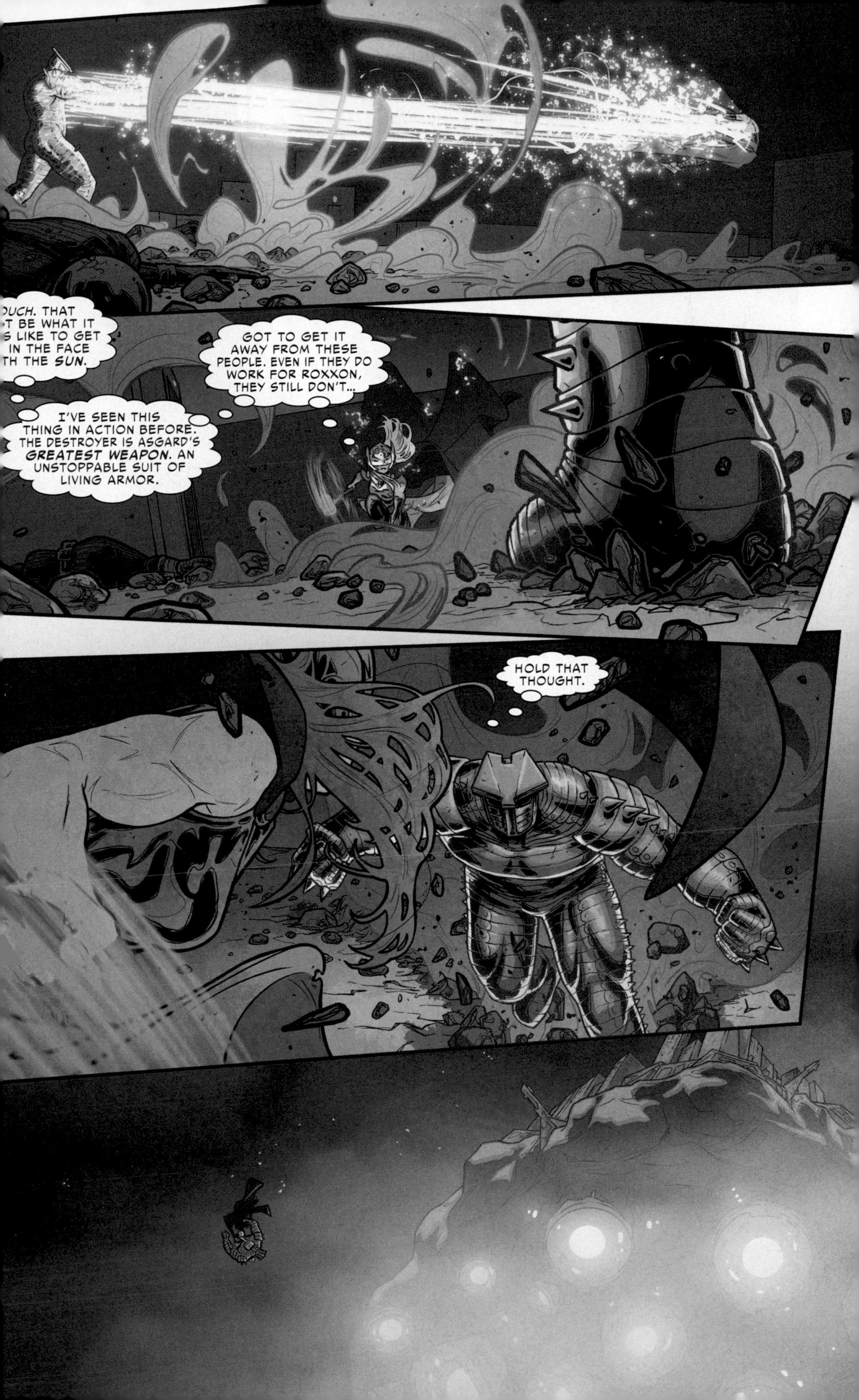

OUCH. THAT T BE WHAT IT S LIKE TO GET IN THE FACE TH THE SUN.
GOT TO GET IT AWAY FROM THESE PEOPLE. EVEN IF THEY DO WORK FOR ROXXON, THEY STILL DON'T...
I'VE SEEN THIS THING IN ACTION BEFORE. THE DESTROYER IS ASGARD'S GREATEST WEAPON. AN UNSTOPPABLE SUIT OF LIVING ARMOR.
HOLD THAT THOUGHT.

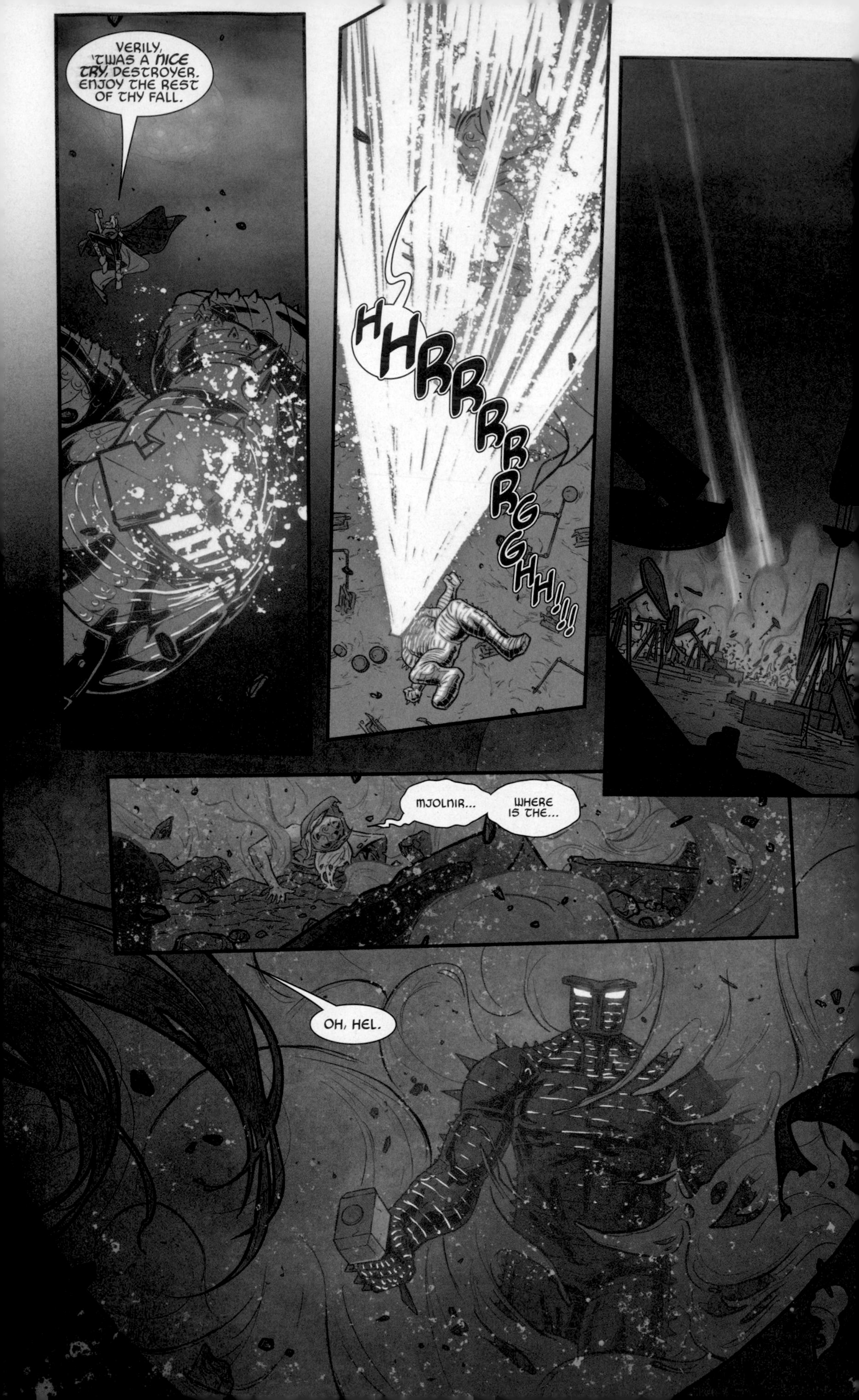
VERILY, 'TWAS A NICE TRY, DESTROYER. ENJOY THE REST OF THY FALL.
HHRRRRRRGGHH!!!
MJOLNIR...
WHERE IS THE...
OH, HEL.

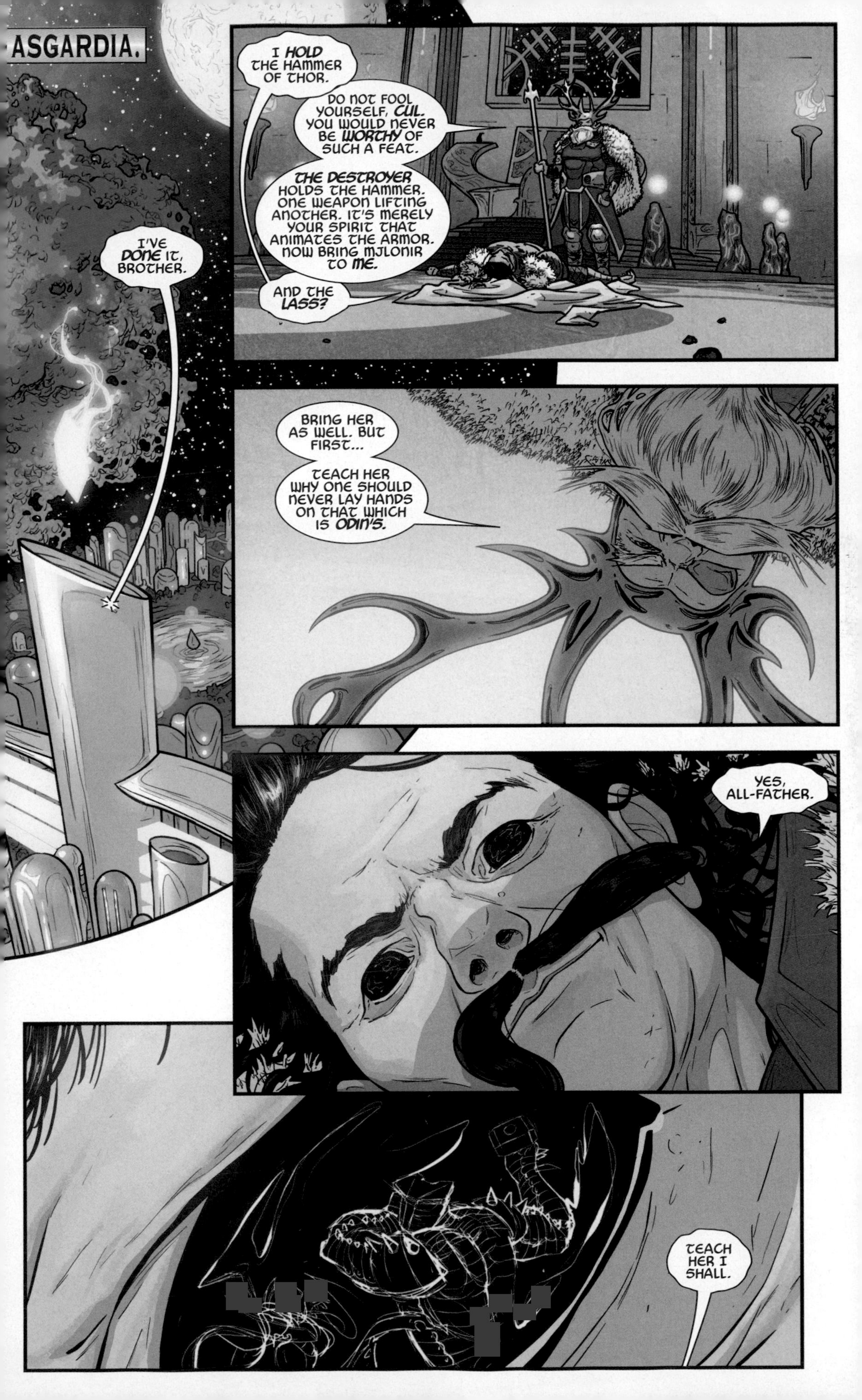
ASGARDIA.
I'VE DONE IT, BROTHER.
I HOLD THE HAMMER OF THOR.
DO NOT FOOL YOURSELF, CUL. YOU WOULD NEVER BE WORTHY OF SUCH A FEAT.
THE DESTROYER HOLDS THE HAMMER. ONE WEAPON LIFTING ANOTHER. IT'S MERELY YOUR SPIRIT THAT ANIMATES THE ARMOR. NOW BRING MJLONIR TO ME.
AND THE LASS?
BRING HER AS WELL. BUT FIRST...
TEACH HER WHY ONE SHOULD NEVER LAY HANDS ON THAT WHICH IS ODIN'S.
YES, ALL-FATHER.
TEACH HER I SHALL.

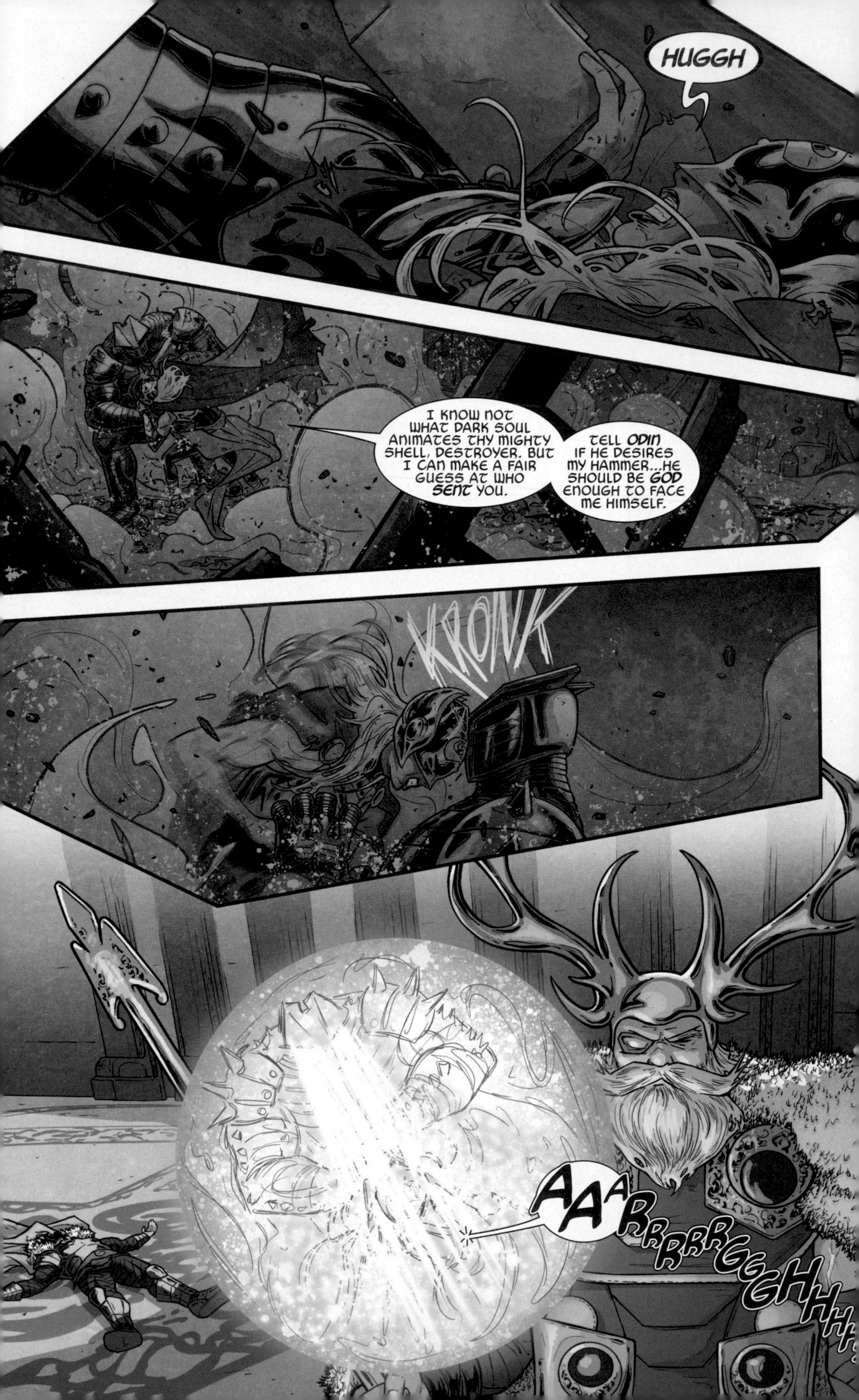
HUGGH
I KNOW NOT WHAT DARK SOUL ANIMATES THY MIGHTY SHELL, DESTROYER. BUT I CAN MAKE A FAIR GUESS AT WHO SENT YOU.
TELL ODIN IF HE DESIRES MY HAMMER...HE SHOULD BE GOD ENOUGH TO FACE ME HIMSELF.
KRONK
AAARRRRRRGGGHHH

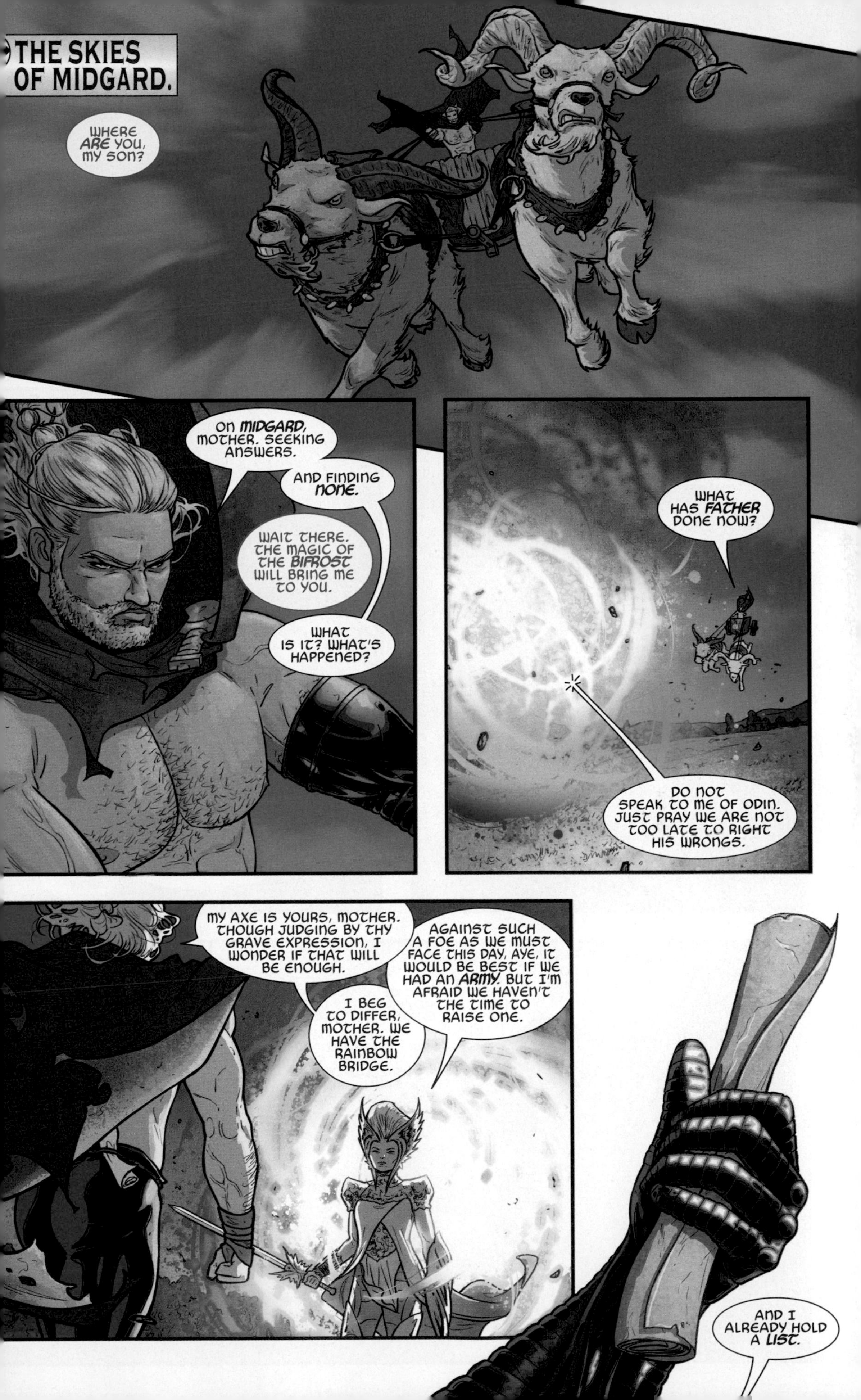
THE SKIES OF MIDGARD.
WHERE ARE YOU, MY SON?
ON MIDGARD, MOTHER. SEEKING ANSWERS.
AND FINDING NONE.
WAIT THERE. THE MAGIC OF THE BIFROST WILL BRING ME TO YOU.
WHAT IS IT? WHAT'S HAPPENED?
WHAT HAS FATHER DONE NOW?
DO NOT SPEAK TO ME OF ODIN. JUST PRAY WE ARE NOT TOO LATE TO RIGHT HIS WRONGS.
MY AXE IS YOURS, MOTHER. THOUGH JUDGING BY THY GRAVE EXPRESSION, I WONDER IF THAT WILL BE ENOUGH.
AGAINST SUCH A FOE AS WE MUST FACE THIS DAY, AYE, IT WOULD BE BEST IF WE HAD AN ARMY. BUT I'M AFRAID WE HAVEN'T THE TIME TO RAISE ONE.
I BEG TO DIFFER, MOTHER. WE HAVE THE RAINBOW BRIDGE.
AND I ALREADY HOLD A LIST.

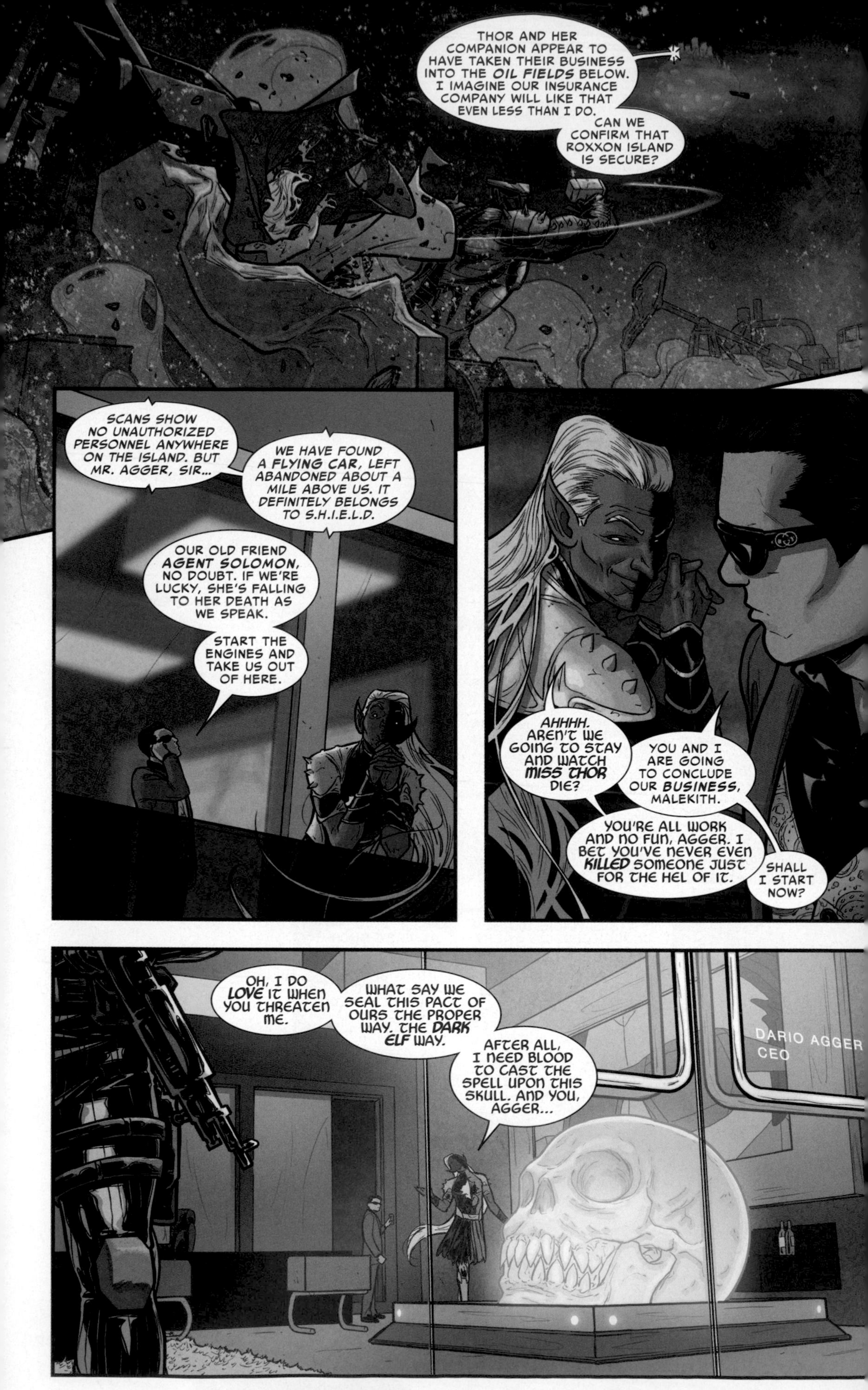
THOR AND HER COMPANION APPEAR TO HAVE TAKEN THEIR BUSINESS INTO THE OIL FIELDS BELOW. I IMAGINE OUR INSURANCE COMPANY WILL LIKE THAT EVEN LESS THAN I DO.
CAN WE CONFIRM THAT ROXXON ISLAND IS SECURE?
SCANS SHOW NO UNAUTHORIZED PERSONNEL ANYWHERE ON THE ISLAND. BUT MR. AGGER, SIR...
WE HAVE FOUND A FLYING CAR, LEFT ABANDONED ABOUT A MILE ABOVE US. IT DEFINITELY BELONGS TO S.H.I.E.L.D.
OUR OLD FRIEND AGENT SOLOMON, NO DOUBT. IF WE'RE LUCKY, SHE'S FALLING TO HER DEATH AS WE SPEAK.
START THE ENGINES AND TAKE US OUT OF HERE.
AHHHH. AREN'T WE GOING TO STAY AND WATCH MISS THOR DIE?
YOU AND I ARE GOING TO CONCLUDE OUR BUSINESS, MALEKITH.
YOU'RE ALL WORK AND NO FUN, AGGER. I BET YOU'VE NEVER EVEN KILLED SOMEONE JUST FOR THE HEL OF IT.
SHALL I START NOW?
OH, I DO LOVE IT WHEN YOU THREATEN ME.
WHAT SAY WE SEAL THIS PACT OF OURS THE PROPER WAY. THE DARK ELF WAY.
AFTER ALL, I NEED BLOOD TO CAST THE SPELL UPON THIS SKULL. AND YOU, AGGER...
DARIO AGGER
CEO

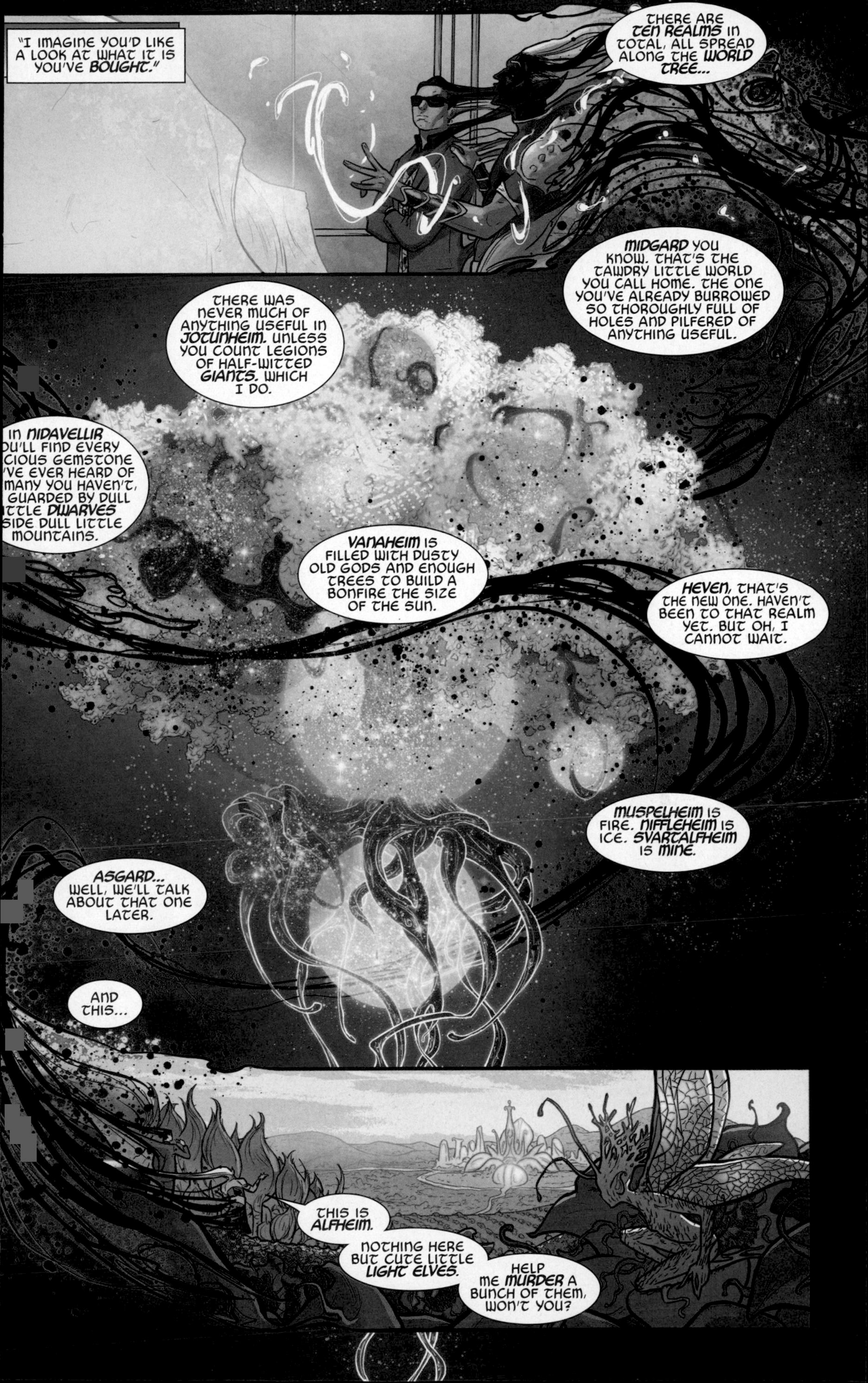
"I IMAGINE YOU'D LIKE A LOOK AT WHAT IT IS YOU'VE BOUGHT."
THERE ARE TEN REALMS IN TOTAL, ALL SPREAD ALONG THE WORLD TREE...
MIDGARD YOU KNOW. THAT'S THE TAWDRY LITTLE WORLD YOU CALL HOME. THE ONE YOU'VE ALREADY BURROWED SO THOROUGHLY FULL OF HOLES AND PILFERED OF ANYTHING USEFUL.
THERE WAS NEVER MUCH OF ANYTHING USEFUL IN JOTUNHEIM. UNLESS YOU COUNT LEGIONS OF HALF-WITTED GIANTS. WHICH I DO.
IN NIDAVELLIR OU'LL FIND EVERY CIOUS GEMSTONE 'VE EVER HEARD OF MANY YOU HAVEN'T, GUARDED BY DULL TTLE DWARVES SIDE DULL LITTLE MOUNTAINS.
VANAHEIM IS FILLED WITH DUSTY OLD GODS AND ENOUGH TREES TO BUILD A BONFIRE THE SIZE OF THE SUN.
HEVEN, THAT'S THE NEW ONE. HAVEN'T BEEN TO THAT REALM YET. BUT OH, I CANNOT WAIT.
MUSPELHEIM IS FIRE. NIFFLEHEIM IS ICE. SVARTALFHEIM IS MINE.
ASGARD... WELL, WE'LL TALK ABOUT THAT ONE LATER.
AND THIS...
THIS IS ALFHEIM.
NOTHING HERE BUT CUTE LITTLE LIGHT ELVES.
HELP ME MURDER A BUNCH OF THEM, WON'T YOU?

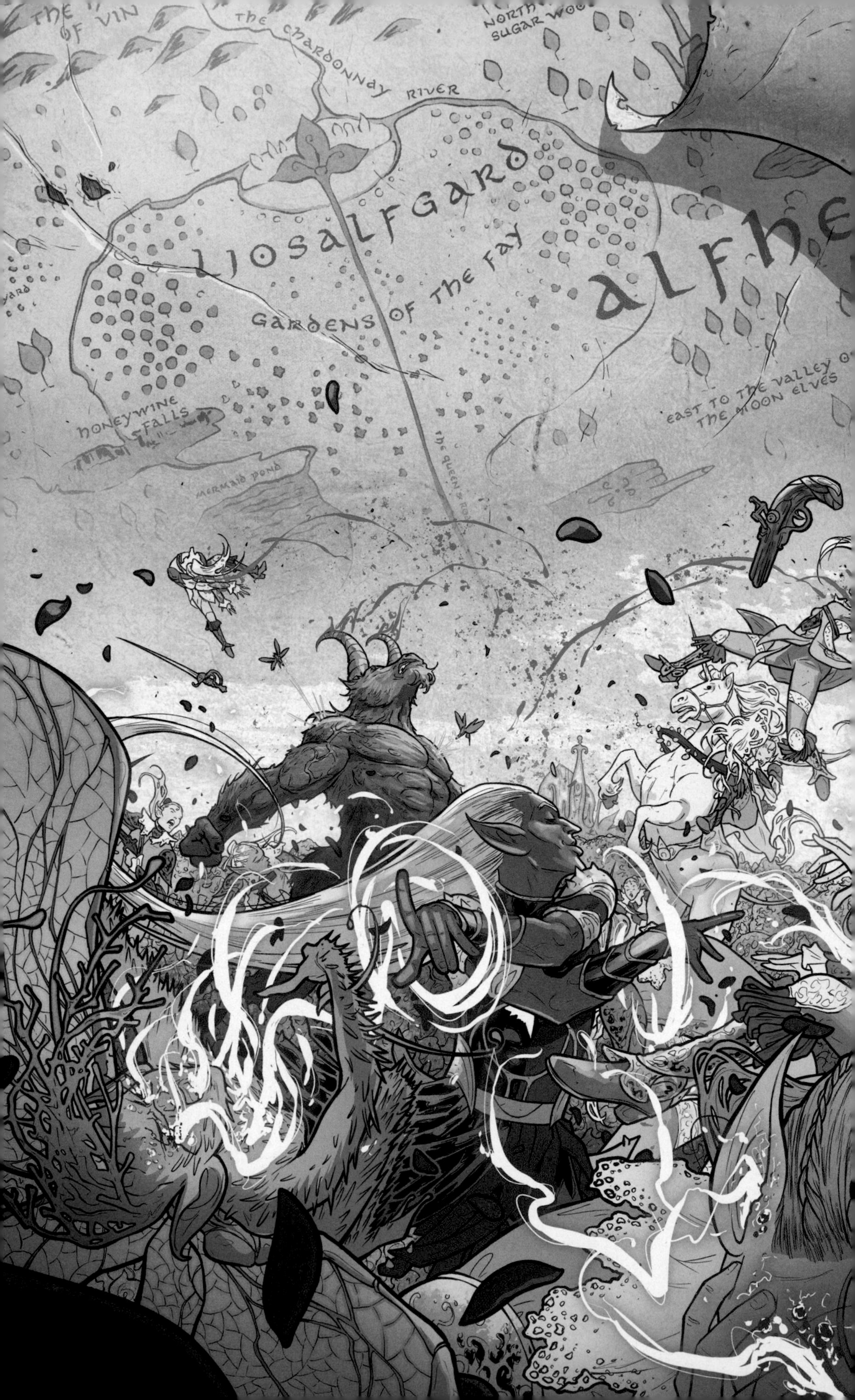
THE CHARDONNAY RIVER
NORTH SUGAR
LIOSALFGARD
GARDENS OF THE FAY
HONEYWINE FALLS
MERMAID POND
EAST TO THE VALLEY
THE MOON ELVES

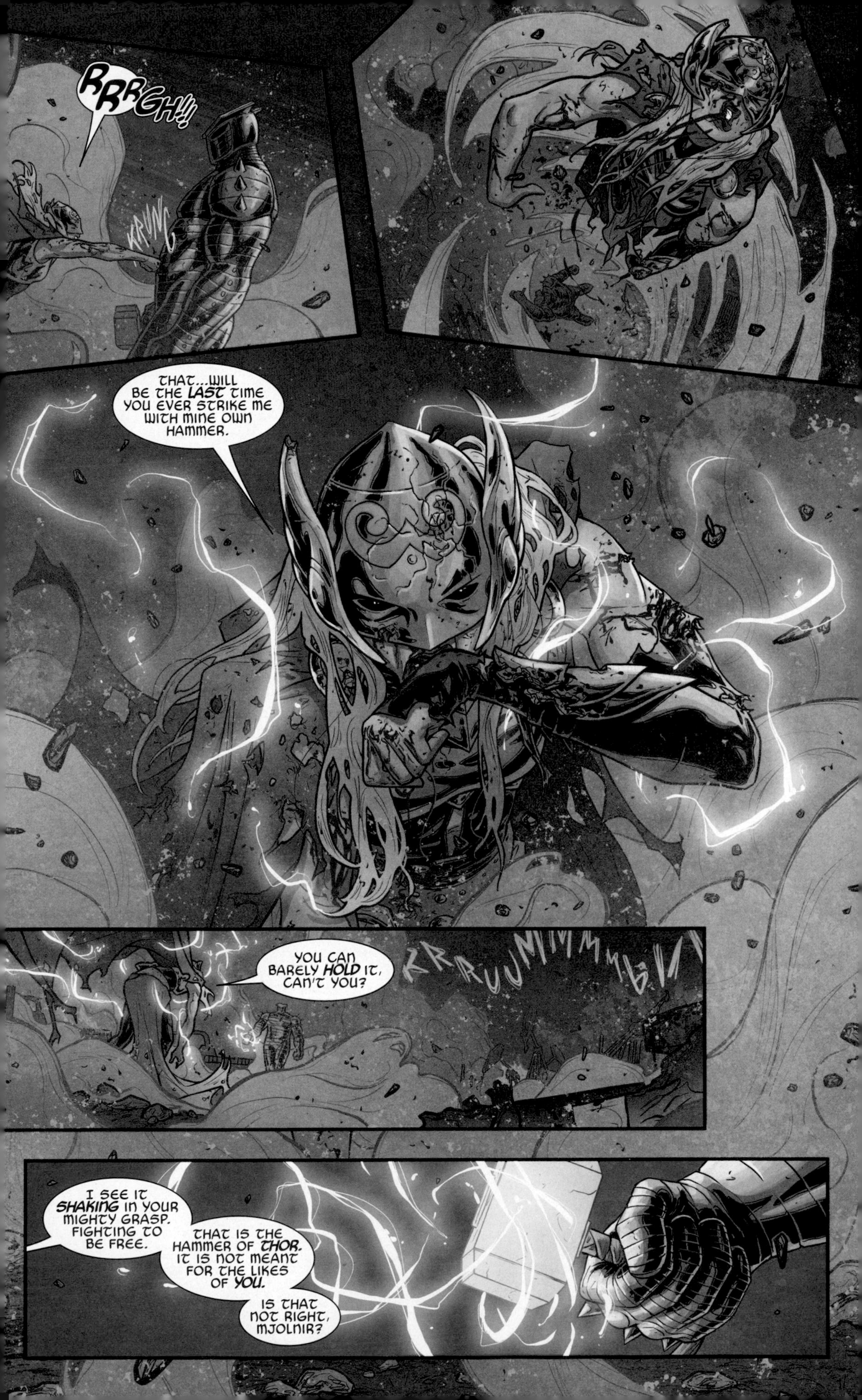
RRRGH!!
KRUNG
THAT...WILL BE THE LAST TIME YOU EVER STRIKE ME WITH MINE OWN HAMMER.
YOU CAN BARELY HOLD IT, CAN'T YOU?
KRRUUMMMMBLL
I SEE IT SHAKING IN YOUR MIGHTY GRASP. FIGHTING TO BE FREE.
THAT IS THE HAMMER OF THOR. IT IS NOT MEANT FOR THE LIKES OF YOU.
IS THAT NOT RIGHT, MJOLNIR?

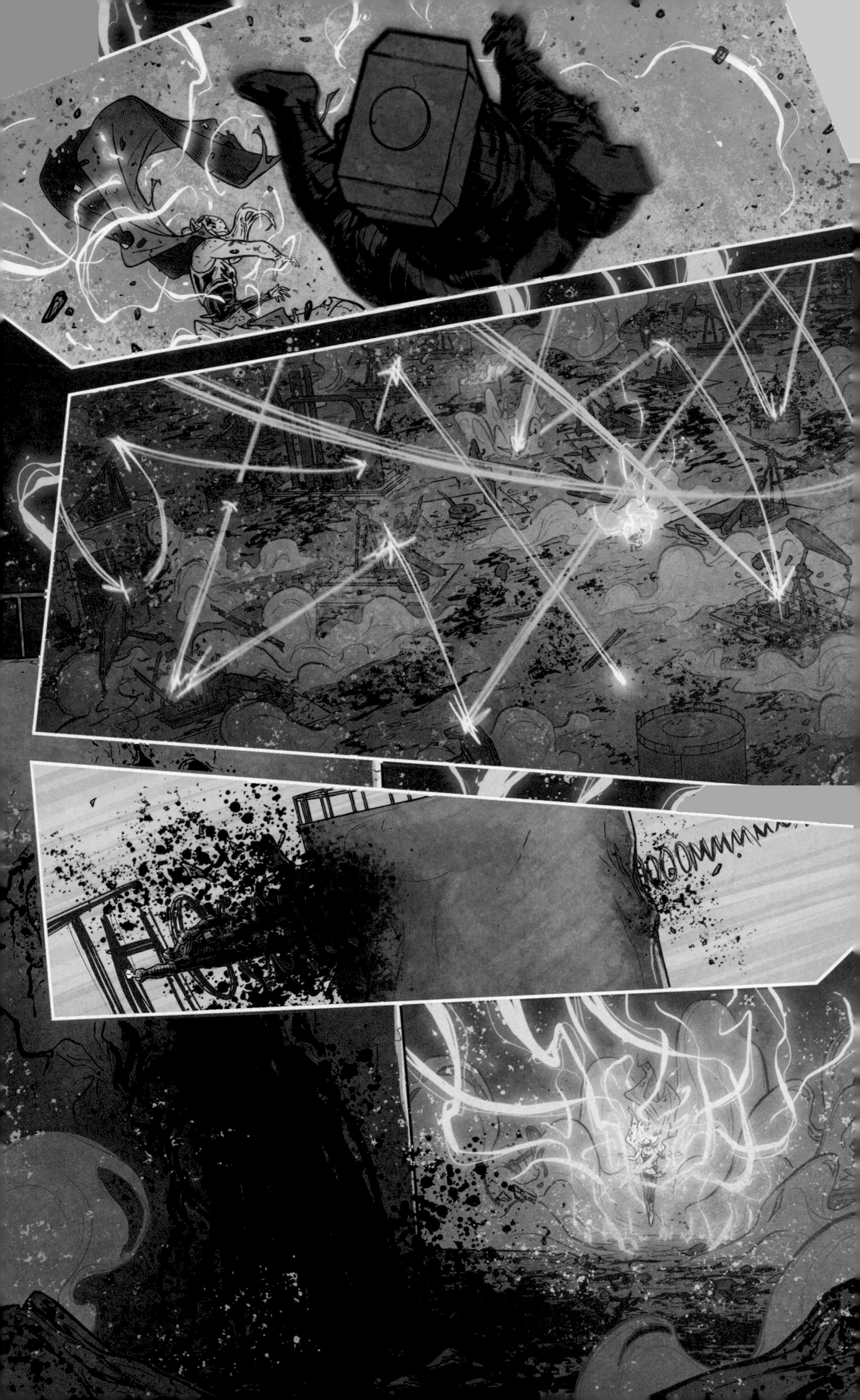

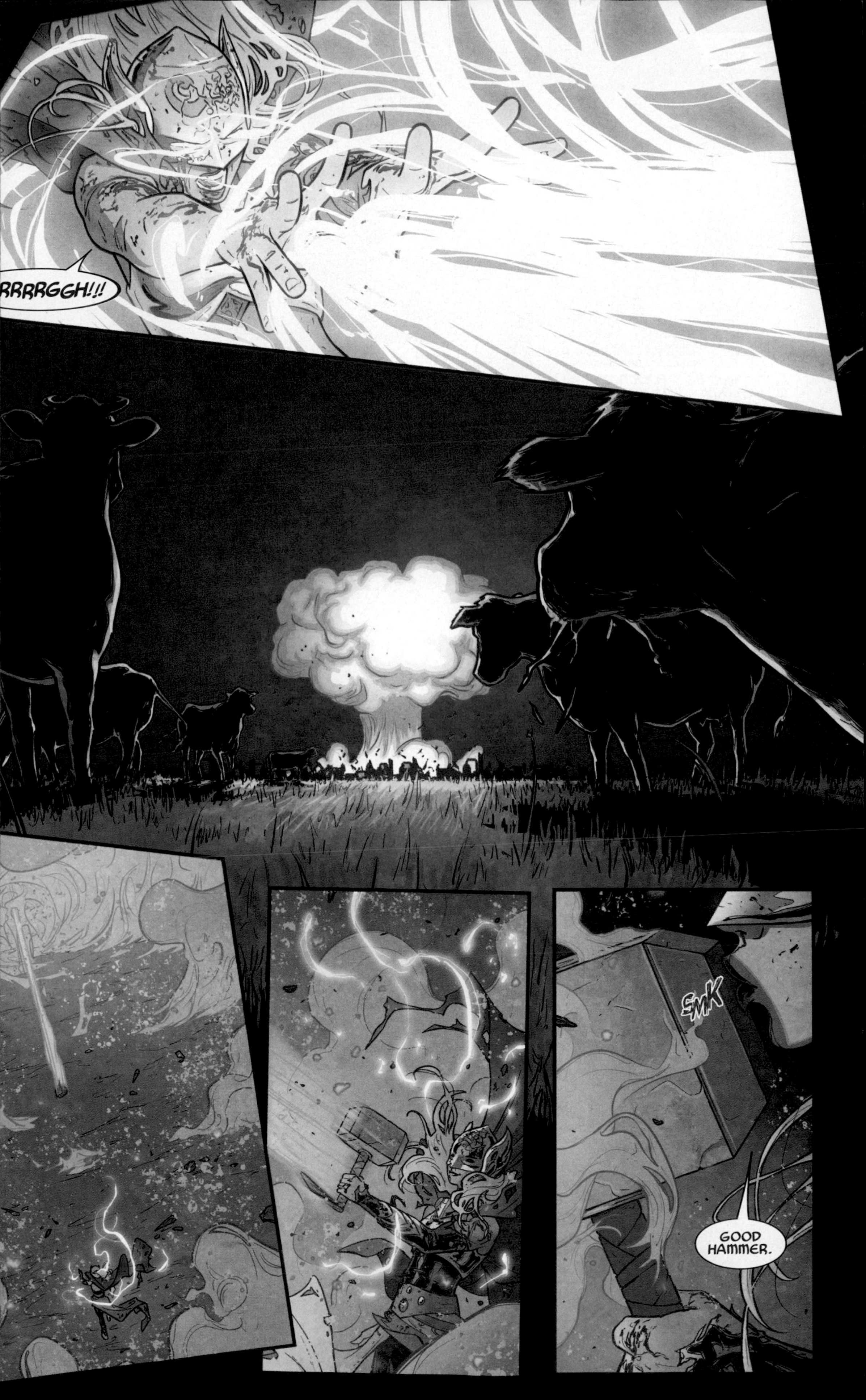
RRRRGGH!!!
SMK
GOOD HAMMER.

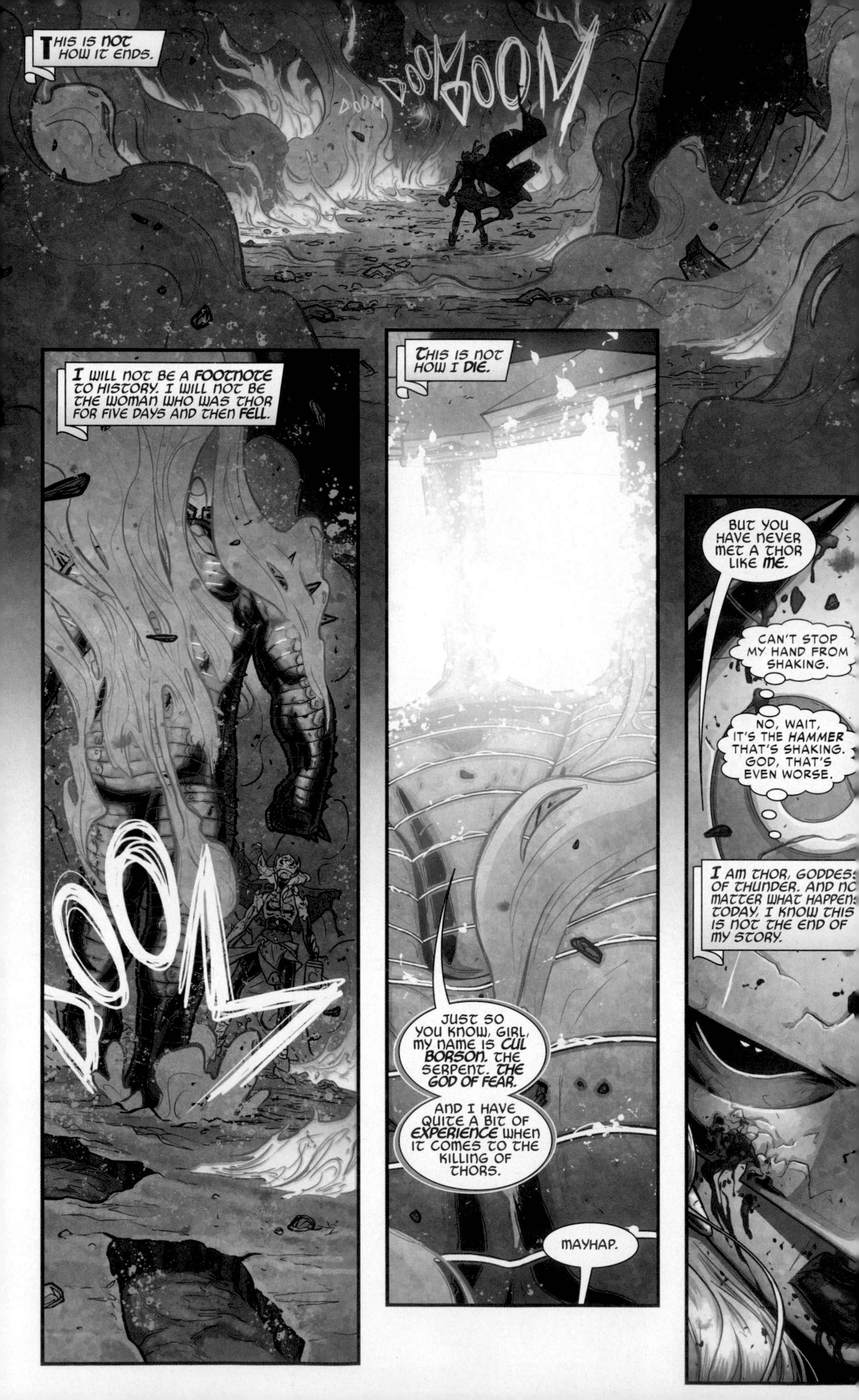
THIS IS NOT HOW IT ENDS.
DOOM DOOM DOOM DOOM
I WILL NOT BE A FOOTNOTE TO HISTORY. I WILL NOT BE THE WOMAN WHO WAS THOR FOR FIVE DAYS AND THEN FELL.
DOOM
THIS IS NOT HOW I DIE.
JUST SO YOU KNOW, GIRL, MY NAME IS CUL BORSON. THE SERPENT. THE GOD OF FEAR.
AND I HAVE QUITE A BIT OF EXPERIENCE WHEN IT COMES TO THE KILLING OF THORS.
MAYHAP.
BUT YOU HAVE NEVER MET A THOR LIKE ME.
CAN'T STOP MY HAND FROM SHAKING.
NO, WAIT, IT'S THE HAMMER THAT'S SHAKING. GOD, THAT'S EVEN WORSE.
I AM THOR, GODDES OF THUNDER. AND NO MATTER WHAT HAPPEN TODAY, I KNOW THIS IS NOT THE END OF MY STORY.

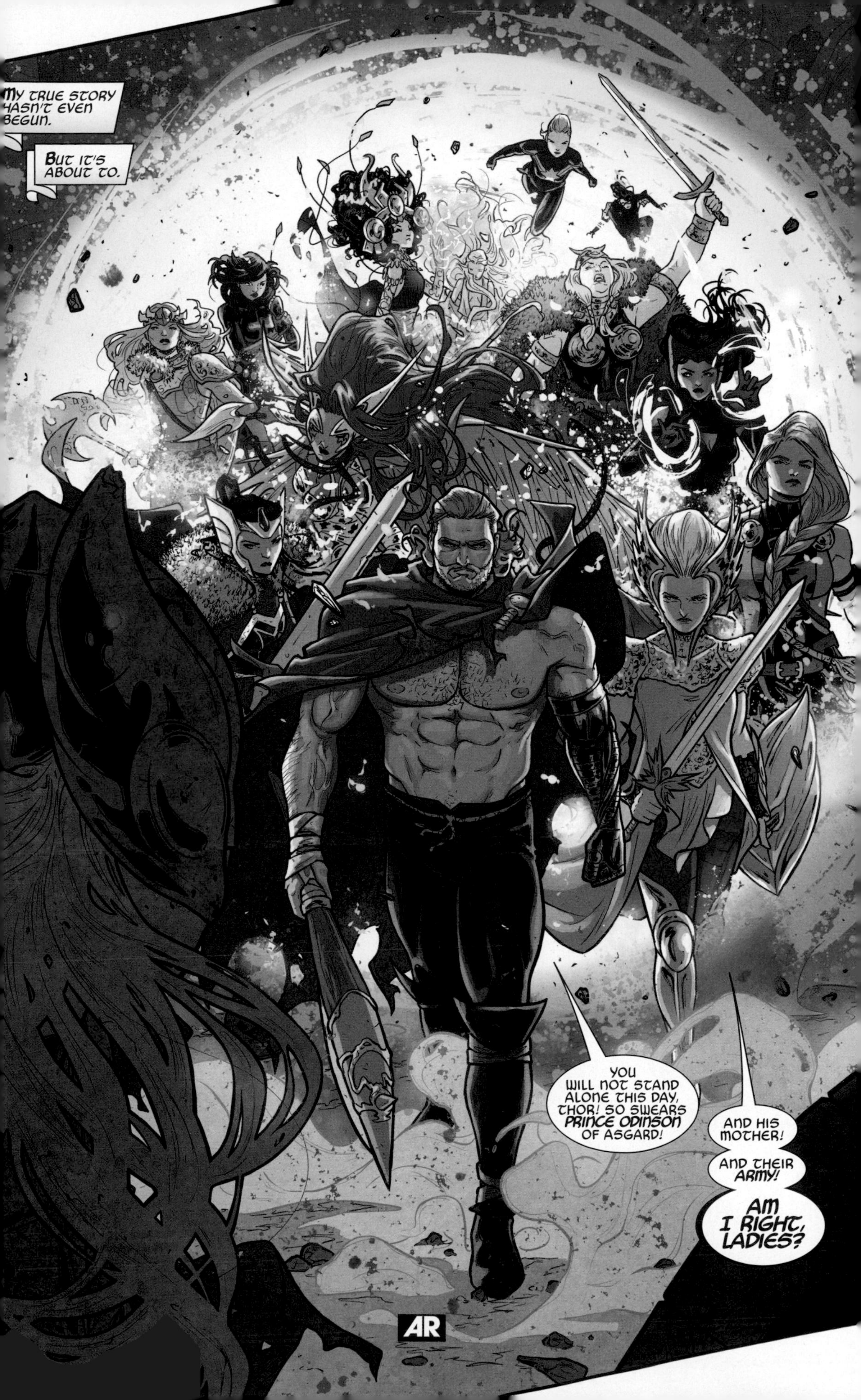

MY TRUE STORY HASN'T EVEN BEGUN.
BUT IT'S ABOUT TO.
YOU WILL NOT STAND ALONE THIS DAY, THOR! SO SWEARS PRINCE ODINSON OF ASGARD!
AND HIS MOTHER!
AND THEIR ARMY!
AM I RIGHT, LADIES?
AR

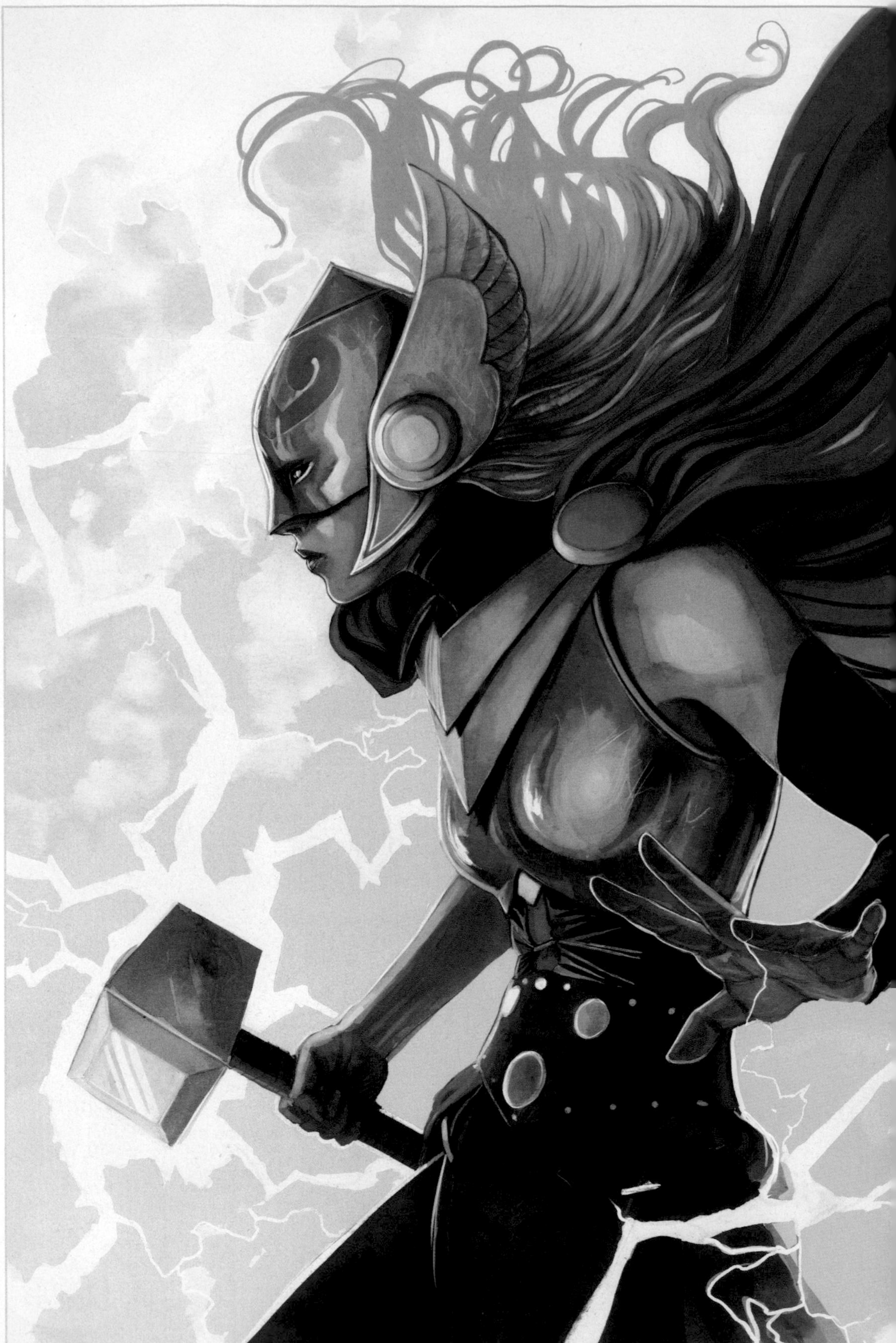

THOR # 6 WOMEN OF MARVEL VARIANT
BY **STEPHANIE HANS**

8

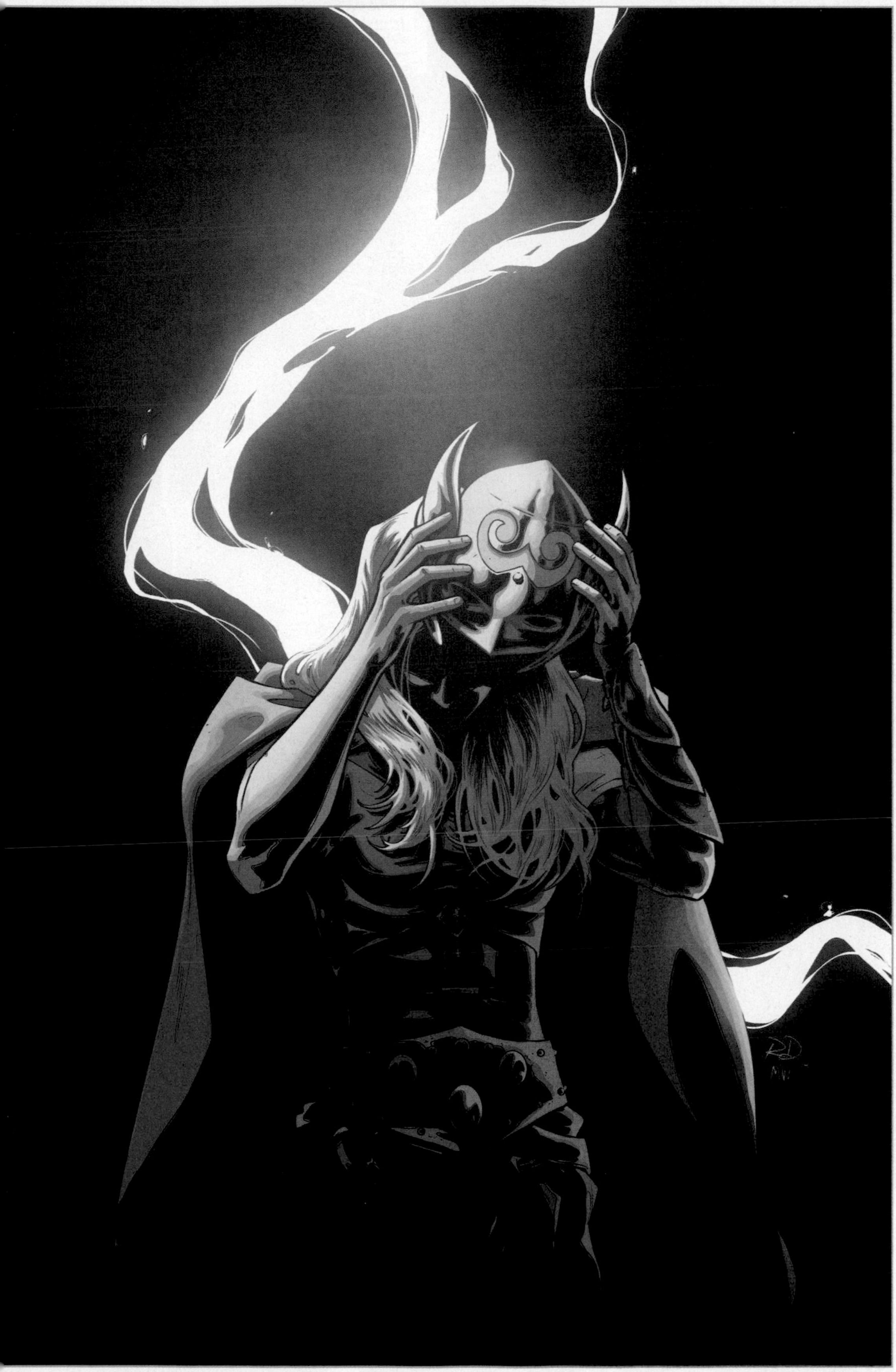

THE WOMAN BENEATH THE MASK

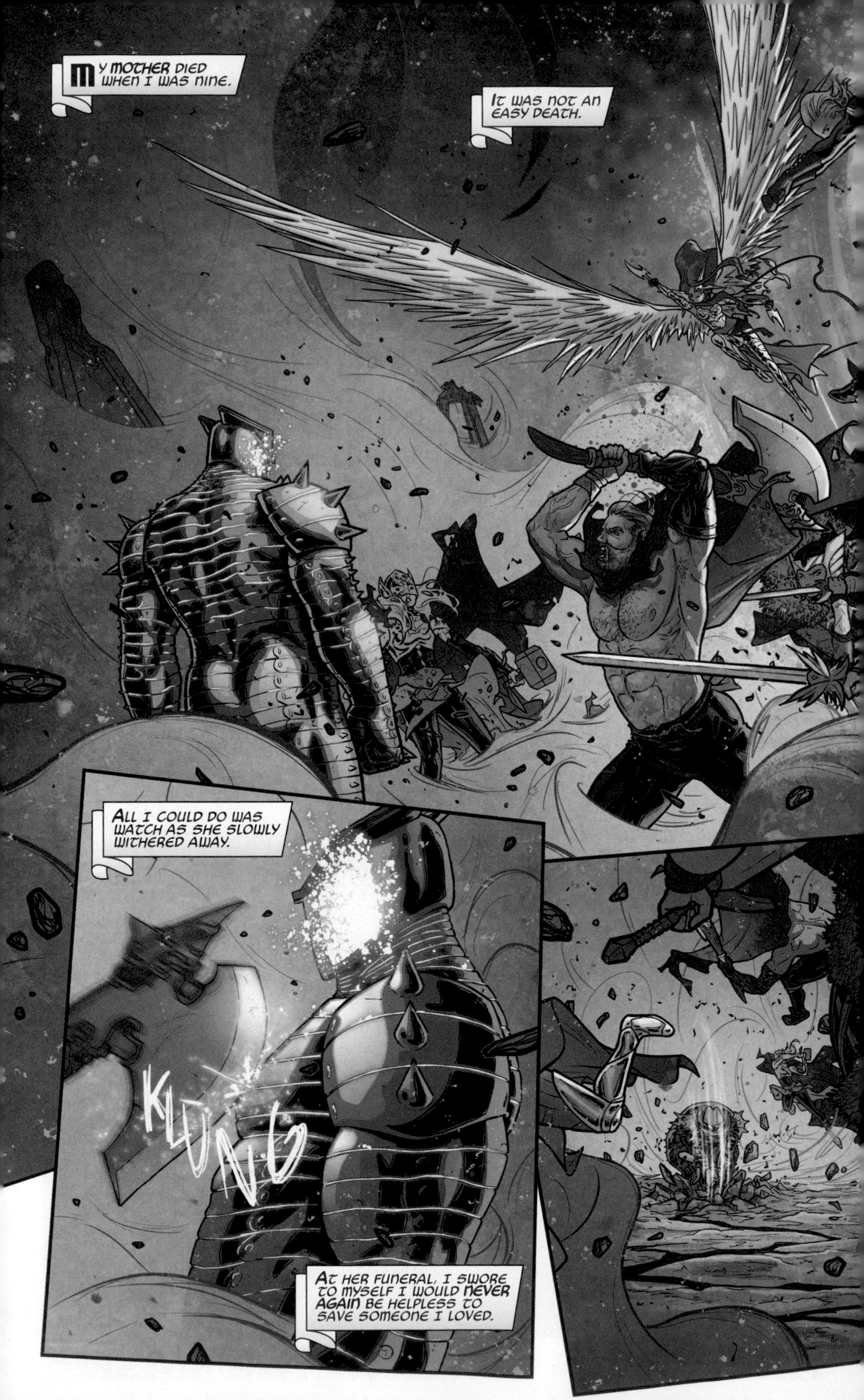

MY MOTHER DIED WHEN I WAS NINE.
IT WAS NOT AN EASY DEATH.
ALL I COULD DO WAS WATCH AS SHE SLOWLY WITHERED AWAY.
KLUNG
AT HER FUNERAL, I SWORE TO MYSELF I WOULD NEVER AGAIN BE HELPLESS TO SAVE SOMEONE I LOVED.

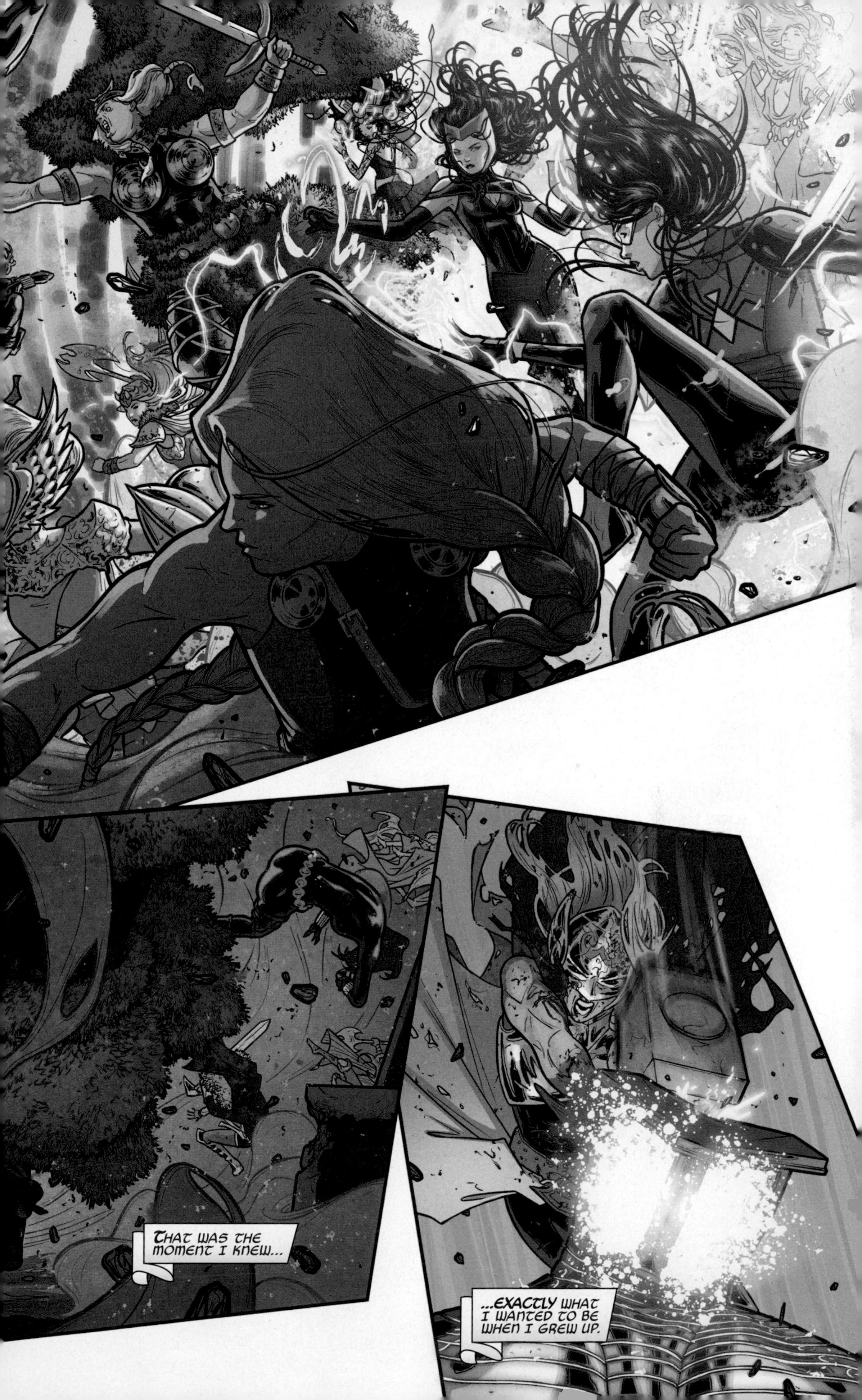
THAT WAS THE MOMENT I KNEW...
...EXACTLY WHAT I WANTED TO BE WHEN I GREW UP.

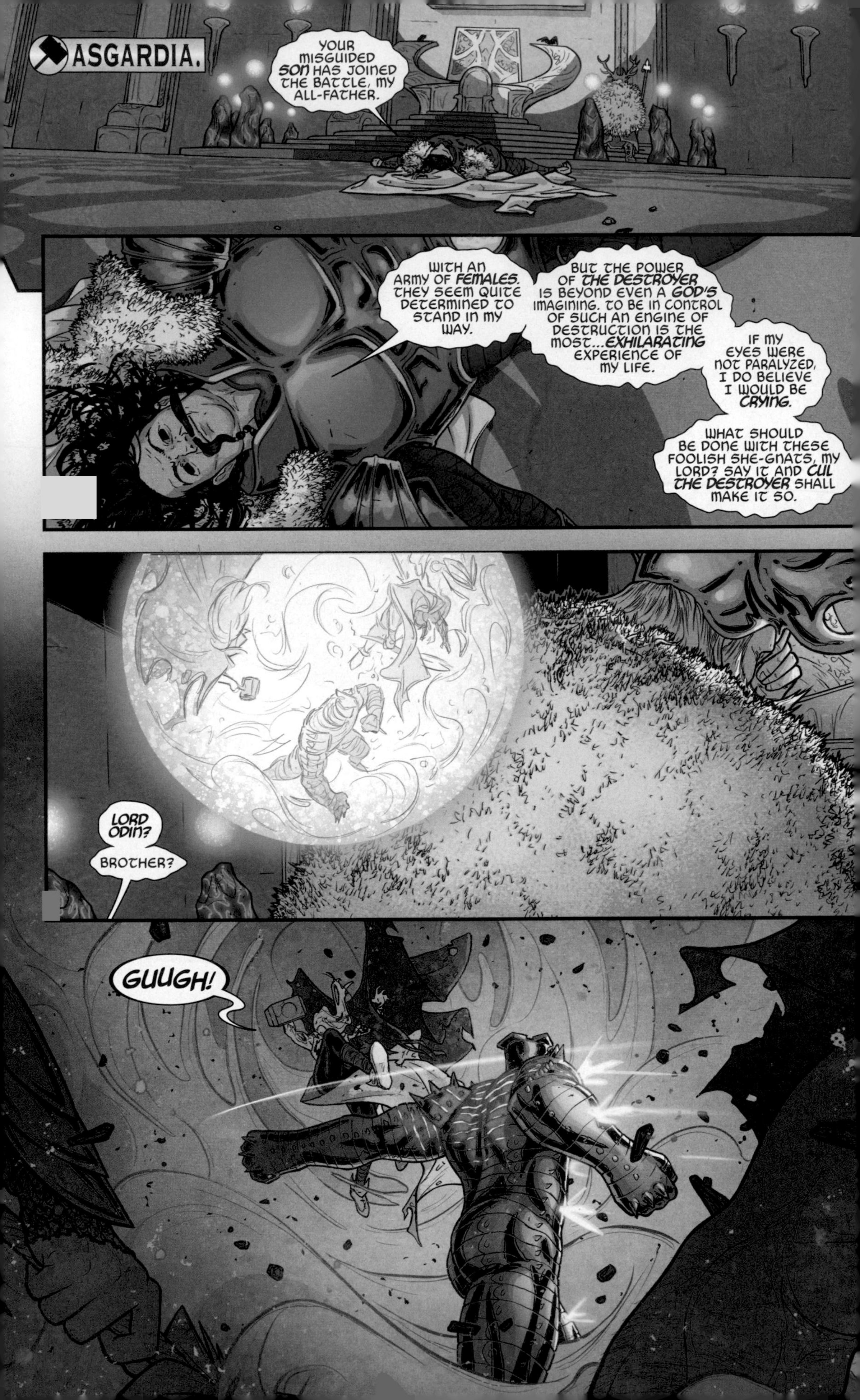
ASGARDIA.
YOUR MISGUIDED SON HAS JOINED THE BATTLE, MY ALL-FATHER.
WITH AN ARMY OF FEMALES. THEY SEEM QUITE DETERMINED TO STAND IN MY WAY.
BUT THE POWER OF THE DESTROYER IS BEYOND EVEN A GOD'S IMAGINING. TO BE IN CONTROL OF SUCH AN ENGINE OF DESTRUCTION IS THE MOST...EXHILARATING EXPERIENCE OF MY LIFE.
IF MY EYES WERE NOT PARALYZED, I DO BELIEVE I WOULD BE CRYING.
WHAT SHOULD BE DONE WITH THESE FOOLISH SHE-GNATS, MY LORD? SAY IT AND CUL THE DESTROYER SHALL MAKE IT SO.
LORD ODIN?
BROTHER?
GUUGH!

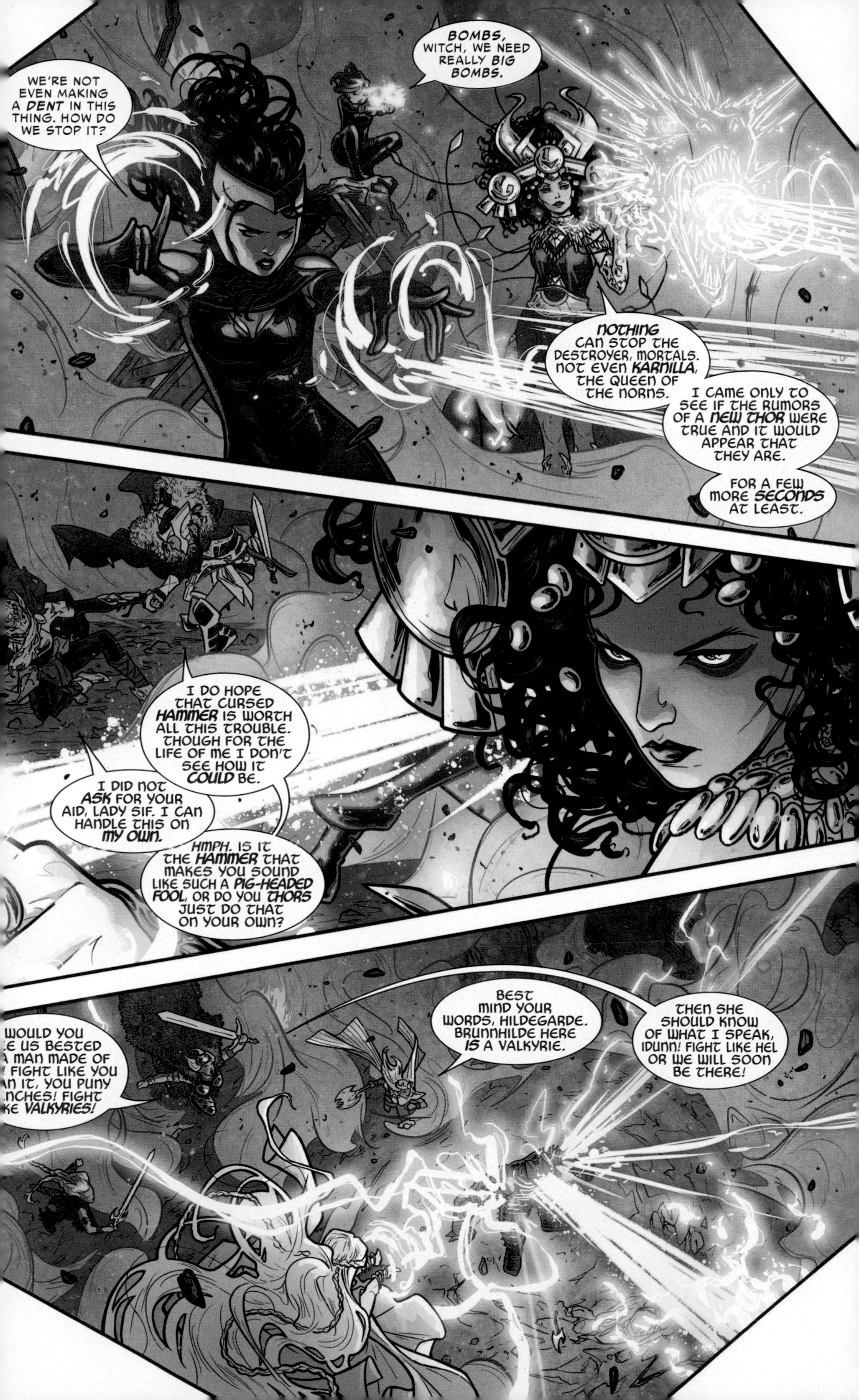
WE'RE NOT EVEN MAKING A DENT IN THIS THING. HOW DO WE STOP IT?
BOMBS, WITCH, WE NEED REALLY BIG BOMBS.
NOTHING CAN STOP THE DESTROYER, MORTALS. NOT EVEN KARNILLA, THE QUEEN OF THE NORNS.
I CAME ONLY TO SEE IF THE RUMORS OF A NEW THOR WERE TRUE AND IT WOULD APPEAR THAT THEY ARE.
FOR A FEW MORE SECONDS AT LEAST.
I DO HOPE THAT CURSED HAMMER IS WORTH ALL THIS TROUBLE. THOUGH FOR THE LIFE OF ME I DON'T SEE HOW IT COULD BE.
I DID NOT ASK FOR YOUR AID, LADY SIF. I CAN HANDLE THIS ON MY OWN.
HMPH. IS IT THE HAMMER THAT MAKES YOU SOUND LIKE SUCH A PIG-HEADED FOOL, OR DO YOU THORS JUST DO THAT ON YOUR OWN?
WOULD YOU E US BESTED A MAN MADE OF FIGHT LIKE YOU AN IT, YOU PUNY NCHES! FIGHT KE VALKYRIES!
BEST MIND YOUR WORDS, HILDEGARDE. BRUNNHILDE HERE IS A VALKYRIE.
THEN SHE SHOULD KNOW OF WHAT I SPEAK, IDUNN! FIGHT LIKE HEL OR WE WILL SOON BE THERE!

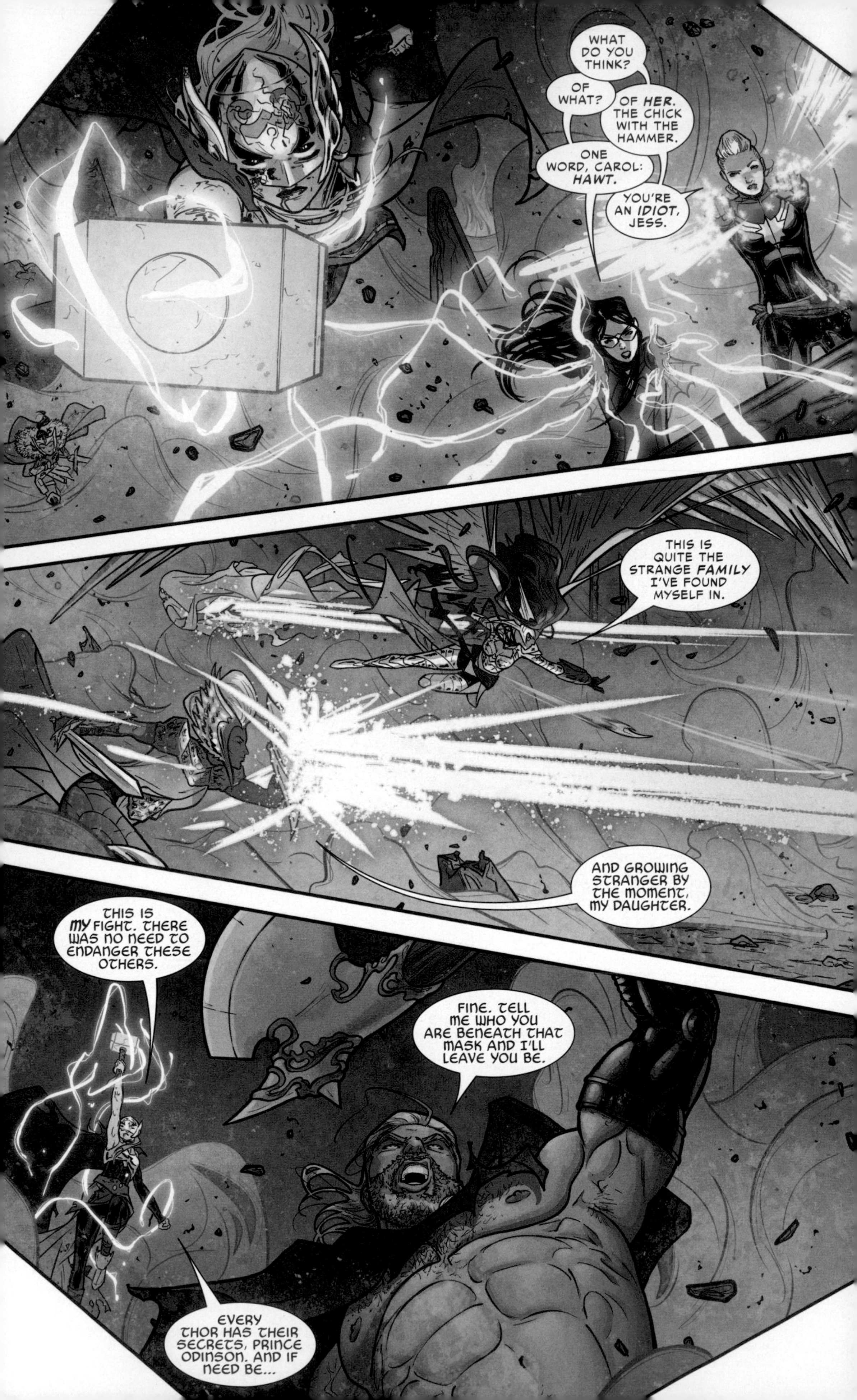
WHAT DO YOU THINK?
OF WHAT?
OF HER. THE CHICK WITH THE HAMMER.
ONE WORD, CAROL: HAWT.
YOU'RE AN IDIOT, JESS.
THIS IS QUITE THE STRANGE FAMILY I'VE FOUND MYSELF IN.
AND GROWING STRANGER BY THE MOMENT, MY DAUGHTER.
THIS IS MY FIGHT. THERE WAS NO NEED TO ENDANGER THESE OTHERS.
FINE. TELL ME WHO YOU ARE BENEATH THAT MASK AND I'LL LEAVE YOU BE.
EVERY THOR HAS THEIR SECRETS, PRINCE ODINSON. AND IF NEED BE...

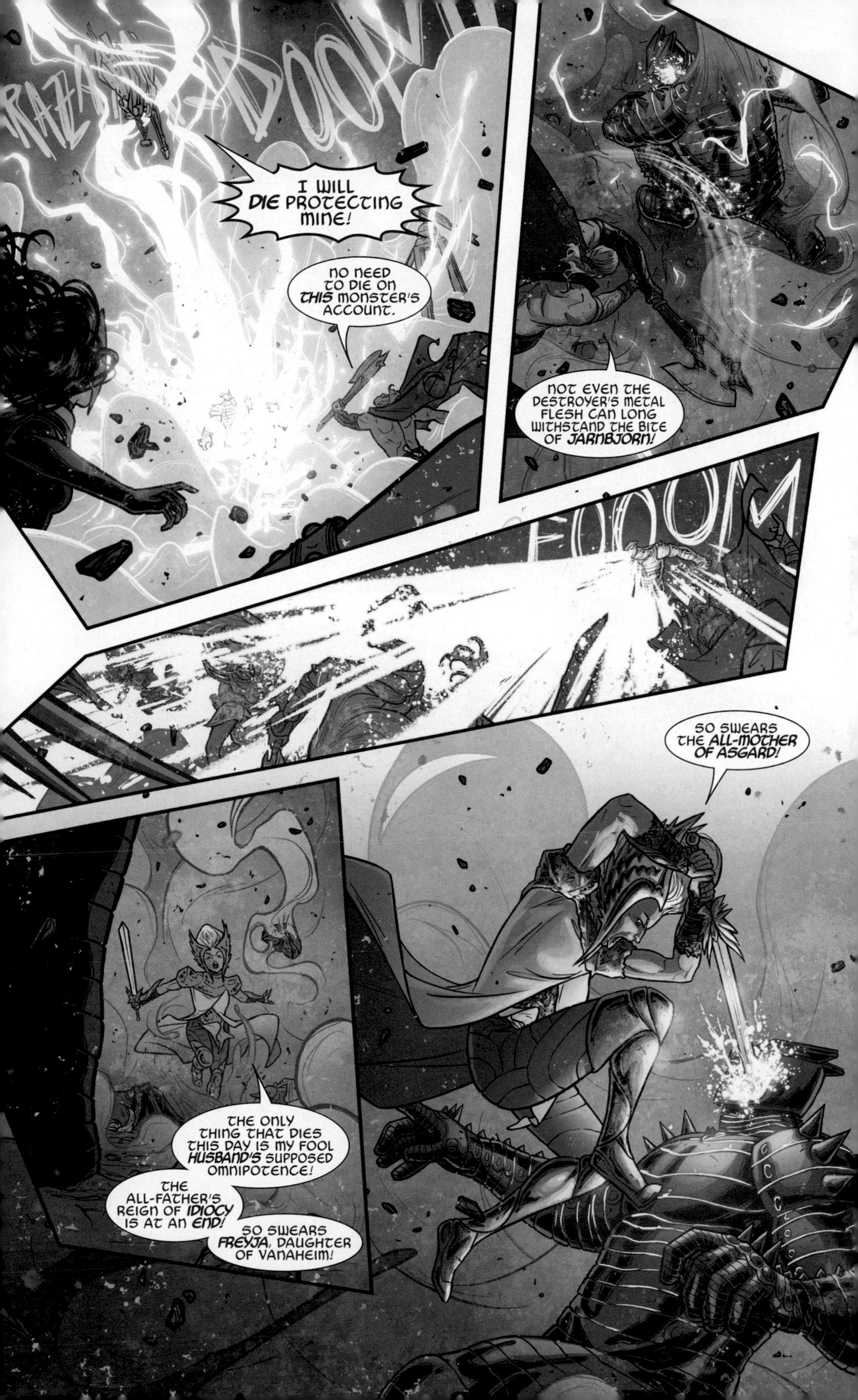

I WILL DIE PROTECTING MINE!
NO NEED TO DIE ON THIS MONSTER'S ACCOUNT.
NOT EVEN THE DESTROYER'S METAL FLESH CAN LONG WITHSTAND THE BITE OF JARNBJORN!
SO SWEARS THE ALL-MOTHER OF ASGARD!
THE ONLY THING THAT DIES THIS DAY IS MY FOOL HUSBAND'S SUPPOSED OMNIPOTENCE!
THE ALL-FATHER'S REIGN OF IDIOCY IS AT AN END!
SO SWEARS FREYJA, DAUGHTER OF VANAHEIM!

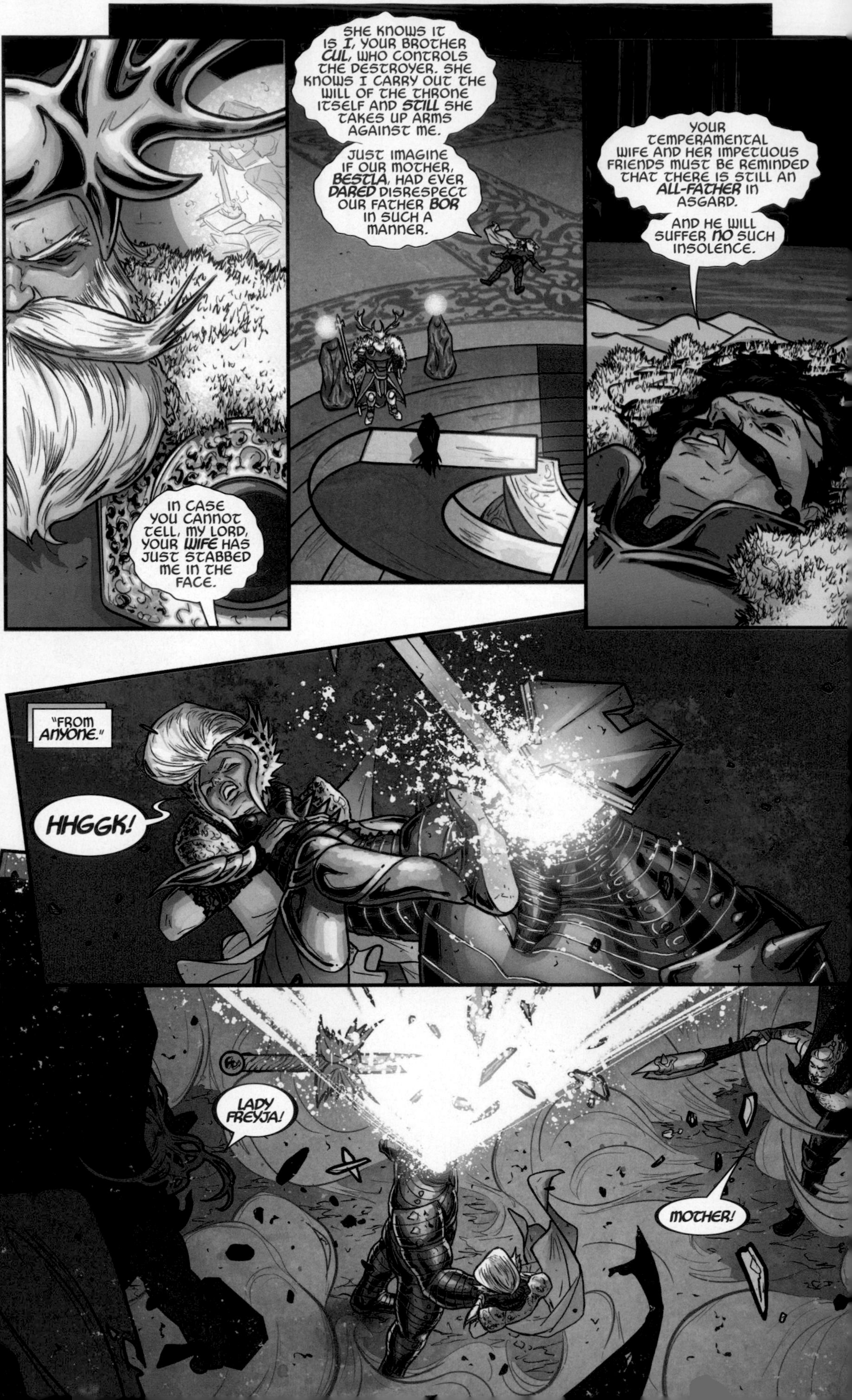
IN CASE YOU CANNOT TELL, MY LORD, YOUR WIFE HAS JUST STABBED ME IN THE FACE.
SHE KNOWS IT IS I, YOUR BROTHER CUL, WHO CONTROLS THE DESTROYER. SHE KNOWS I CARRY OUT THE WILL OF THE THRONE ITSELF AND STILL SHE TAKES UP ARMS AGAINST ME.
JUST IMAGINE IF OUR MOTHER, BESTLA, HAD EVER DARED DISRESPECT OUR FATHER BOR IN SUCH A MANNER.
YOUR TEMPERAMENTAL WIFE AND HER IMPETUOUS FRIENDS MUST BE REMINDED THAT THERE IS STILL AN ALL-FATHER IN ASGARD.
AND HE WILL SUFFER NO SUCH INSOLENCE.
"FROM ANYONE."
HHGGK!
LADY FREYJA!
MOTHER!

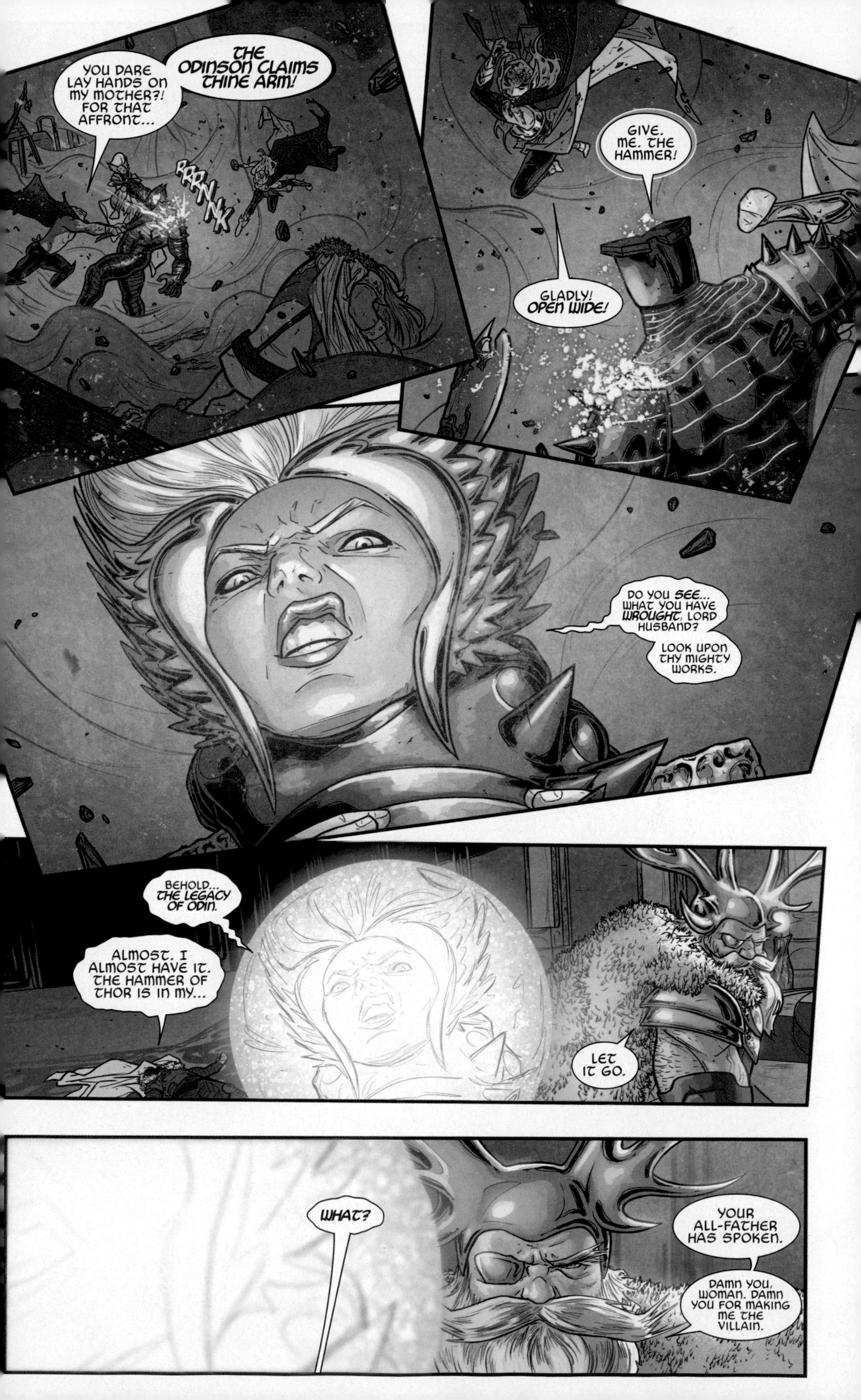

YOU DARE LAY HANDS ON MY MOTHER?! FOR THAT AFFRONT...
THE ODINSON CLAIMS THINE ARM!
RRRNNK
GIVE. ME. THE HAMMER!
GLADLY! OPEN WIDE!
DO YOU SEE... WHAT YOU HAVE WROUGHT, LORD HUSBAND?
LOOK UPON THY MIGHTY WORKS.
BEHOLD... THE LEGACY OF ODIN.
ALMOST. I ALMOST HAVE IT. THE HAMMER OF THOR IS IN MY...
LET IT GO.
WHAT?
YOUR ALL-FATHER HAS SPOKEN.
DAMN YOU, WOMAN. DAMN YOU FOR MAKING ME THE VILLAIN.

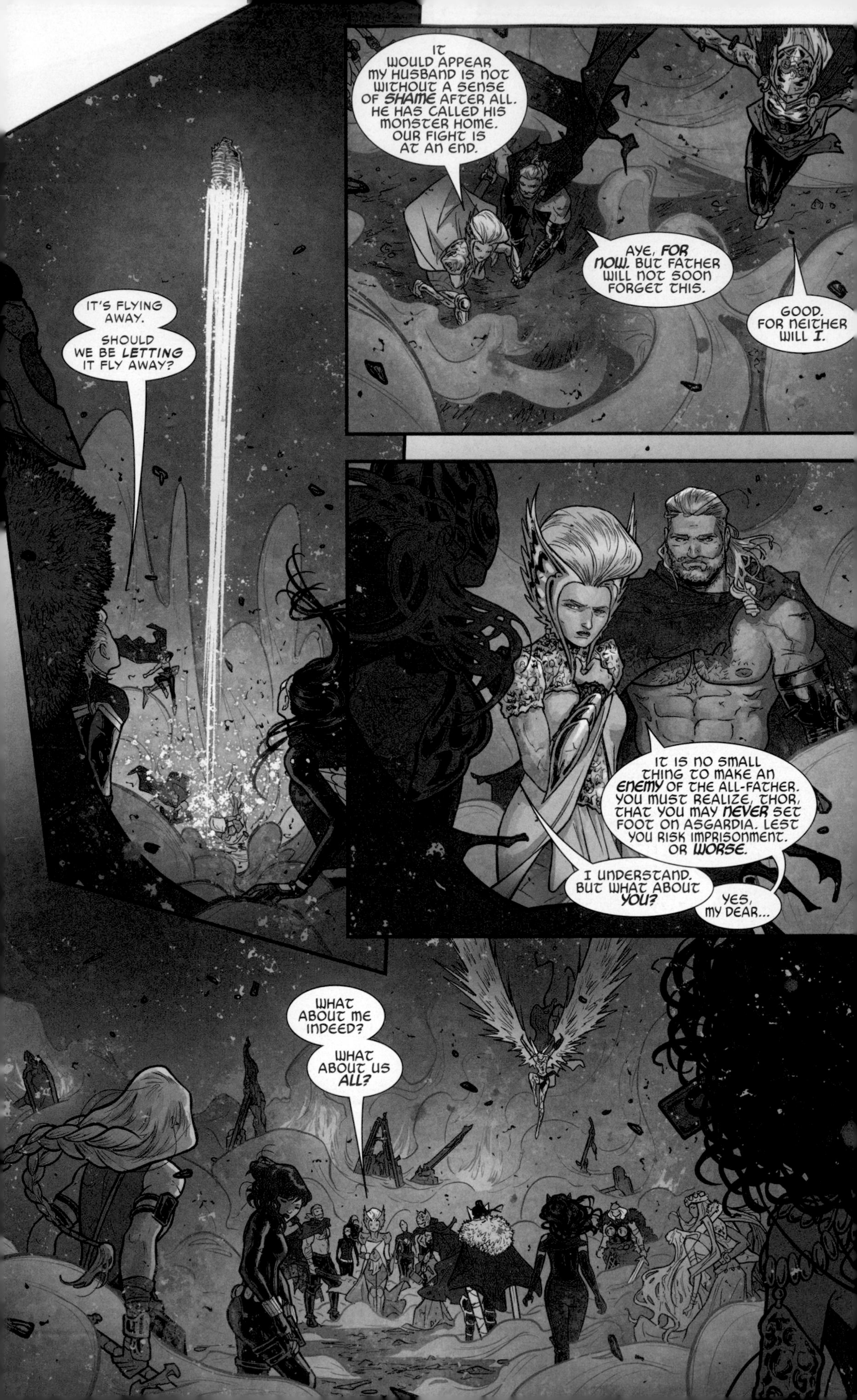
IT'S FLYING AWAY.
SHOULD WE BE LETTING IT FLY AWAY?
IT WOULD APPEAR MY HUSBAND IS NOT WITHOUT A SENSE OF SHAME AFTER ALL. HE HAS CALLED HIS MONSTER HOME. OUR FIGHT IS AT AN END.
AYE, FOR NOW. BUT FATHER WILL NOT SOON FORGET THIS.
GOOD. FOR NEITHER WILL I.
IT IS NO SMALL THING TO MAKE AN ENEMY OF THE ALL-FATHER. YOU MUST REALIZE, THOR, THAT YOU MAY NEVER SET FOOT ON ASGARDIA. LEST YOU RISK IMPRISONMENT. OR WORSE.
I UNDERSTAND. BUT WHAT ABOUT YOU?
YES, MY DEAR...
WHAT ABOUT ME INDEED?
WHAT ABOUT US ALL?

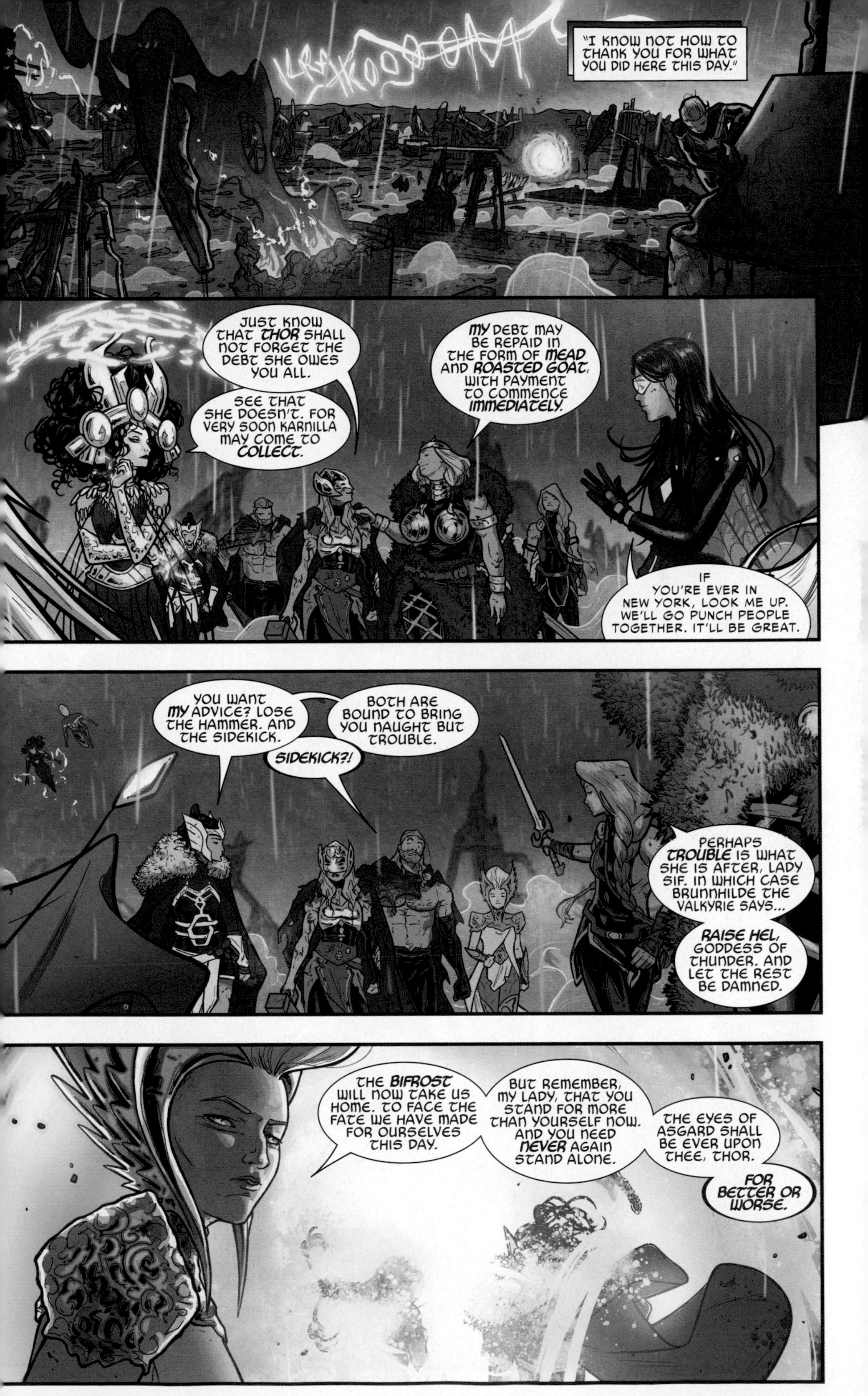
KLRAKKOOOOM
"I KNOW NOT HOW TO THANK YOU FOR WHAT YOU DID HERE THIS DAY."
JUST KNOW THAT THOR SHALL NOT FORGET THE DEBT SHE OWES YOU ALL.
SEE THAT SHE DOESN'T. FOR VERY SOON KARNILLA MAY COME TO COLLECT.
MY DEBT MAY BE REPAID IN THE FORM OF MEAD AND ROASTED GOAT, WITH PAYMENT TO COMMENCE IMMEDIATELY.
IF YOU'RE EVER IN NEW YORK, LOOK ME UP. WE'LL GO PUNCH PEOPLE TOGETHER. IT'LL BE GREAT.
YOU WANT MY ADVICE? LOSE THE HAMMER. AND THE SIDEKICK.
BOTH ARE BOUND TO BRING YOU NAUGHT BUT TROUBLE.
SIDEKICK?!
PERHAPS TROUBLE IS WHAT SHE IS AFTER, LADY SIF. IN WHICH CASE BRUNNHILDE THE VALKYRIE SAYS...
RAISE HEL, GODDESS OF THUNDER. AND LET THE REST BE DAMNED.
THE BIFROST WILL NOW TAKE US HOME. TO FACE THE FATE WE HAVE MADE FOR OURSELVES THIS DAY.
BUT REMEMBER, MY LADY, THAT YOU STAND FOR MORE THAN YOURSELF NOW. AND YOU NEED NEVER STAND ALONE.
THE EYES OF ASGARD SHALL BE EVER UPON THEE, THOR.
FOR BETTER OR WORSE.

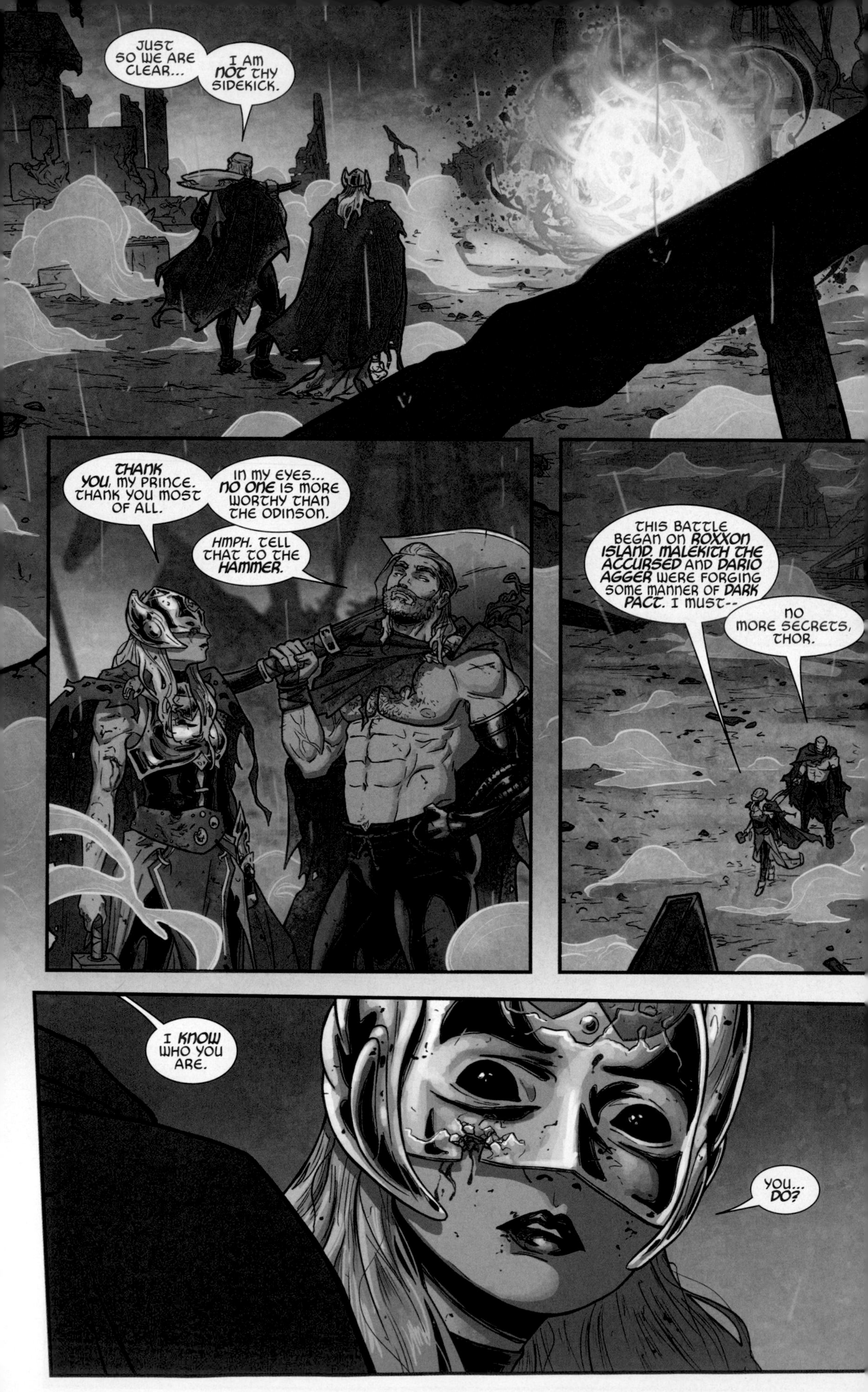
JUST SO WE ARE CLEAR...
I AM NOT THY SIDEKICK.
THANK YOU, MY PRINCE. THANK YOU MOST OF ALL.
IN MY EYES... NO ONE IS MORE WORTHY THAN THE ODINSON.
HMPH. TELL THAT TO THE HAMMER.
THIS BATTLE BEGAN ON ROXXON ISLAND. MALEKITH THE ACCURSED AND DARIO AGGER WERE FORGING SOME MANNER OF DARK PACT. I MUST--
NO MORE SECRETS, THOR.
I KNOW WHO YOU ARE.
YOU... DO?

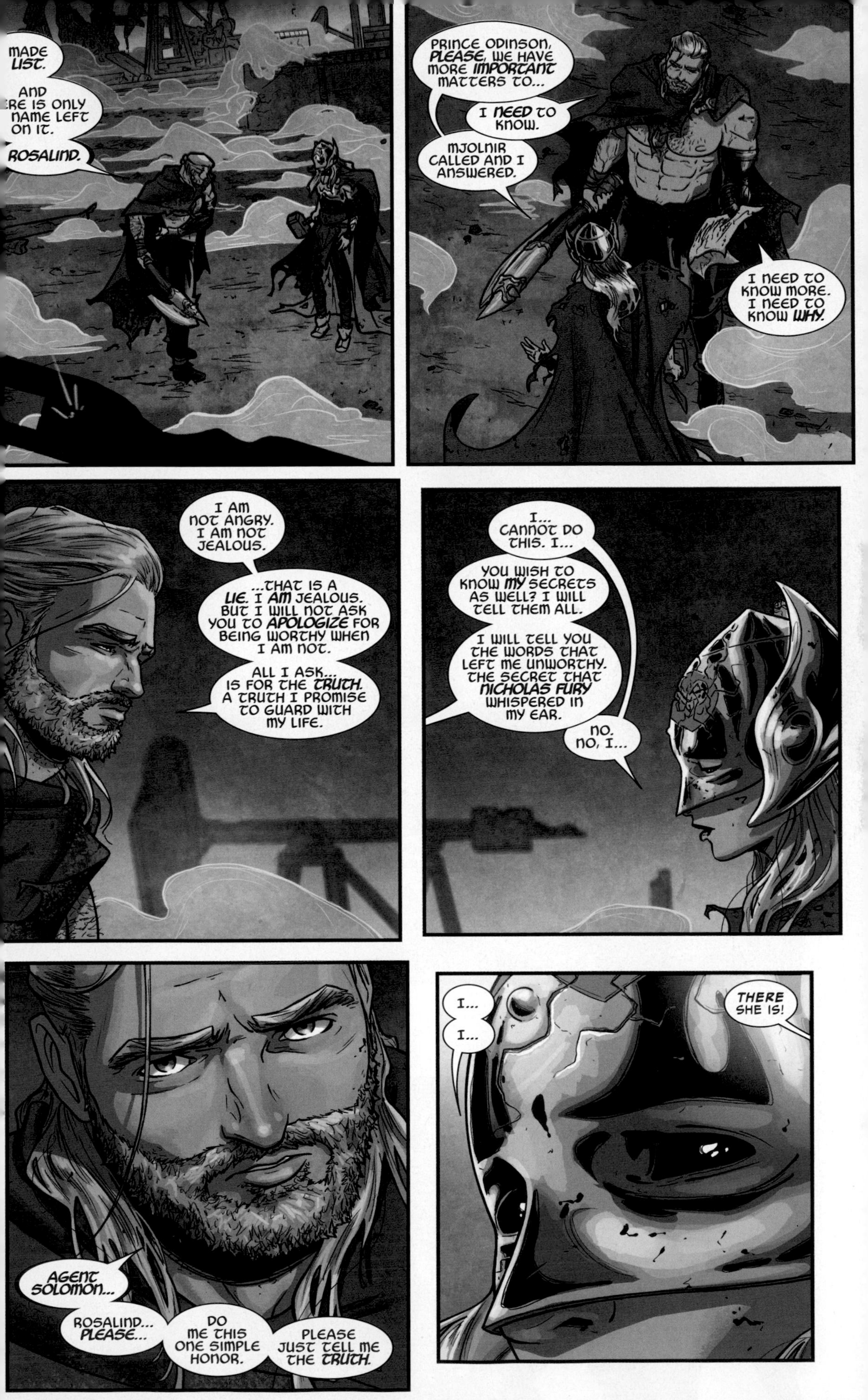
MADE
LIST.
AND
ERE IS ONLY
NAME LEFT
ON IT.
ROSALIND.
PRINCE ODINSON, PLEASE, WE HAVE MORE IMPORTANT MATTERS TO...
I NEED TO KNOW.
MJOLNIR CALLED AND I ANSWERED.
I NEED TO KNOW MORE. I NEED TO KNOW WHY.
I AM NOT ANGRY. I AM NOT JEALOUS.
...THAT IS A LIE. I AM JEALOUS. BUT I WILL NOT ASK YOU TO APOLOGIZE FOR BEING WORTHY WHEN I AM NOT.
ALL I ASK... IS FOR THE TRUTH. A TRUTH I PROMISE TO GUARD WITH MY LIFE.
I... CANNOT DO THIS. I...
YOU WISH TO KNOW MY SECRETS AS WELL? I WILL TELL THEM ALL.
I WILL TELL YOU THE WORDS THAT LEFT ME UNWORTHY. THE SECRET THAT NICHOLAS FURY WHISPERED IN MY EAR.
NO. NO, I...
AGENT SOLOMON...
ROSALIND... PLEASE...
DO ME THIS ONE SIMPLE HONOR.
PLEASE JUST TELL ME THE TRUTH.
I...
I...
THERE SHE IS!

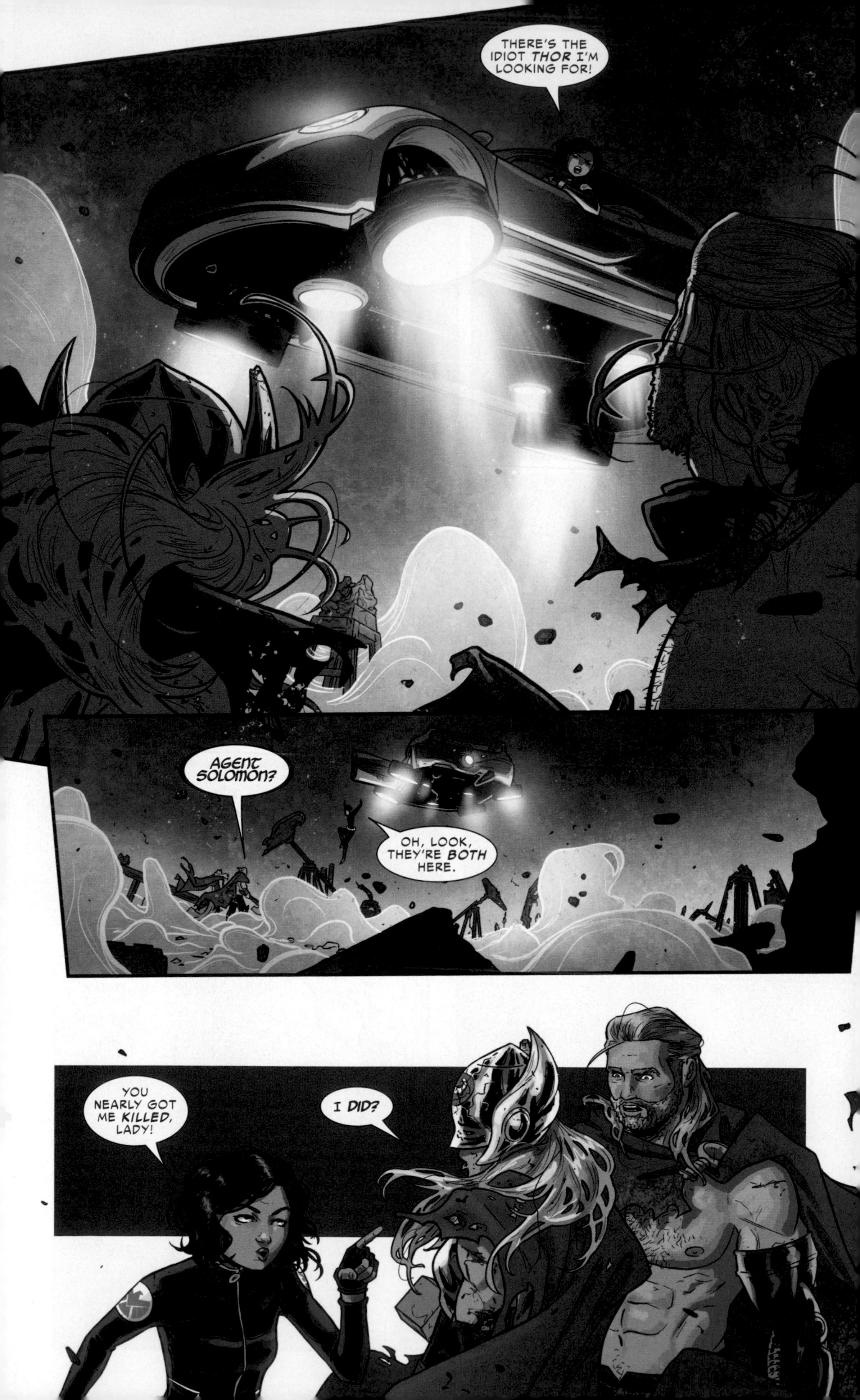
THERE'S THE IDIOT THOR I'M LOOKING FOR!
AGENT SOLOMON?
OH, LOOK, THEY'RE BOTH HERE.
YOU NEARLY GOT ME KILLED, LADY!
I DID?

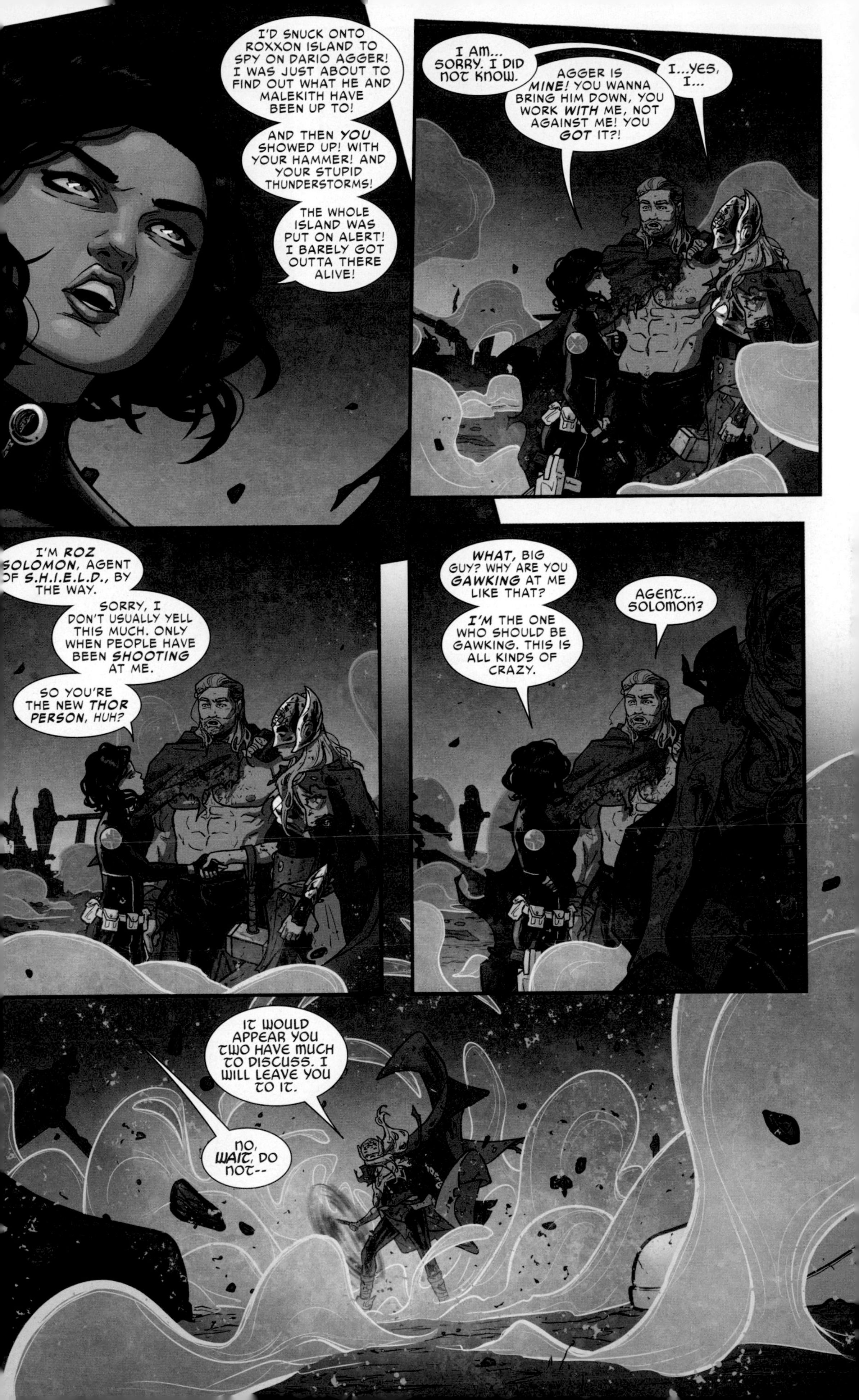
I'D SNUCK ONTO ROXXON ISLAND TO SPY ON DARIO AGGER! I WAS JUST ABOUT TO FIND OUT WHAT HE AND MALEKITH HAVE BEEN UP TO!
AND THEN YOU SHOWED UP! WITH YOUR HAMMER! AND YOUR STUPID THUNDERSTORMS!
THE WHOLE ISLAND WAS PUT ON ALERT! I BARELY GOT OUTTA THERE ALIVE!
I AM... SORRY. I DID NOT KNOW.
AGGER IS MINE! YOU WANNA BRING HIM DOWN, YOU WORK WITH ME, NOT AGAINST ME! YOU GOT IT?!
I...YES, I...
I'M ROZ SOLOMON, AGENT OF S.H.I.E.L.D., BY THE WAY.
SORRY, I DON'T USUALLY YELL THIS MUCH. ONLY WHEN PEOPLE HAVE BEEN SHOOTING AT ME.
SO YOU'RE THE NEW THOR PERSON, HUH?
WHAT, BIG GUY? WHY ARE YOU GAWKING AT ME LIKE THAT?
I'M THE ONE WHO SHOULD BE GAWKING. THIS IS ALL KINDS OF CRAZY.
AGENT... SOLOMON?
IT WOULD APPEAR YOU TWO HAVE MUCH TO DISCUSS. I WILL LEAVE YOU TO IT.
NO, WAIT, DO NOT--

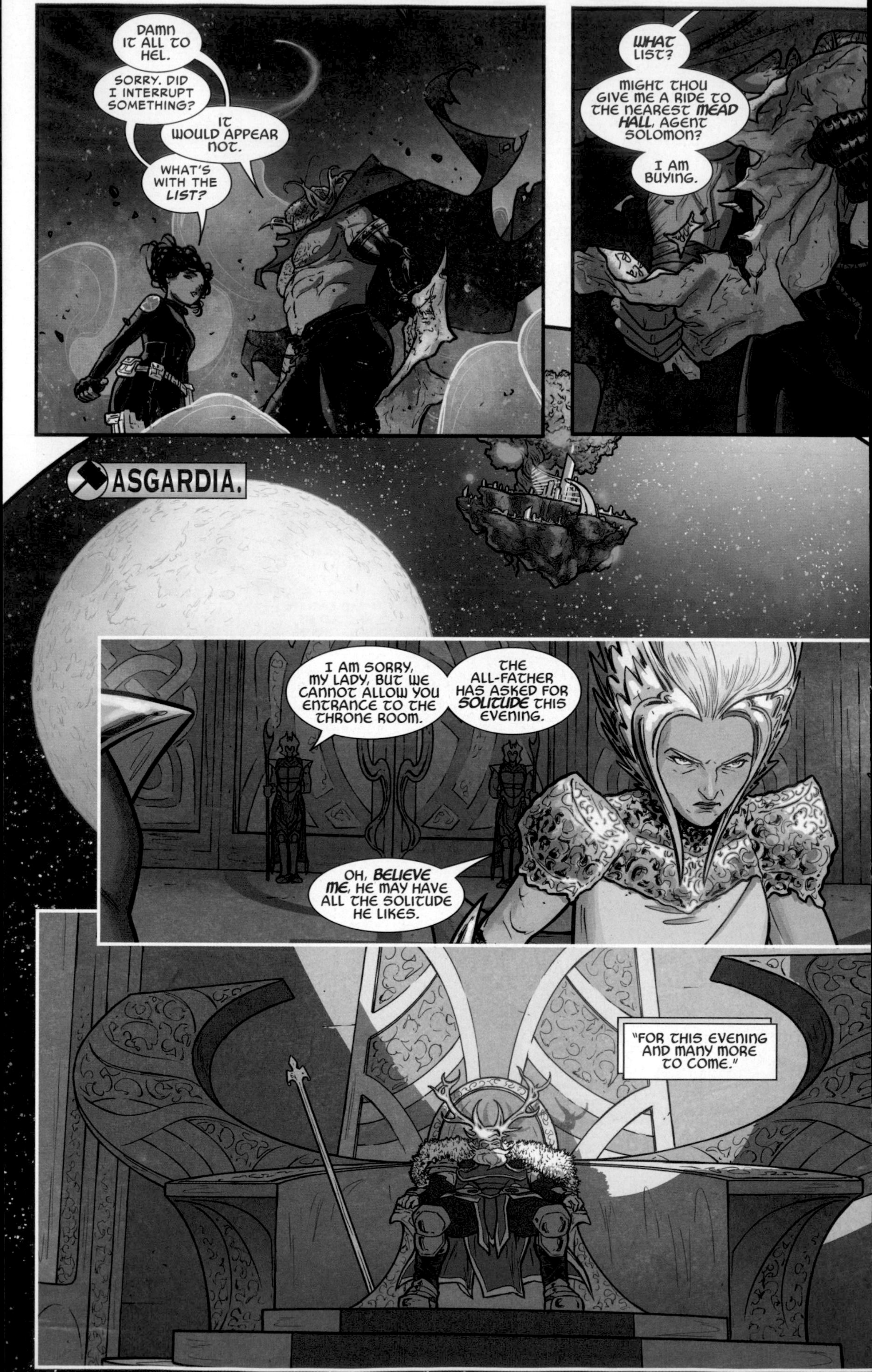

DAMN IT ALL TO HEL.
SORRY. DID I INTERRUPT SOMETHING?
IT WOULD APPEAR NOT.
WHAT'S WITH THE *LIST?*
WHAT LIST?
MIGHT THOU GIVE ME A RIDE TO THE NEAREST *MEAD HALL*, AGENT SOLOMON?
I AM BUYING.
ASGARDIA.
I AM SORRY, MY LADY, BUT WE CANNOT ALLOW YOU ENTRANCE TO THE THRONE ROOM.
THE ALL-FATHER HAS ASKED FOR *SOLITUDE* THIS EVENING.
OH, *BELIEVE ME*, HE MAY HAVE ALL THE SOLITUDE HE LIKES.
"FOR THIS EVENING AND MANY MORE TO COME."

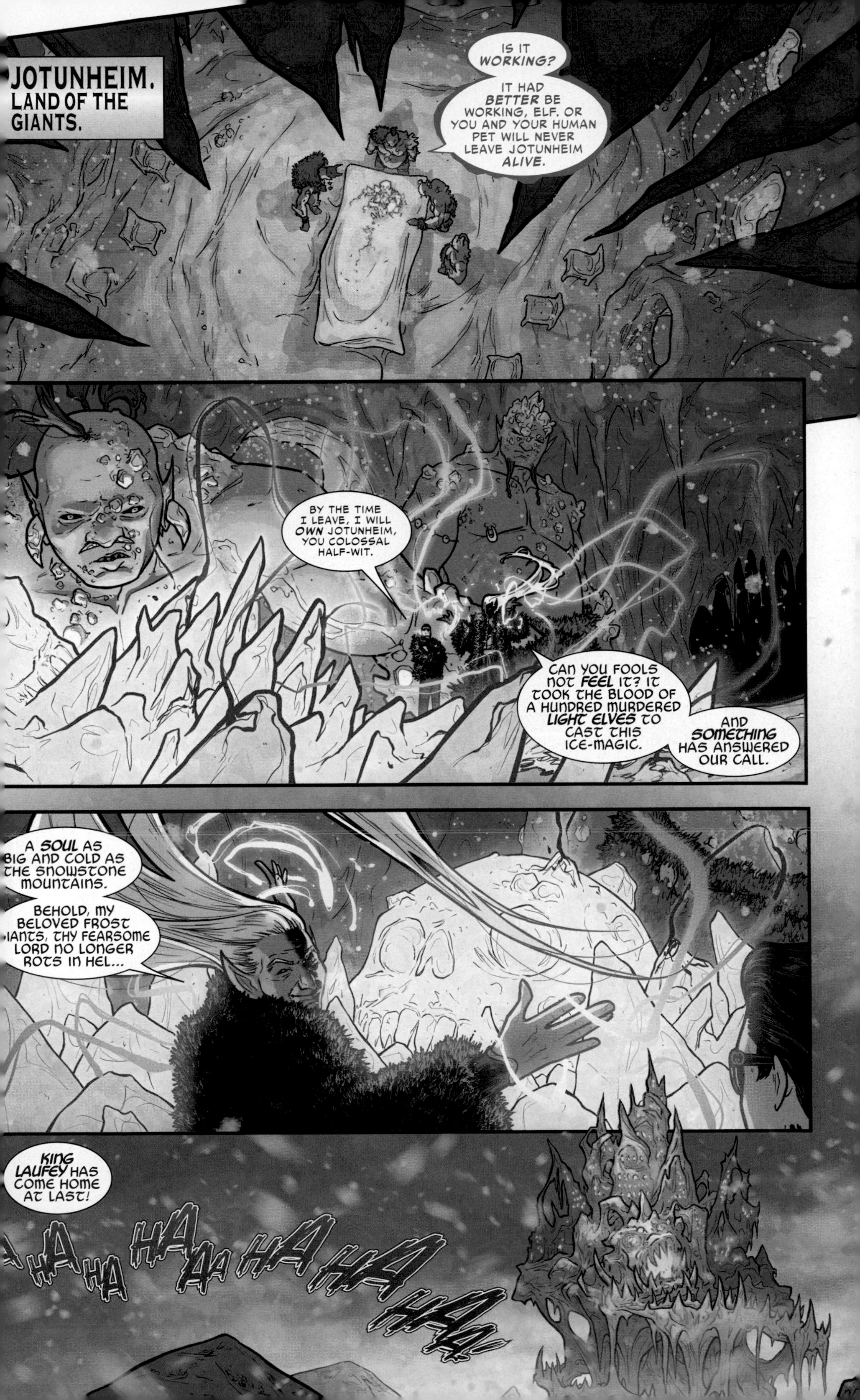
JOTUNHEIM. LAND OF THE GIANTS.
IS IT WORKING?
IT HAD BETTER BE WORKING, ELF. OR YOU AND YOUR HUMAN PET WILL NEVER LEAVE JOTUNHEIM ALIVE.
BY THE TIME I LEAVE, I WILL OWN JOTUNHEIM, YOU COLOSSAL HALF-WIT.
CAN YOU FOOLS NOT FEEL IT? IT TOOK THE BLOOD OF A HUNDRED MURDERED LIGHT ELVES TO CAST THIS ICE-MAGIC.
AND SOMETHING HAS ANSWERED OUR CALL.
A SOUL AS BIG AND COLD AS THE SNOWSTONE MOUNTAINS.
BEHOLD, MY BELOVED FROST GIANTS, THY FEARSOME LORD NO LONGER ROTS IN HEL...
KING LAUFEY HAS COME HOME AT LAST!
HA HA HA HA HA HA HA HA HA HA HA

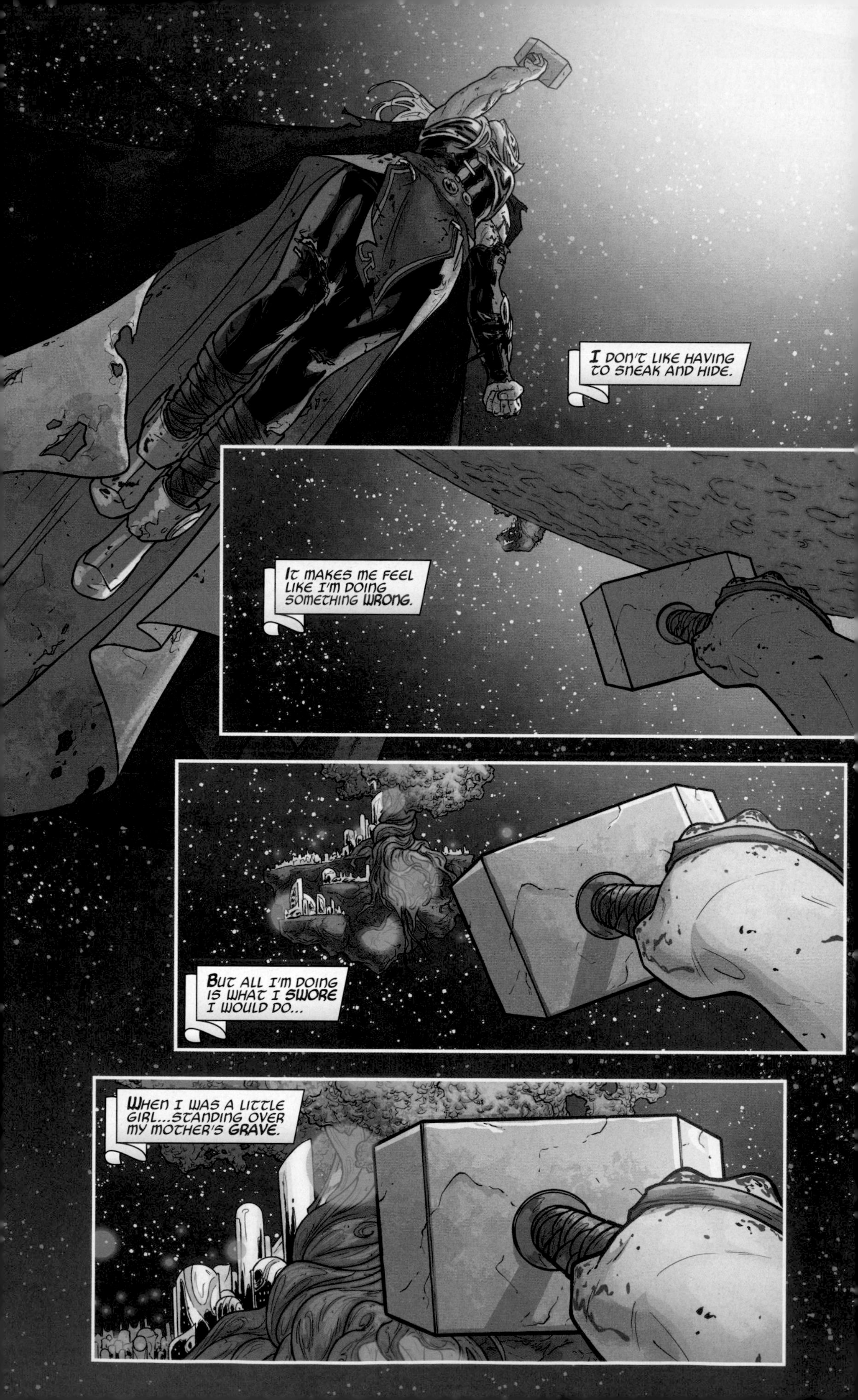
I DON'T LIKE HAVING TO SNEAK AND HIDE.
IT MAKES ME FEEL LIKE I'M DOING SOMETHING WRONG.
BUT ALL I'M DOING IS WHAT I SWORE I WOULD DO...
WHEN I WAS A LITTLE GIRL...STANDING OVER MY MOTHER'S GRAVE.

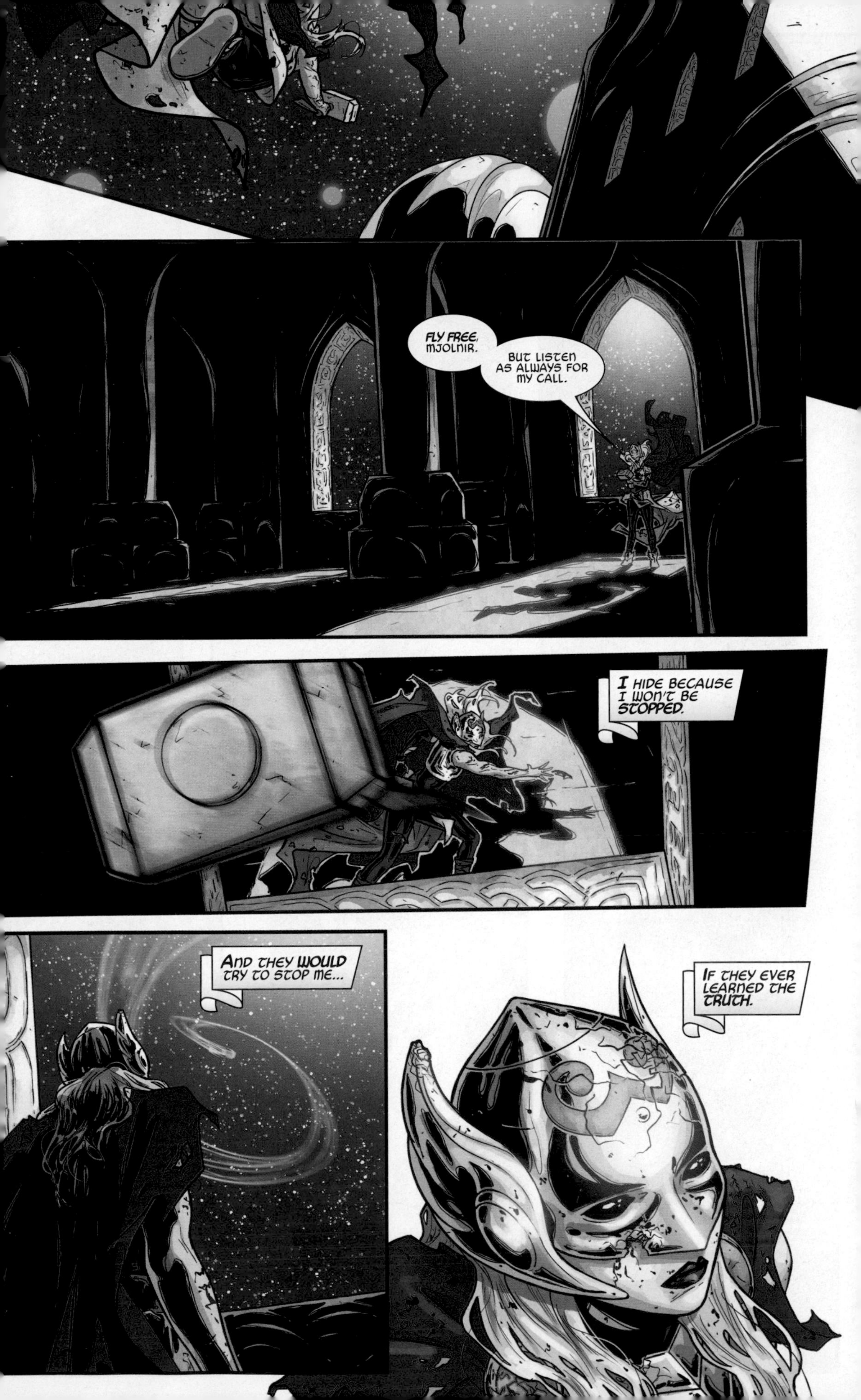
FLY FREE, MJOLNIR.
BUT LISTEN AS ALWAYS FOR MY CALL.
I HIDE BECAUSE I WON'T BE STOPPED.
AND THEY WOULD TRY TO STOP ME...
IF THEY EVER LEARNED THE TRUTH.

THE WORLD NEEDS A THOR. THAT'S ALL THAT REALLY MATTERS.

WE NEED A GOD WHO UNDERSTANDS WHAT IT MEANS TO BE HUMBLED. TO BE MORTAL.

A GOD WHO KNOWS HOW PRECIOUS LIFE IS. HOW DELICATE.

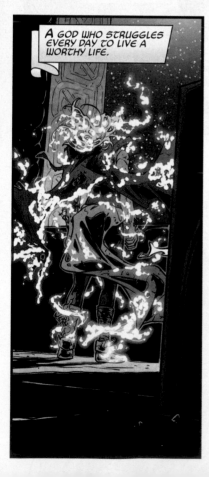

A GOD WHO STRUGGLES EVERY DAY TO LIVE A WORTHY LIFE.

WHO SUFFERS SO THAT NO ONE ELSE WILL HAVE TO.

A GOD WHO LOVES THE EARTH ENOUGH TO DIE FOR IT.

UGGHH

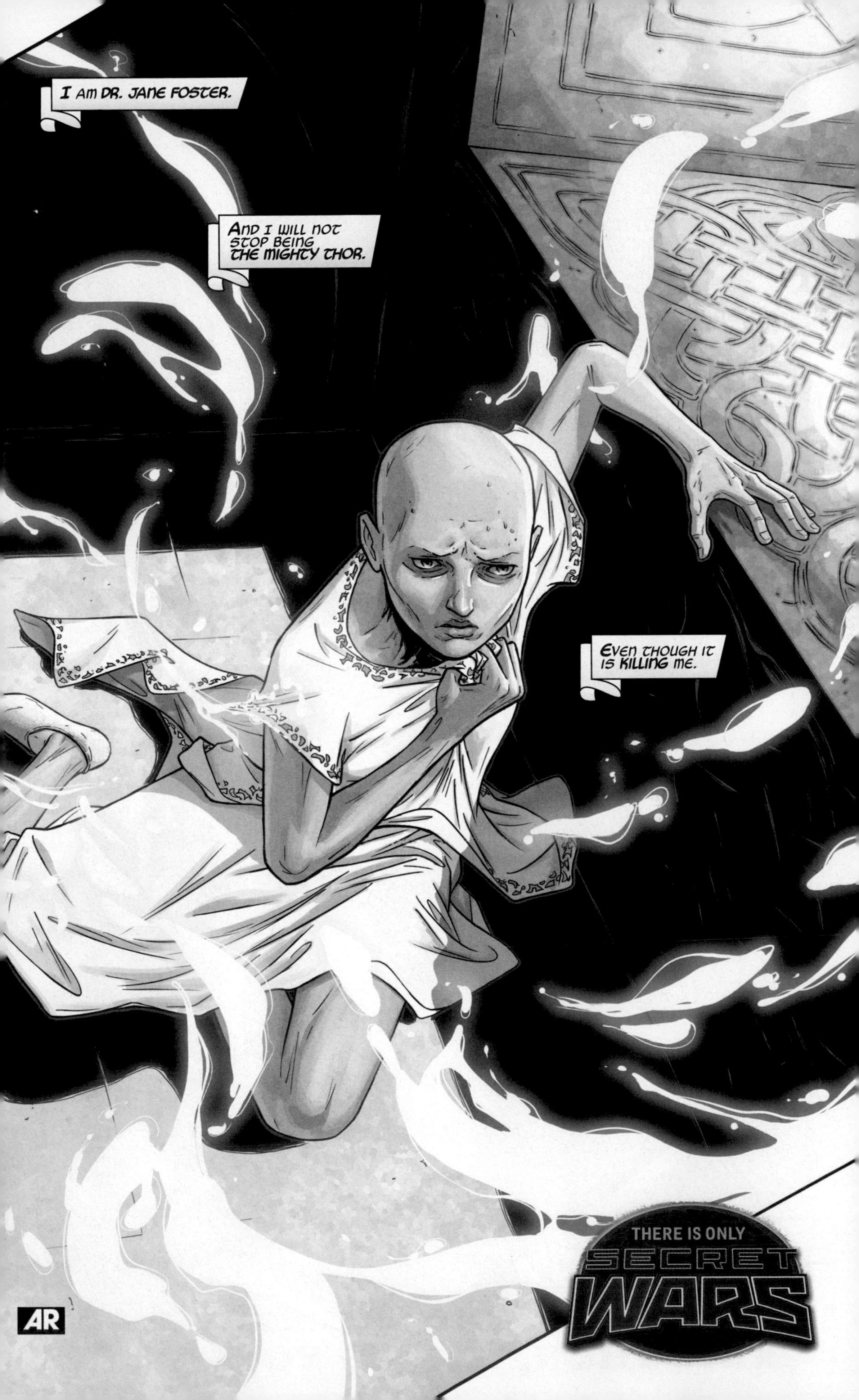

I AM DR. JANE FOSTER.
AND I WILL NOT STOP BEING THE MIGHTY THOR.
EVEN THOUGH IT IS KILLING ME.
THERE IS ONLY SECRET WARS
AR

— ANNUAL 1 —

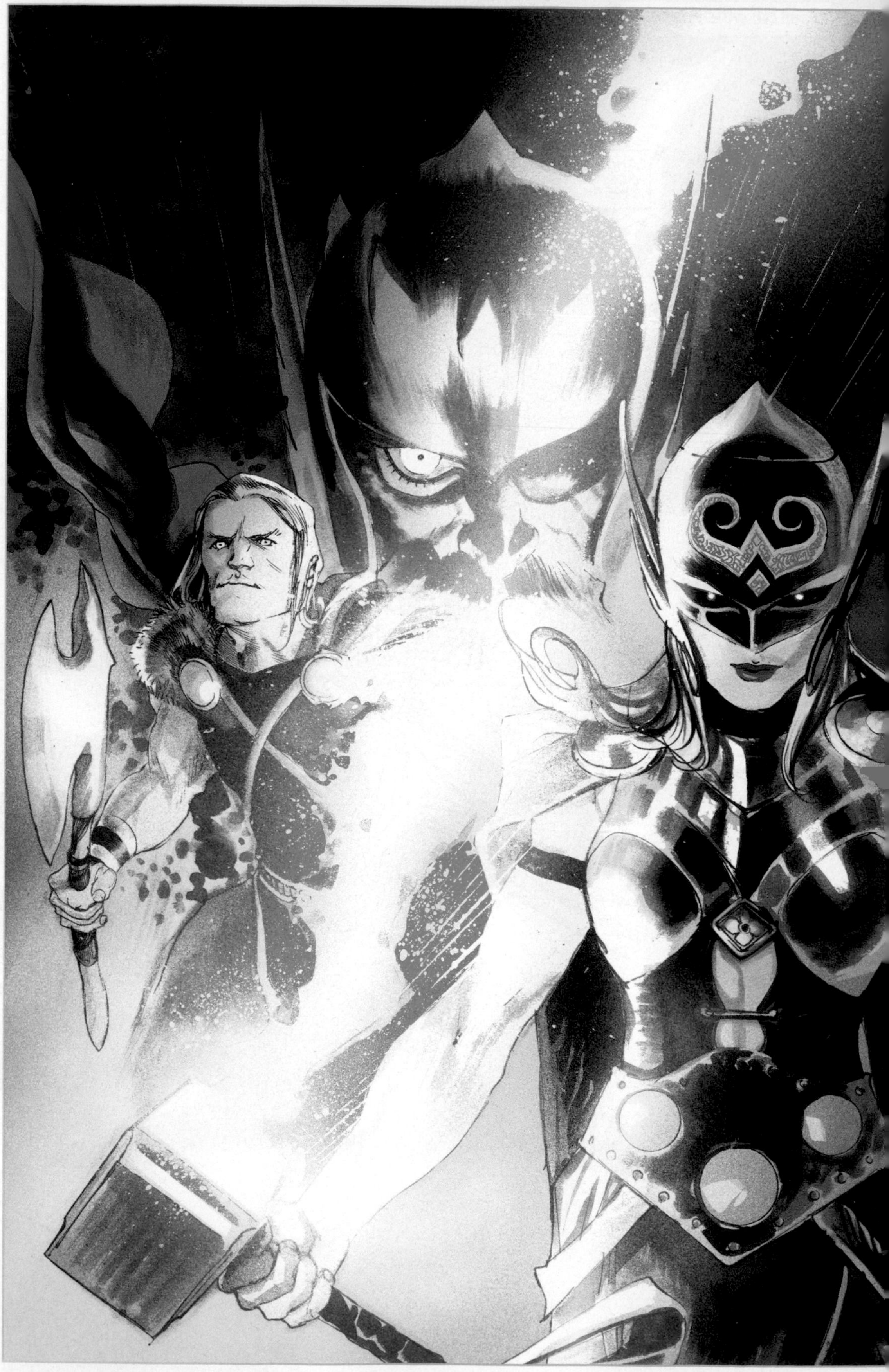

KING THOR, THOR & YOUNG THOR

KING THOR

THE GOD OF THUNDER OF THE FAR FUTURE. HE RULES ASGARD AND HAS THREE GRANDDAUGHTERS—FRIGG, ELLISIV, AND ATLI—KNOWN AS THE GIRLS OF THUNDER. TOGETHER, THEY RECENTLY HELPED BRING LIFE BACK TO EARTH AFTER IT HAD BEEN DEAD AND BARREN FOR QUITE SOME TIME.

JASON AARON WRITER
TIMOTHY TRUMAN ARTIST
FRANK MARTIN COLORIST
JOE SABINO LETTERER
JON MOISAN ASSISTANT EDITOR
WIL MOSS EDITOR

THOR

THE GODDESS OF THUNDER OF THE PRESENT. RECENTLY, AFTER THOR FOUND HIMSELF SUDDENLY UNWORTHY TO LIFT MJOLNIR, A MYSTERIOUS WOMAN WAS ABLE TO LIFT THE ENCHANTED HAMMER, BECOMING THE NEW THOR! HER TRUE IDENTITY REMAINS A SECRET TO ALL.

NOELLE STEVENSON WRITER
MARGUERITE SAUVAGE ARTIST
JOE SABINO LETTERER
JON MOISAN ASSISTANT EDITOR
WIL MOSS EDITOR

YOUNG THOR

THE GOD OF THUNDER OF THE DISTANT PAST. THIS THOR IS NOT YET WORTHY TO WIELD MJOLNIR. HE IS WORSHIPPED BY VIKINGS AND BELOVED BY HIS FELLOW ASGARDIANS, BUT IS BEST KNOWN FOR HIS MEAD-FUELED ESCAPADES.

CM PUNK WRITER
ROB GUILLORY ARTIST
JOE SABINO LETTERER
JON MOISAN EDITOR
WIL MOSS CONSULTING EDITOR

RAFAEL ALBUQUERQUE COVER ARTIST
ROB GUILLORY; MARGUERITE SAUVAGE VARIANT COVER ARTISTS

AXEL ALONSO EDITOR IN CHIEF
JOE QUESADA CHIEF CREATIVE OFFICER
DAN BUCKLEY PUBLISHER
ALAN FINE EXECUTIVE PRODUCER

THOR CREATED BY STAN LEE, LARRY LIEBER & JACK KIRBY

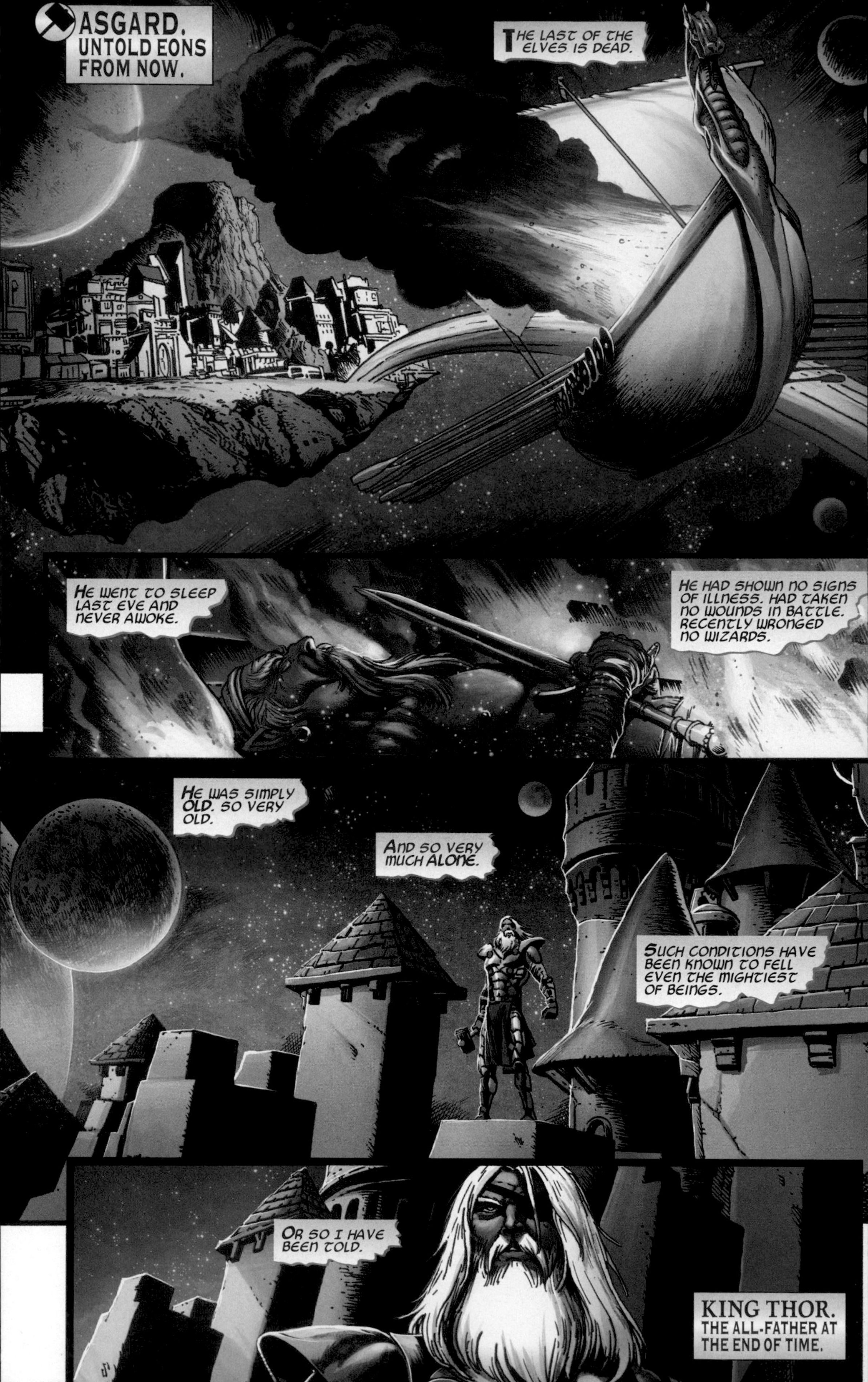
ASGARD. UNTOLD EONS FROM NOW.
THE LAST OF THE ELVES IS DEAD.
HE WENT TO SLEEP LAST EVE AND NEVER AWOKE.
HE HAD SHOWN NO SIGNS OF ILLNESS. HAD TAKEN NO WOUNDS IN BATTLE. RECENTLY WRONGED NO WIZARDS.
HE WAS SIMPLY OLD. SO VERY OLD.
AND SO VERY MUCH ALONE.
SUCH CONDITIONS HAVE BEEN KNOWN TO FELL EVEN THE MIGHTIEST OF BEINGS.
OR SO I HAVE BEEN TOLD.
KING THOR. THE ALL-FATHER AT THE END OF TIME.

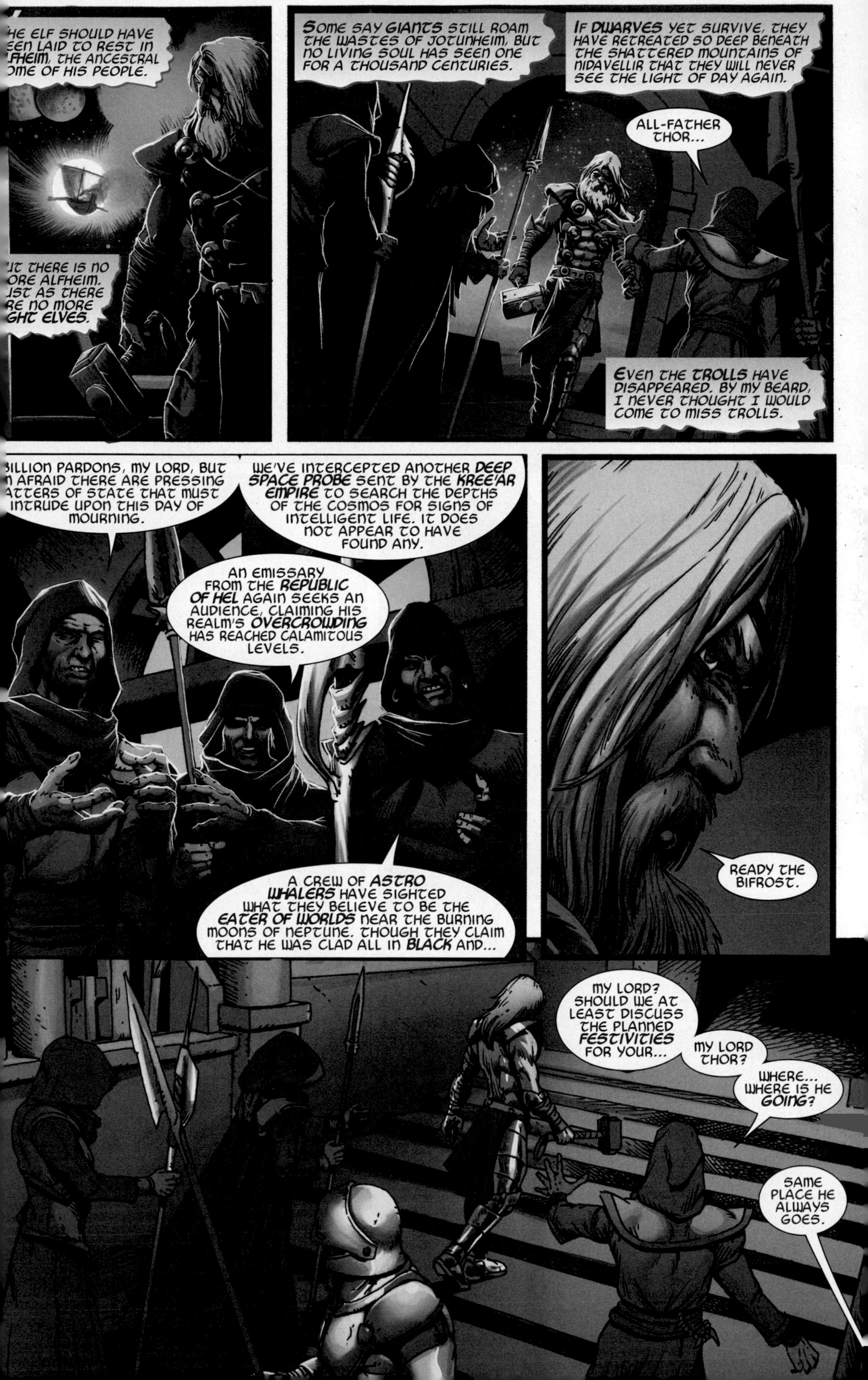

HE ELF SHOULD HAVE
EEN LAID TO REST IN
LFHEIM, THE ANCESTRAL
OME OF HIS PEOPLE.
UT THERE IS NO
ORE ALFHEIM.
UST AS THERE
RE NO MORE
GHT ELVES.
SOME SAY GIANTS STILL ROAM THE WASTES OF JOTUNHEIM, BUT NO LIVING SOUL HAS SEEN ONE FOR A THOUSAND CENTURIES.
IF DWARVES YET SURVIVE, THEY HAVE RETREATED SO DEEP BENEATH THE SHATTERED MOUNTAINS OF NIDAVELLIR THAT THEY WILL NEVER SEE THE LIGHT OF DAY AGAIN.
ALL-FATHER THOR...
EVEN THE TROLLS HAVE DISAPPEARED. BY MY BEARD, I NEVER THOUGHT I WOULD COME TO MISS TROLLS.
BILLION PARDONS, MY LORD, BUT
N AFRAID THERE ARE PRESSING
ATTERS OF STATE THAT MUST
INTRUDE UPON THIS DAY OF
MOURNING.
WE'VE INTERCEPTED ANOTHER DEEP SPACE PROBE SENT BY THE KREE'AR EMPIRE TO SEARCH THE DEPTHS OF THE COSMOS FOR SIGNS OF INTELLIGENT LIFE. IT DOES NOT APPEAR TO HAVE FOUND ANY.
AN EMISSARY FROM THE REPUBLIC OF HEL AGAIN SEEKS AN AUDIENCE, CLAIMING HIS REALM'S OVERCROWDING HAS REACHED CALAMITOUS LEVELS.
A CREW OF ASTRO WHALERS HAVE SIGHTED WHAT THEY BELIEVE TO BE THE EATER OF WORLDS NEAR THE BURNING MOONS OF NEPTUNE. THOUGH THEY CLAIM THAT HE WAS CLAD ALL IN BLACK AND...
READY THE BIFROST.
MY LORD? SHOULD WE AT LEAST DISCUSS THE PLANNED FESTIVITIES FOR YOUR...
MY LORD THOR?
WHERE... WHERE IS HE GOING?
SAME PLACE HE ALWAYS GOES.

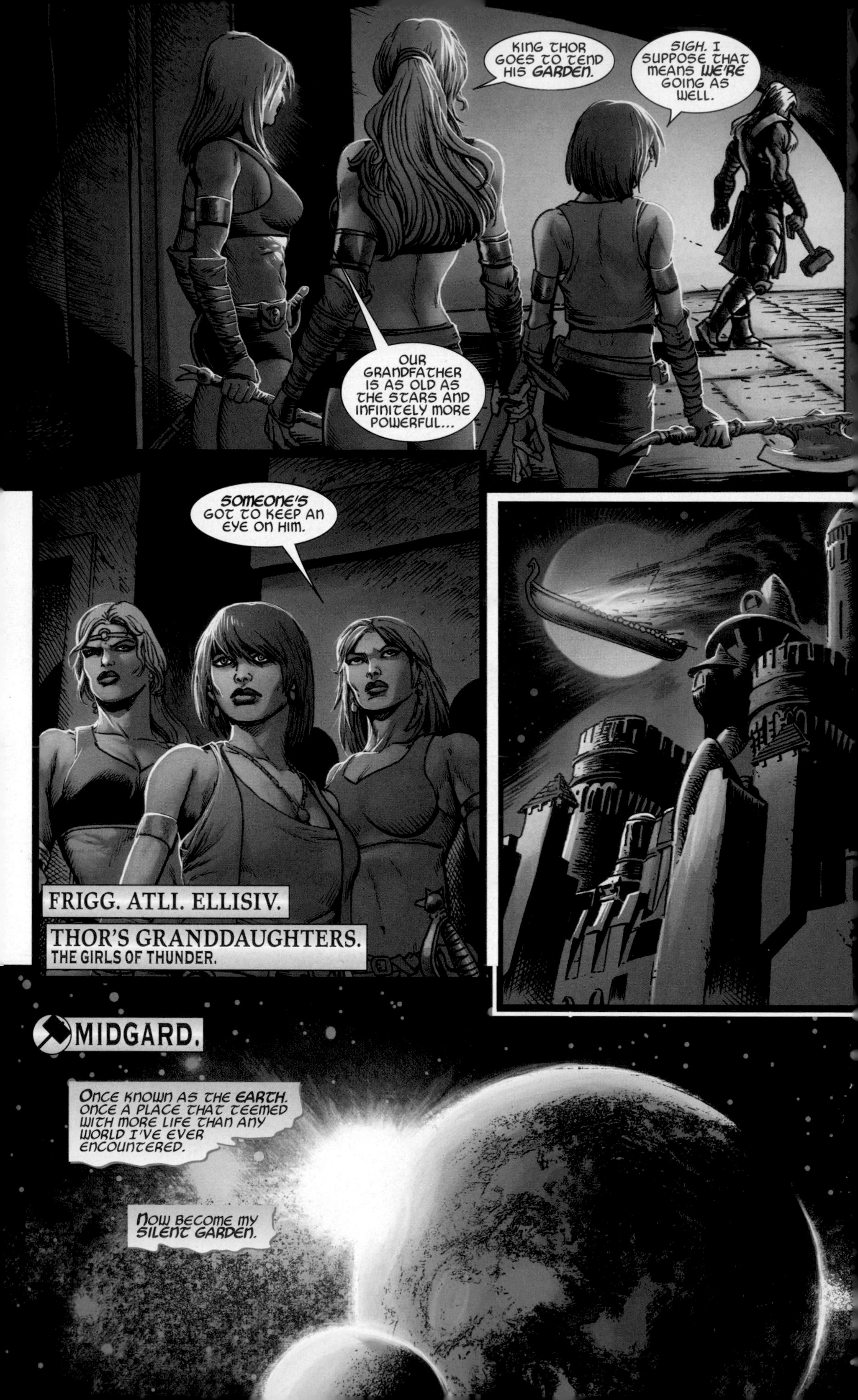
KING THOR GOES TO TEND HIS GARDEN.
SIGH. I SUPPOSE THAT MEANS WE'RE GOING AS WELL.
OUR GRANDFATHER IS AS OLD AS THE STARS AND INFINITELY MORE POWERFUL...
SOMEONE'S GOT TO KEEP AN EYE ON HIM.
FRIGG. ATLI. ELLISIV.
THOR'S GRANDDAUGHTERS.
THE GIRLS OF THUNDER.
MIDGARD.
ONCE KNOWN AS THE EARTH. ONCE A PLACE THAT TEEMED WITH MORE LIFE THAN ANY WORLD I'VE EVER ENCOUNTERED.
NOW BECOME MY SILENT GARDEN.

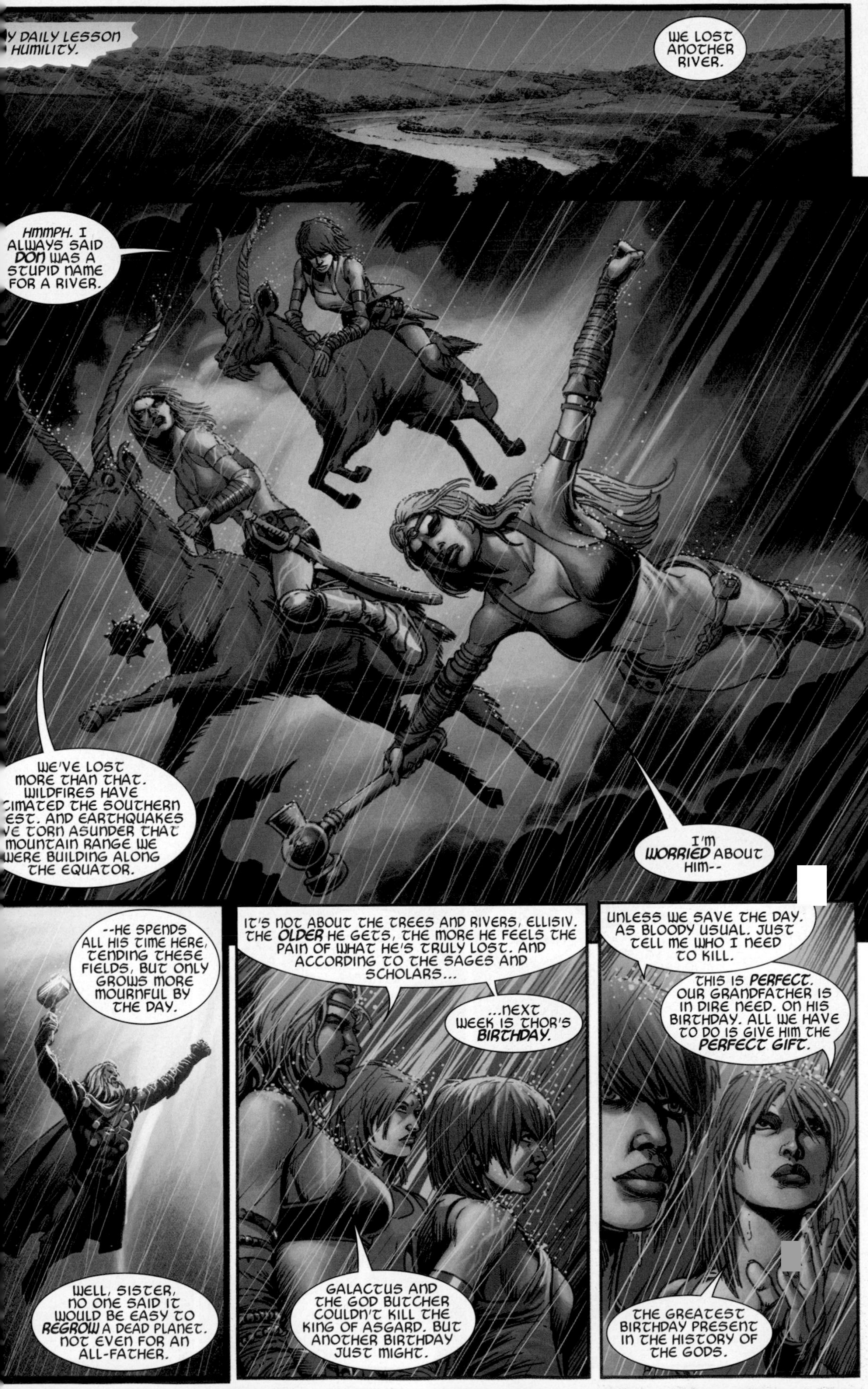
Y DAILY LESSON HUMILITY.
WE LOST ANOTHER RIVER.
HMMPH. I ALWAYS SAID DON WAS A STUPID NAME FOR A RIVER.
WE'VE LOST MORE THAN THAT. WILDFIRES HAVE CIMATED THE SOUTHERN EST. AND EARTHQUAKES VE TORN ASUNDER THAT MOUNTAIN RANGE WE WERE BUILDING ALONG THE EQUATOR.
I'M WORRIED ABOUT HIM--
--HE SPENDS ALL HIS TIME HERE, TENDING THESE FIELDS, BUT ONLY GROWS MORE MOURNFUL BY THE DAY.
WELL, SISTER, NO ONE SAID IT WOULD BE EASY TO REGROW A DEAD PLANET. NOT EVEN FOR AN ALL-FATHER.
IT'S NOT ABOUT THE TREES AND RIVERS, ELLISIV. THE OLDER HE GETS, THE MORE HE FEELS THE PAIN OF WHAT HE'S TRULY LOST. AND ACCORDING TO THE SAGES AND SCHOLARS...
...NEXT WEEK IS THOR'S BIRTHDAY.
GALACTUS AND THE GOD BUTCHER COULDN'T KILL THE KING OF ASGARD. BUT ANOTHER BIRTHDAY JUST MIGHT.
UNLESS WE SAVE THE DAY. AS BLOODY USUAL. JUST TELL ME WHO I NEED TO KILL.
THIS IS PERFECT. OUR GRANDFATHER IS IN DIRE NEED. ON HIS BIRTHDAY. ALL WE HAVE TO DO IS GIVE HIM THE PERFECT GIFT.
THE GREATEST BIRTHDAY PRESENT IN THE HISTORY OF THE GODS.

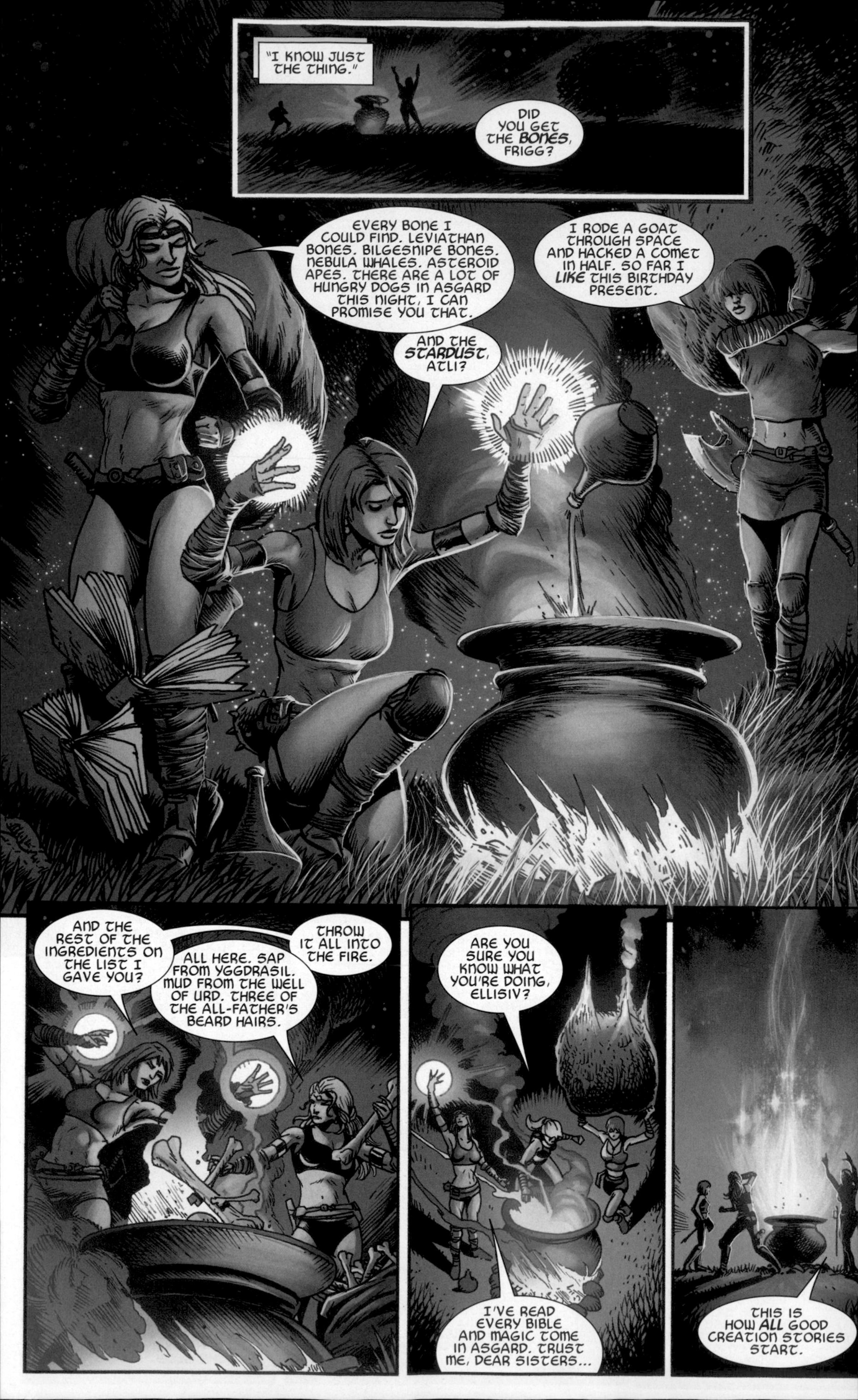
"I KNOW JUST THE THING."
DID YOU GET THE BONES, FRIGG?
EVERY BONE I COULD FIND. LEVIATHAN BONES. BILGESNIPE BONES. NEBULA WHALES. ASTEROID APES. THERE ARE A LOT OF HUNGRY DOGS IN ASGARD THIS NIGHT, I CAN PROMISE YOU THAT.
I RODE A GOAT THROUGH SPACE AND HACKED A COMET IN HALF. SO FAR I LIKE THIS BIRTHDAY PRESENT.
AND THE STARDUST, ATLI?
AND THE REST OF THE INGREDIENTS ON THE LIST I GAVE YOU?
ALL HERE. SAP FROM YGGDRASIL. MUD FROM THE WELL OF URD. THREE OF THE ALL-FATHER'S BEARD HAIRS.
THROW IT ALL INTO THE FIRE.
ARE YOU SURE YOU KNOW WHAT YOU'RE DOING, ELLISIV?
I'VE READ EVERY BIBLE AND MAGIC TOME IN ASGARD. TRUST ME, DEAR SISTERS...
THIS IS HOW ALL GOOD CREATION STORIES START.

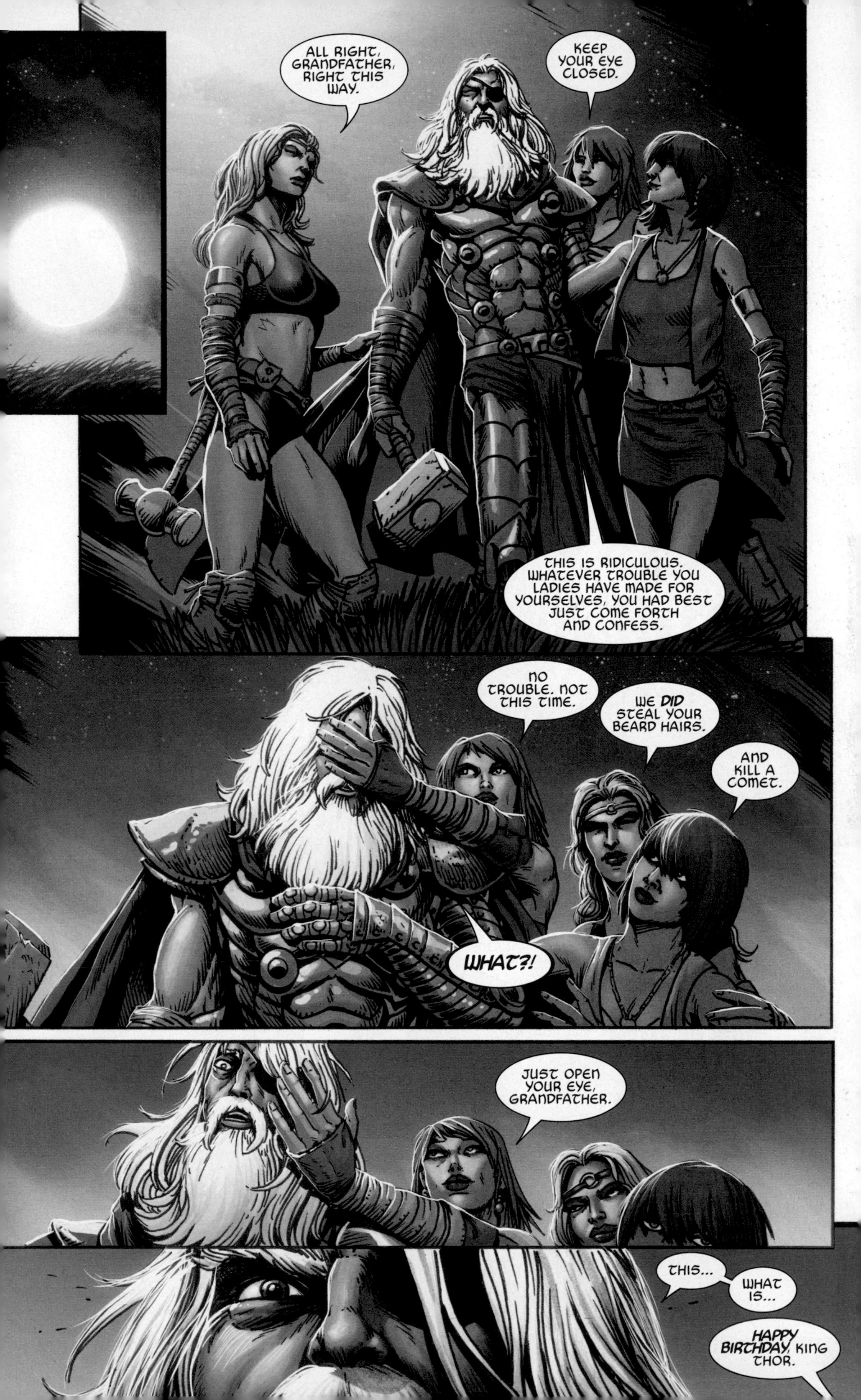
ALL RIGHT, GRANDFATHER, RIGHT THIS WAY.
KEEP YOUR EYE CLOSED.
THIS IS RIDICULOUS. WHATEVER TROUBLE YOU LADIES HAVE MADE FOR YOURSELVES, YOU HAD BEST JUST COME FORTH AND CONFESS.
NO TROUBLE. NOT THIS TIME.
WE **DID** STEAL YOUR BEARD HAIRS.
AND KILL A COMET.
WHAT?!
JUST OPEN YOUR EYE, GRANDFATHER.
THIS...
WHAT IS...
HAPPY BIRTHDAY, KING THOR.

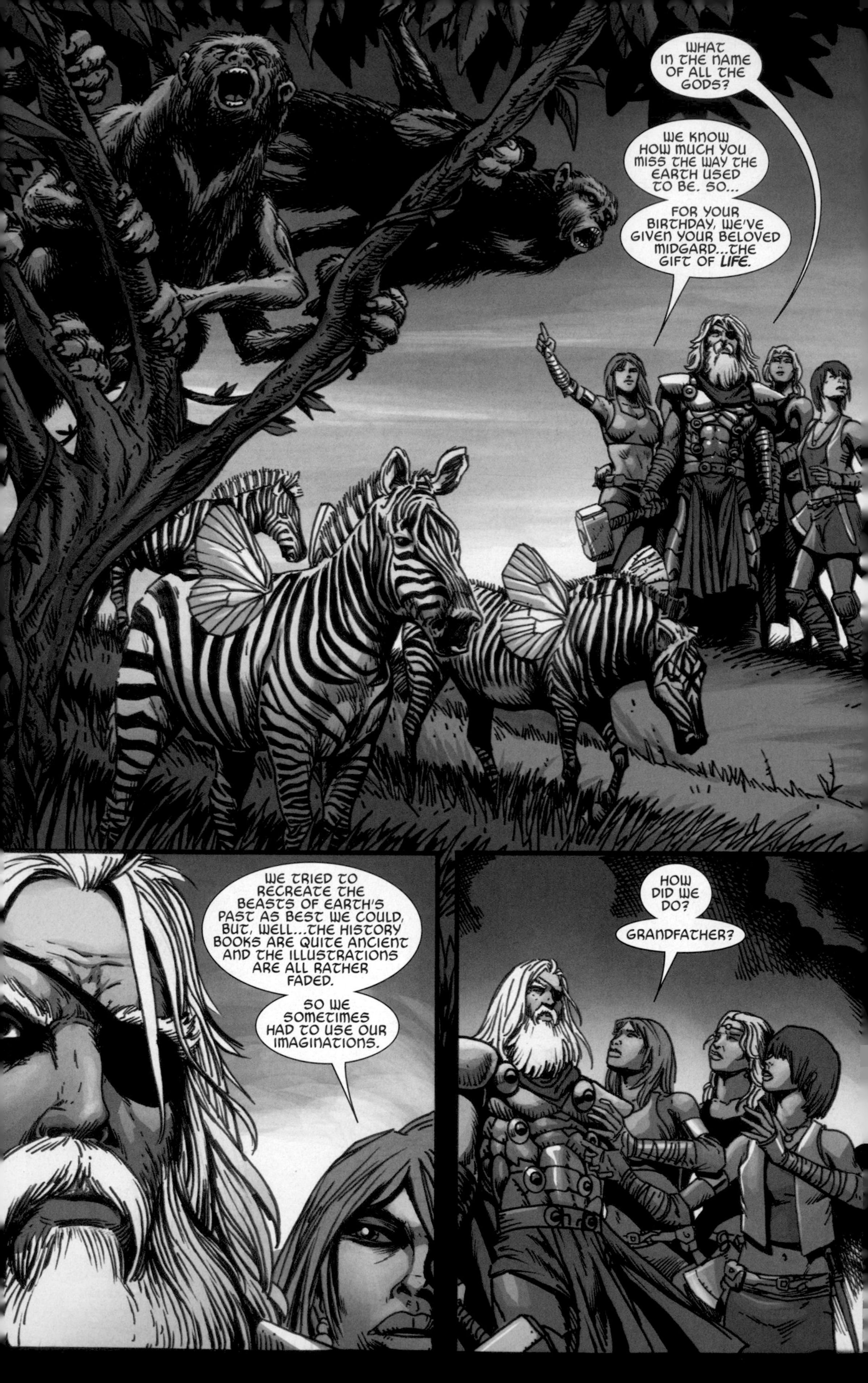
WHAT IN THE NAME OF ALL THE GODS?
WE KNOW HOW MUCH YOU MISS THE WAY THE EARTH USED TO BE. SO...
FOR YOUR BIRTHDAY, WE'VE GIVEN YOUR BELOVED MIDGARD...THE GIFT OF **LIFE.**
WE TRIED TO RECREATE THE BEASTS OF EARTH'S PAST AS BEST WE COULD, BUT, WELL...THE HISTORY BOOKS ARE QUITE ANCIENT AND THE ILLUSTRATIONS ARE ALL RATHER FADED.
SO WE SOMETIMES HAD TO USE OUR IMAGINATIONS.
HOW DID WE DO?
GRANDFATHER?

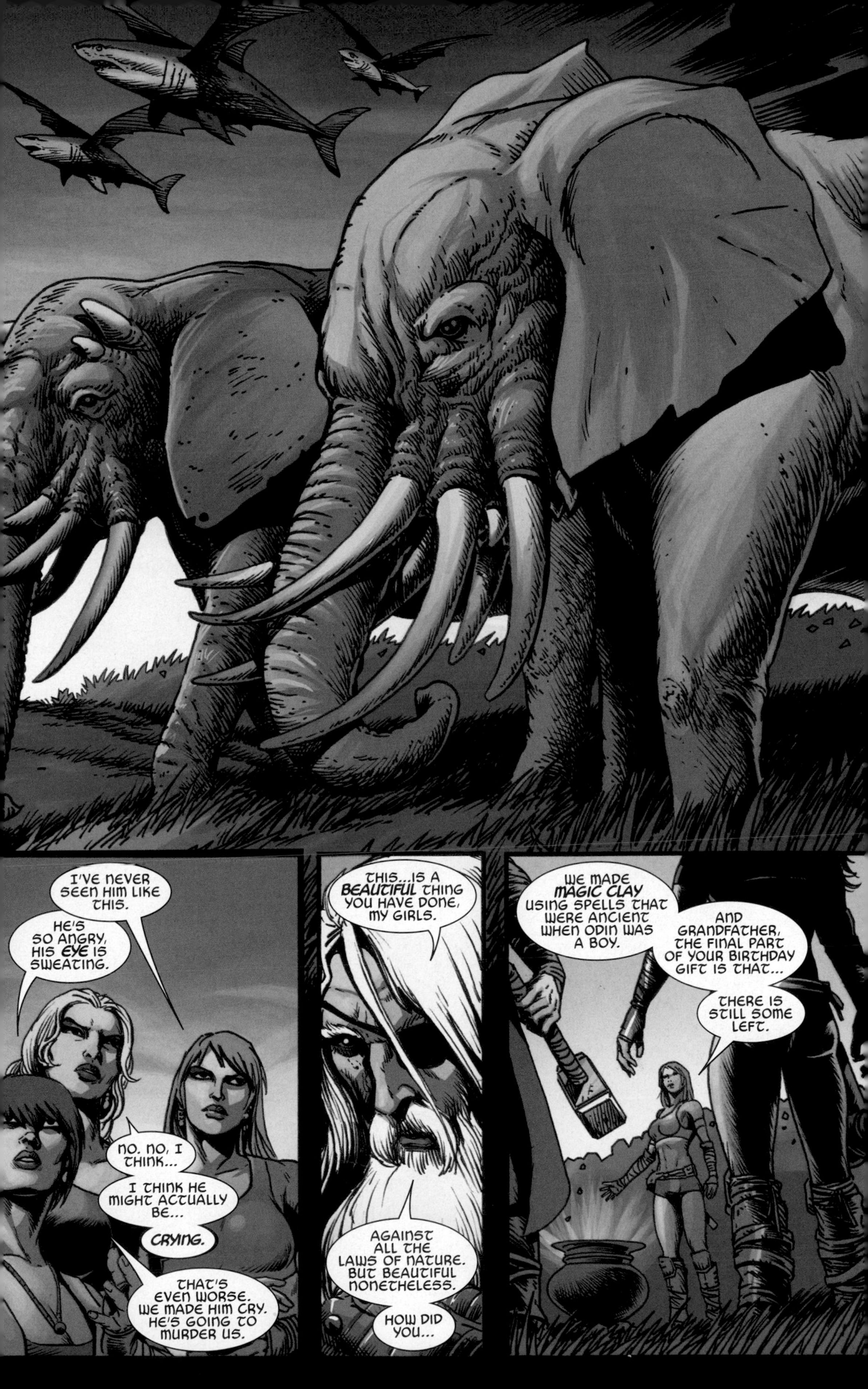

I'VE NEVER SEEN HIM LIKE THIS.
HE'S SO ANGRY, HIS EYE IS SWEATING.
NO. NO, I THINK...
I THINK HE MIGHT ACTUALLY BE...
CRYING.
THAT'S EVEN WORSE. WE MADE HIM CRY. HE'S GOING TO MURDER US.
THIS...IS A BEAUTIFUL THING YOU HAVE DONE, MY GIRLS.
AGAINST ALL THE LAWS OF NATURE. BUT BEAUTIFUL NONETHELESS.
HOW DID YOU...
WE MADE MAGIC CLAY USING SPELLS THAT WERE ANCIENT WHEN ODIN WAS A BOY.
AND GRANDFATHER, THE FINAL PART OF YOUR BIRTHDAY GIFT IS THAT...
THERE IS STILL SOME LEFT.

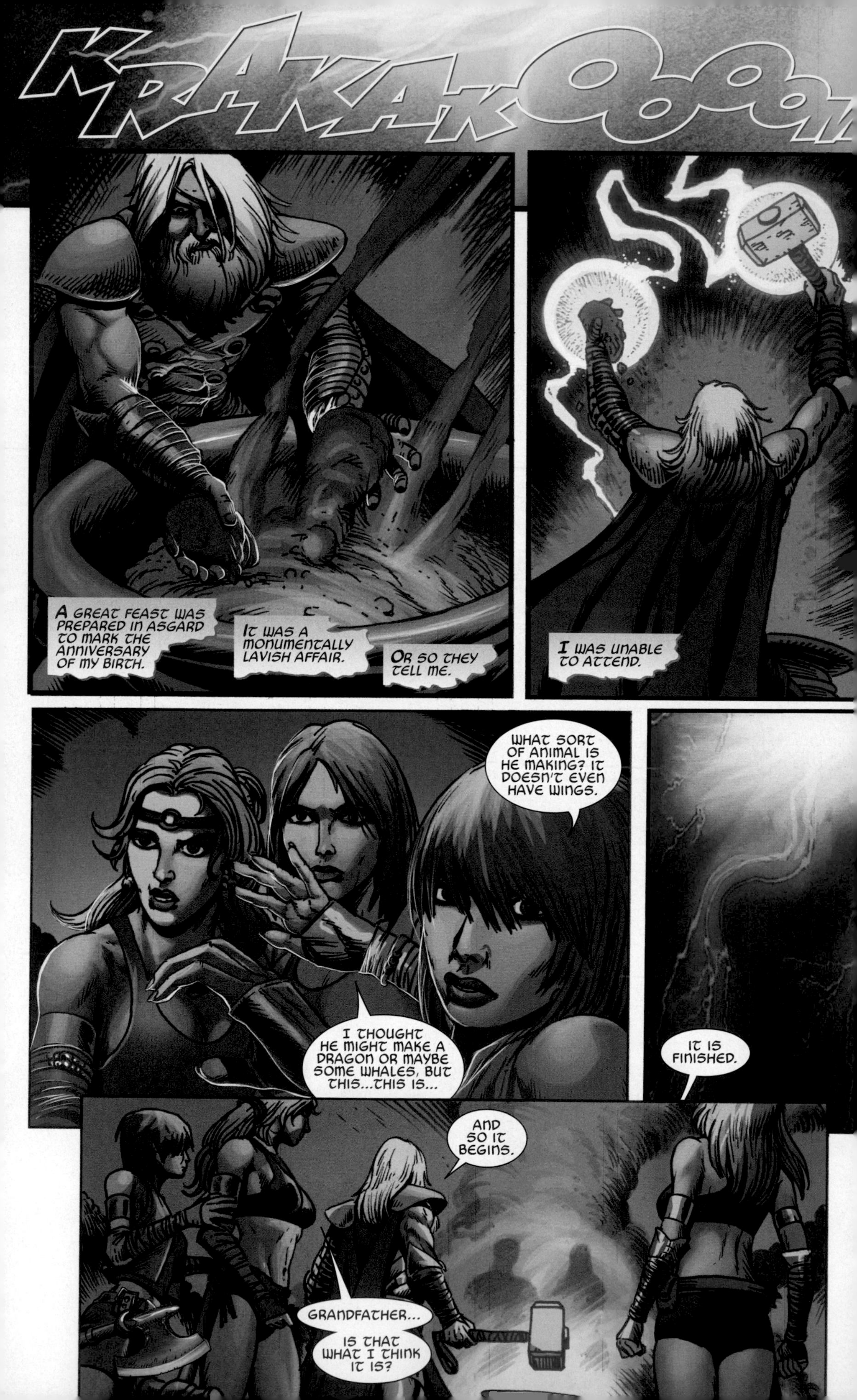
KRAKAKOOOOM
A GREAT FEAST WAS PREPARED IN ASGARD TO MARK THE ANNIVERSARY OF MY BIRTH.
IT WAS A MONUMENTALLY LAVISH AFFAIR.
OR SO THEY TELL ME.
I WAS UNABLE TO ATTEND.
WHAT SORT OF ANIMAL IS HE MAKING? IT DOESN'T EVEN HAVE WINGS.
I THOUGHT HE MIGHT MAKE A DRAGON OR MAYBE SOME WHALES, BUT THIS...THIS IS...
IT IS FINISHED.
AND SO IT BEGINS.
GRANDFATHER...
IS THAT WHAT I THINK IT IS?

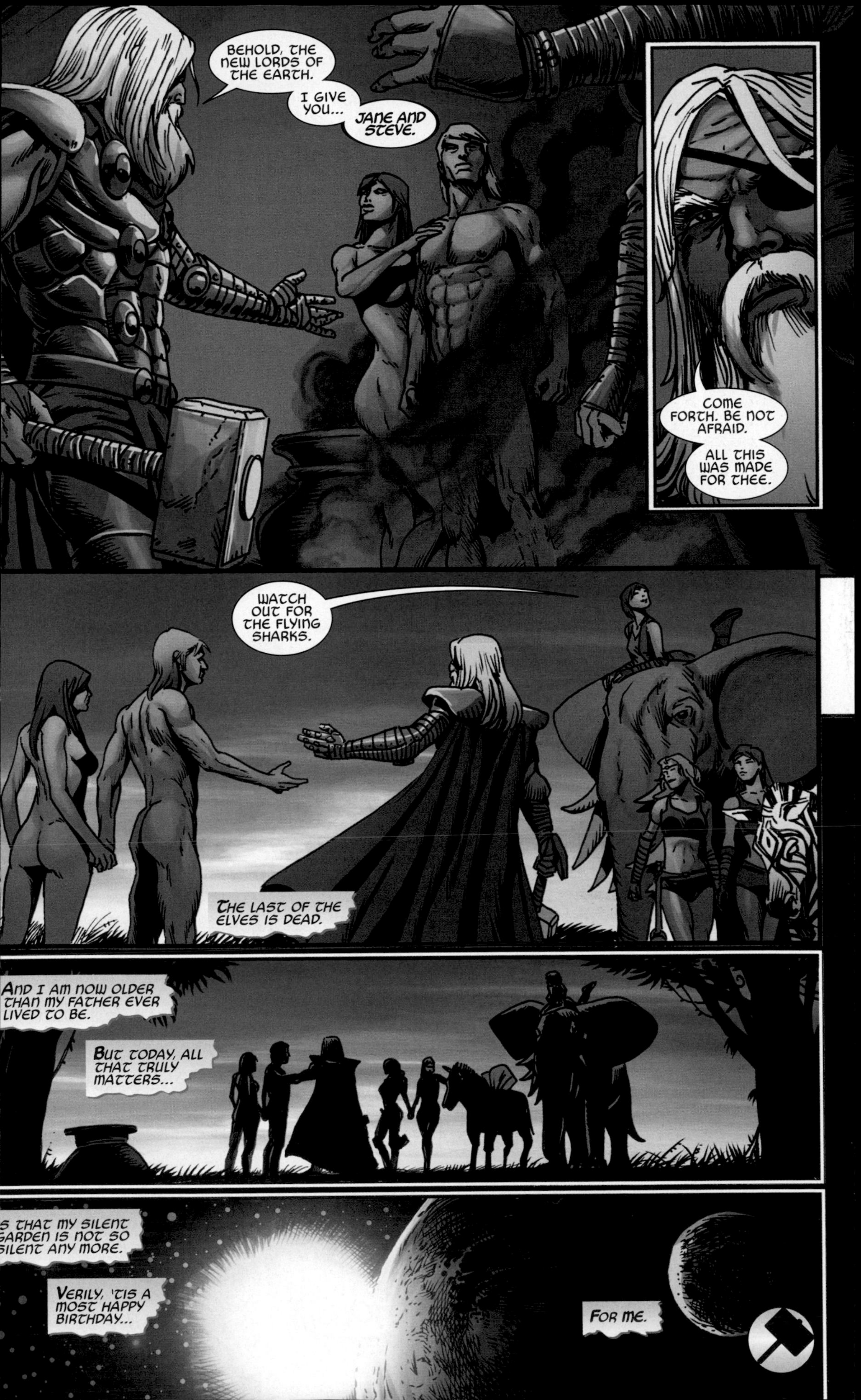
BEHOLD, THE NEW LORDS OF THE EARTH.
I GIVE YOU...
JANE AND STEVE.
COME FORTH. BE NOT AFRAID.
ALL THIS WAS MADE FOR THEE.
WATCH OUT FOR THE FLYING SHARKS.
THE LAST OF THE ELVES IS DEAD.
AND I AM NOW OLDER THAN MY FATHER EVER LIVED TO BE.
BUT TODAY, ALL THAT TRULY MATTERS...
S THAT MY SILENT GARDEN IS NOT SO SILENT ANY MORE.
VERILY, 'TIS A MOST HAPPY BIRTHDAY...
FOR ME.

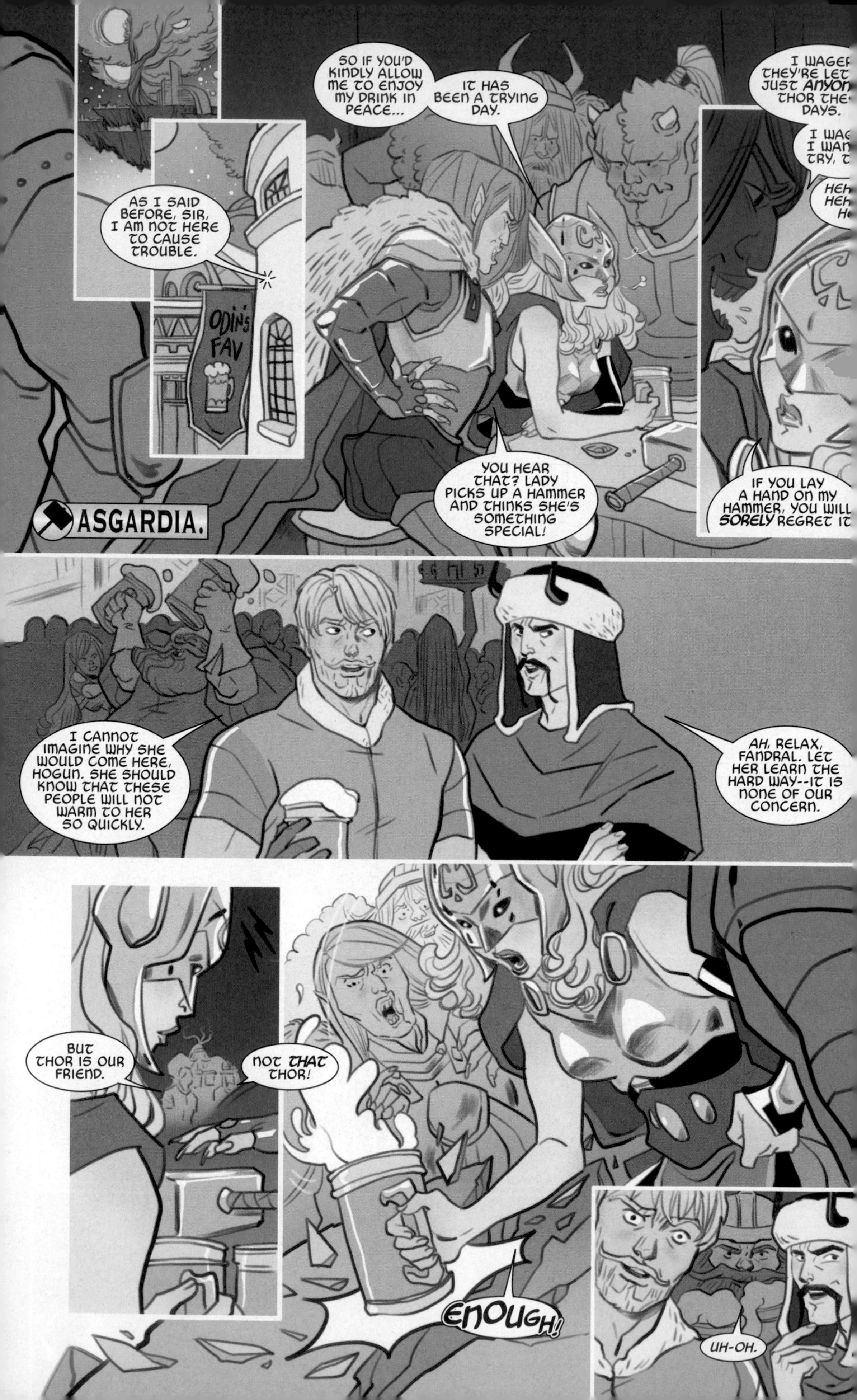
ODIN'S FAV
AS I SAID BEFORE, SIR, I AM NOT HERE TO CAUSE TROUBLE.
ASGARDIA.
SO IF YOU'D KINDLY ALLOW ME TO ENJOY MY DRINK IN PEACE...
IT HAS BEEN A TRYING DAY.
YOU HEAR THAT? LADY PICKS UP A HAMMER AND THINKS SHE'S SOMETHING SPECIAL!
I WAGER THEY'RE LET JUST ANYONE THOR THESE DAYS.
IF YOU LAY A HAND ON MY HAMMER, YOU WILL SORELY REGRET IT.
I CANNOT IMAGINE WHY SHE WOULD COME HERE, HOGUN. SHE SHOULD KNOW THAT THESE PEOPLE WILL NOT WARM TO HER SO QUICKLY.
AH, RELAX, FANDRAL. LET HER LEARN THE HARD WAY--IT IS NONE OF OUR CONCERN.
BUT THOR IS OUR FRIEND.
NOT THAT THOR!
ENOUGH!
UH-OH.

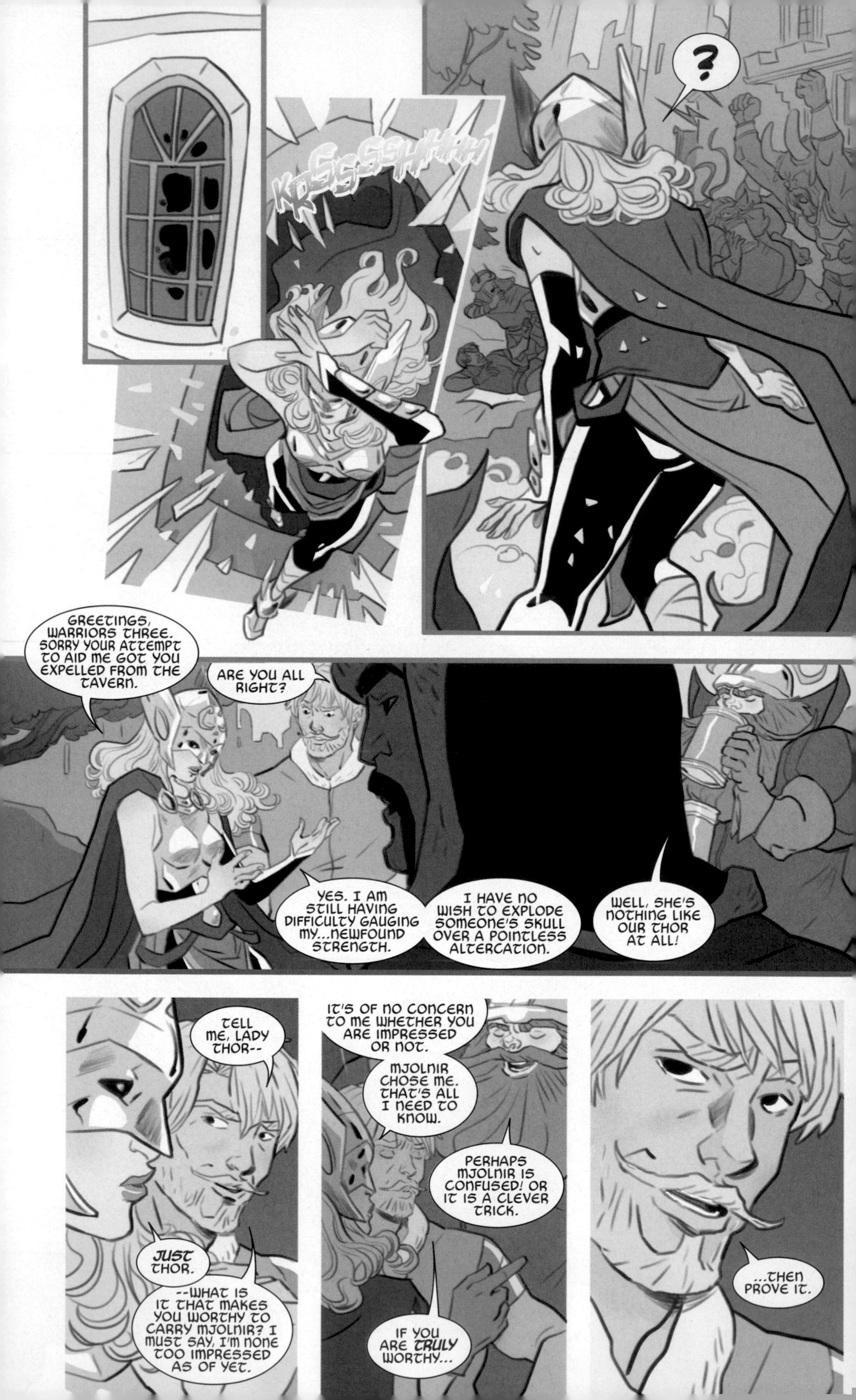
KRSSSSHHH
?
GREETINGS, WARRIORS THREE. SORRY YOUR ATTEMPT TO AID ME GOT YOU EXPELLED FROM THE TAVERN.
ARE YOU ALL RIGHT?
YES. I AM STILL HAVING DIFFICULTY GAUGING MY...NEWFOUND STRENGTH.
I HAVE NO WISH TO EXPLODE SOMEONE'S SKULL OVER A POINTLESS ALTERCATION.
WELL, SHE'S NOTHING LIKE OUR THOR AT ALL!
TELL ME, LADY THOR--
JUST THOR.
--WHAT IS IT THAT MAKES YOU WORTHY TO CARRY MJOLNIR? I MUST SAY, I'M NONE TOO IMPRESSED AS OF YET.
IT'S OF NO CONCERN TO ME WHETHER YOU ARE IMPRESSED OR NOT.
MJOLNIR CHOSE ME. THAT'S ALL I NEED TO KNOW.
PERHAPS MJOLNIR IS CONFUSED! OR IT IS A CLEVER TRICK.
IF YOU ARE TRULY WORTHY...
...THEN PROVE IT.

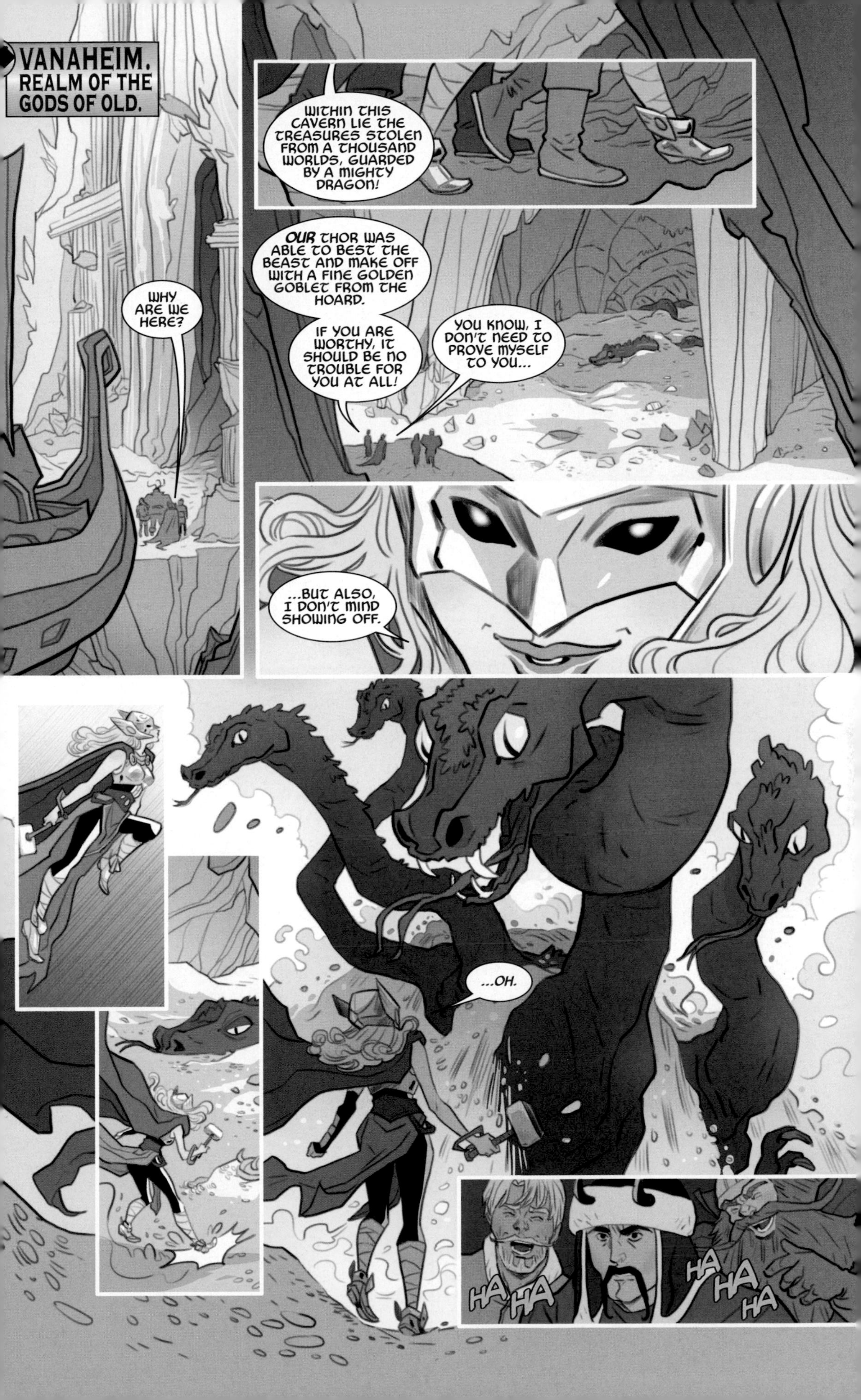
VANAHEIM. REALM OF THE GODS OF OLD.
WHY ARE WE HERE?
WITHIN THIS CAVERN LIE THE TREASURES STOLEN FROM A THOUSAND WORLDS, GUARDED BY A MIGHTY DRAGON!
OUR THOR WAS ABLE TO BEST THE BEAST AND MAKE OFF WITH A FINE GOLDEN GOBLET FROM THE HOARD.
IF YOU ARE WORTHY, IT SHOULD BE NO TROUBLE FOR YOU AT ALL!
YOU KNOW, I DON'T NEED TO PROVE MYSELF TO YOU...
...BUT ALSO, I DON'T MIND SHOWING OFF.
...OH.
HA HA
HA HA HA

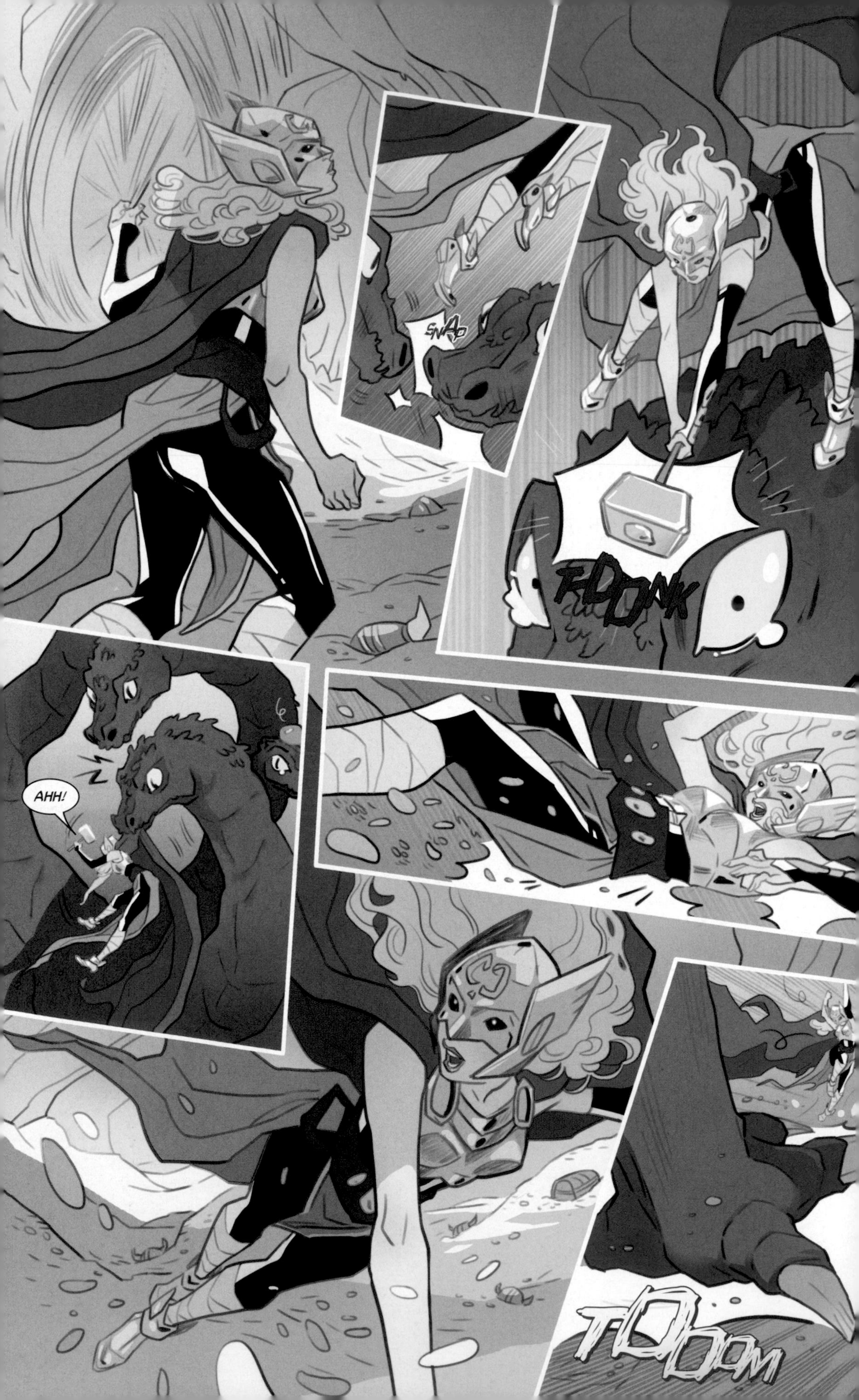
SNAP
TOONK
AHH!
TOOOM

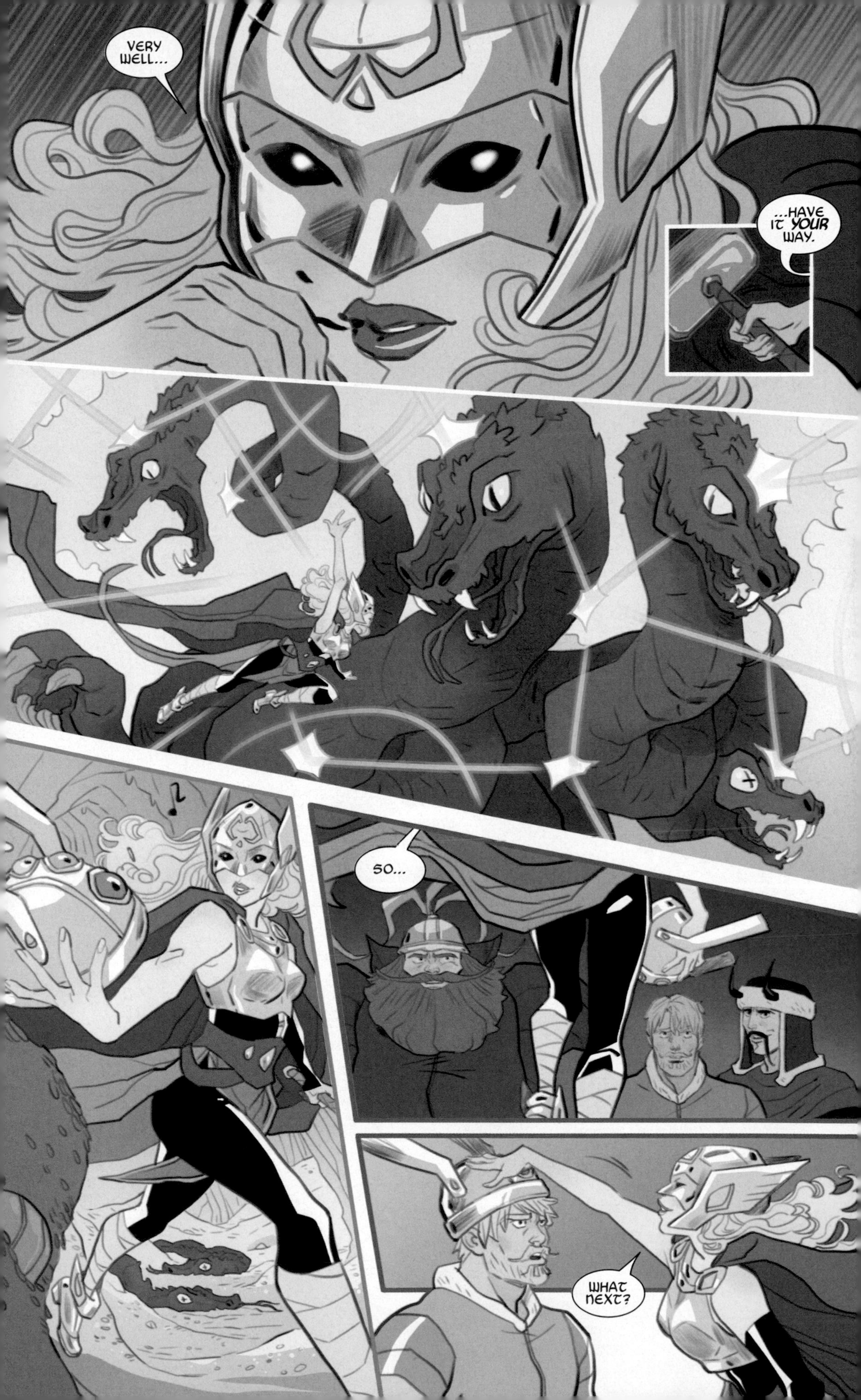
VERY WELL...
...HAVE IT YOUR WAY.
SO...
WHAT NEXT?

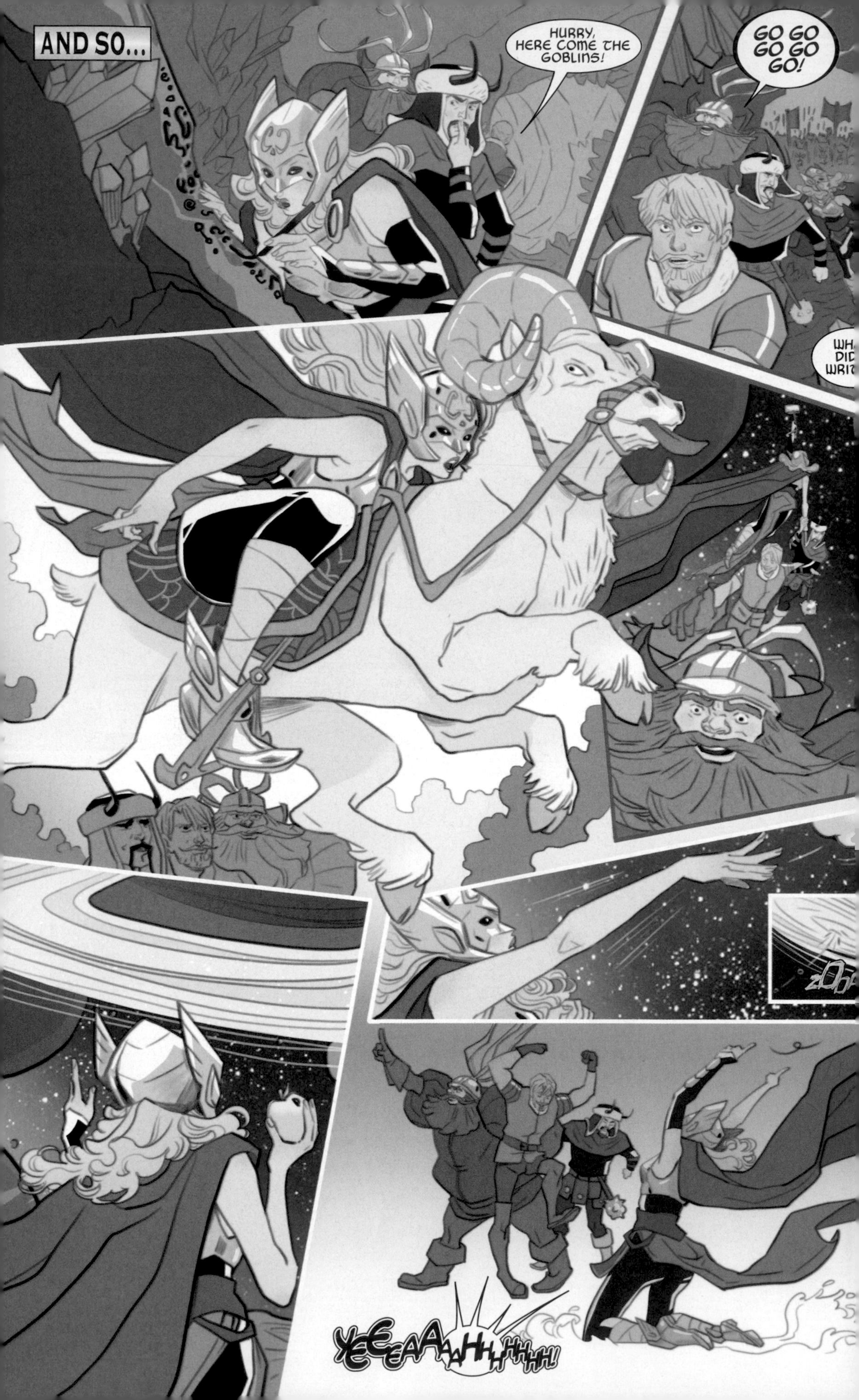
AND SO...
HURRY, HERE COME THE GOBLINS!
GO GO GO GO GO!
YEEEAAAAHHHHHHHH!

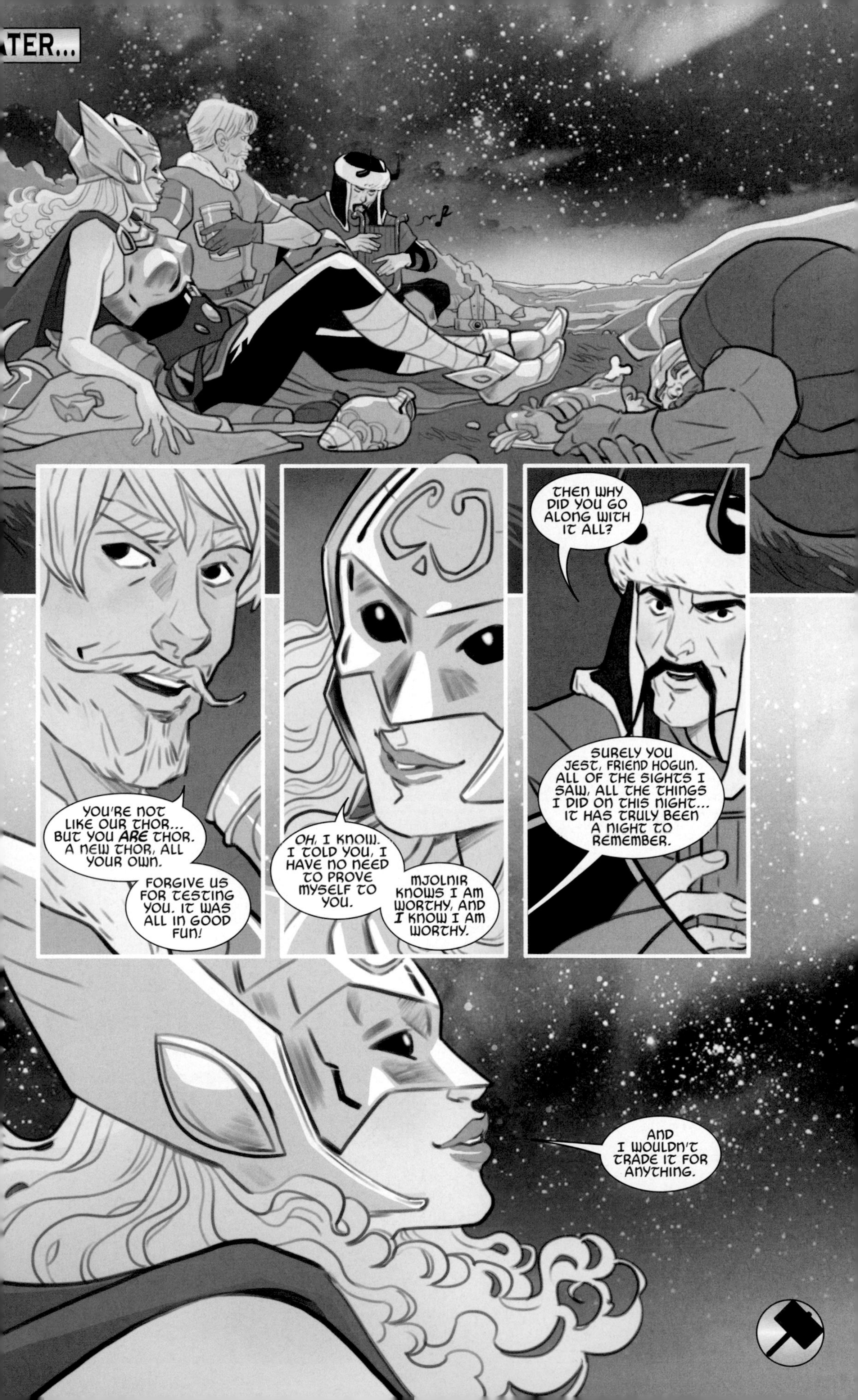

TER...
YOU'RE NOT LIKE OUR THOR... BUT YOU ARE THOR. A NEW THOR, ALL YOUR OWN.
FORGIVE US FOR TESTING YOU. IT WAS ALL IN GOOD FUN!
OH, I KNOW. I TOLD YOU, I HAVE NO NEED TO PROVE MYSELF TO YOU.
MJOLNIR KNOWS I AM WORTHY, AND I KNOW I AM WORTHY.
THEN WHY DID YOU GO ALONG WITH IT ALL?
SURELY YOU JEST, FRIEND HOGUN. ALL OF THE SIGHTS I SAW, ALL THE THINGS I DID ON THIS NIGHT... IT HAS TRULY BEEN A NIGHT TO REMEMBER.
AND I WOULDN'T TRADE IT FOR ANYTHING.

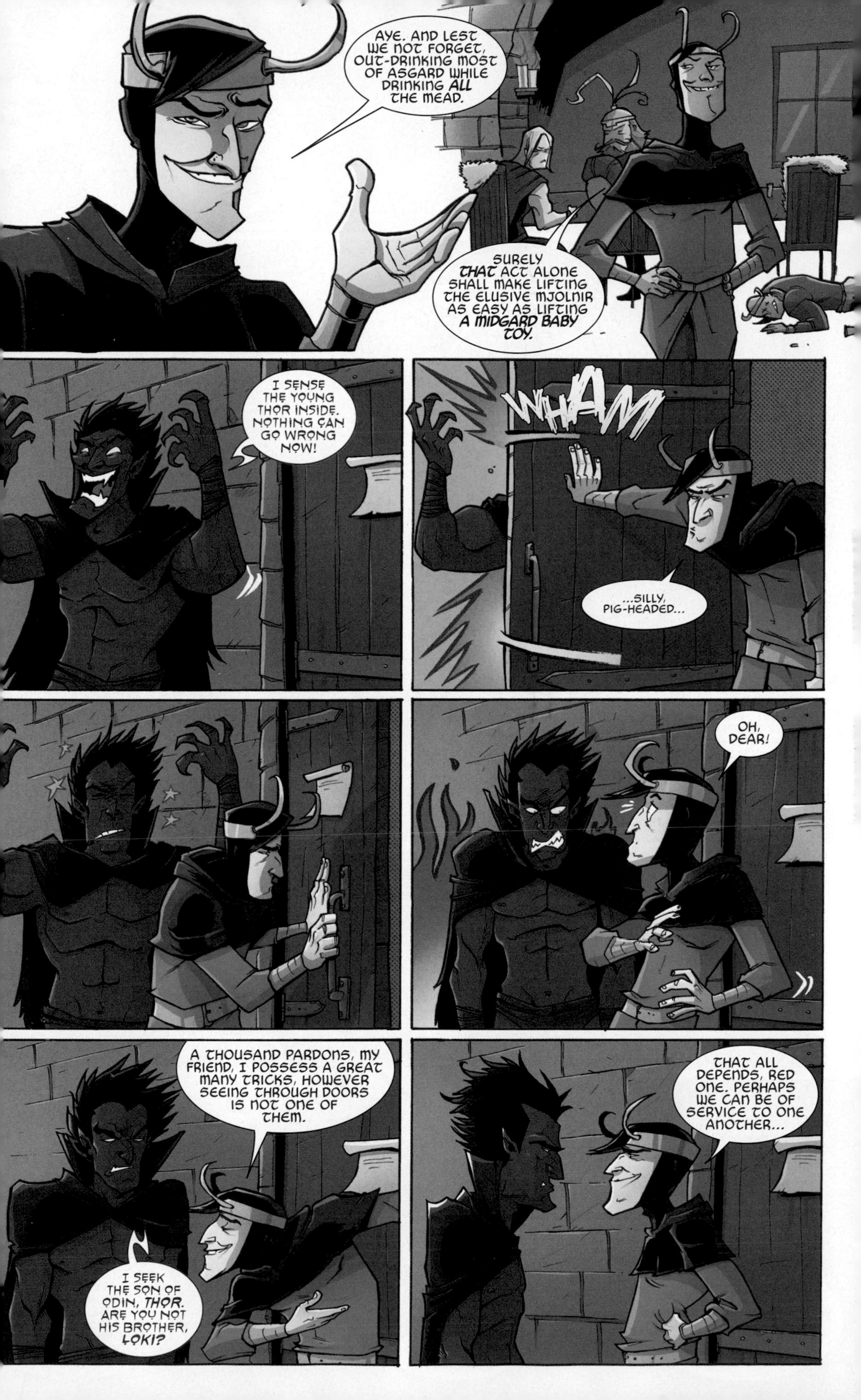
AYE. AND LEST WE NOT FORGET, OUT-DRINKING MOST OF ASGARD WHILE DRINKING ALL THE MEAD.
SURELY THAT ACT ALONE SHALL MAKE LIFTING THE ELUSIVE MJOLNIR AS EASY AS LIFTING A MIDGARD BABY TOY.
I SENSE THE YOUNG THOR INSIDE. NOTHING CAN GO WRONG NOW!
WHAM
...SILLY, PIG-HEADED...
OH, DEAR!
I SEEK THE SON OF ODIN, THOR. ARE YOU NOT HIS BROTHER, LOKI?
A THOUSAND PARDONS, MY FRIEND, I POSSESS A GREAT MANY TRICKS, HOWEVER SEEING THROUGH DOORS IS NOT ONE OF THEM.
THAT ALL DEPENDS, RED ONE. PERHAPS WE CAN BE OF SERVICE TO ONE ANOTHER...

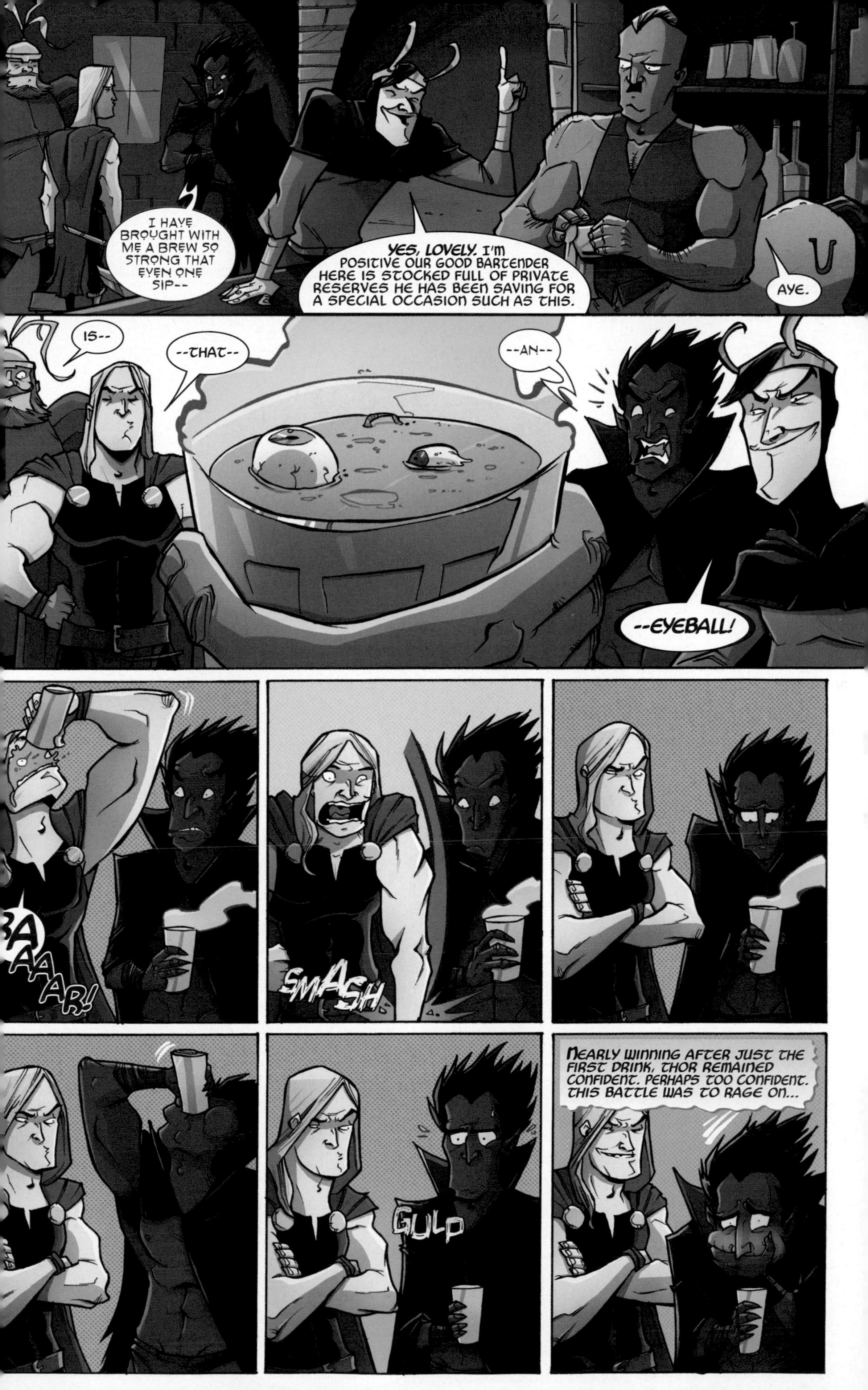

I HAVE BROUGHT WITH ME A BREW SO STRONG THAT EVEN ONE SIP--
YES, LOVELY. I'M POSITIVE OUR GOOD BARTENDER HERE IS STOCKED FULL OF PRIVATE RESERVES HE HAS BEEN SAVING FOR A SPECIAL OCCASION SUCH AS THIS.
AYE.
IS--
--THAT--
--AN--
--EYEBALL!
BAAAAAR!
SMASH
GULP
NEARLY WINNING AFTER JUST THE FIRST DRINK, THOR REMAINED CONFIDENT. PERHAPS TOO CONFIDENT. THIS BATTLE WAS TO RAGE ON...

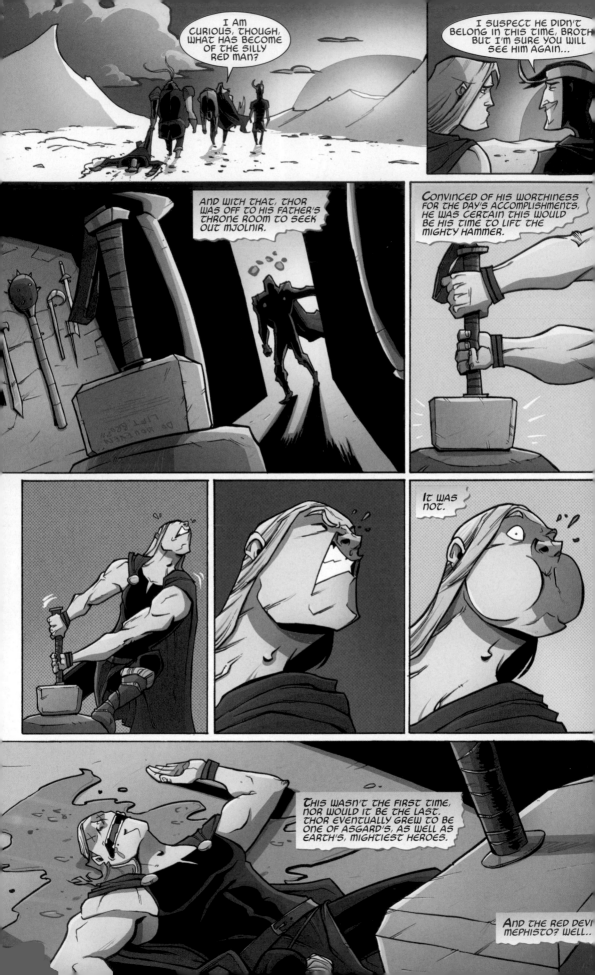

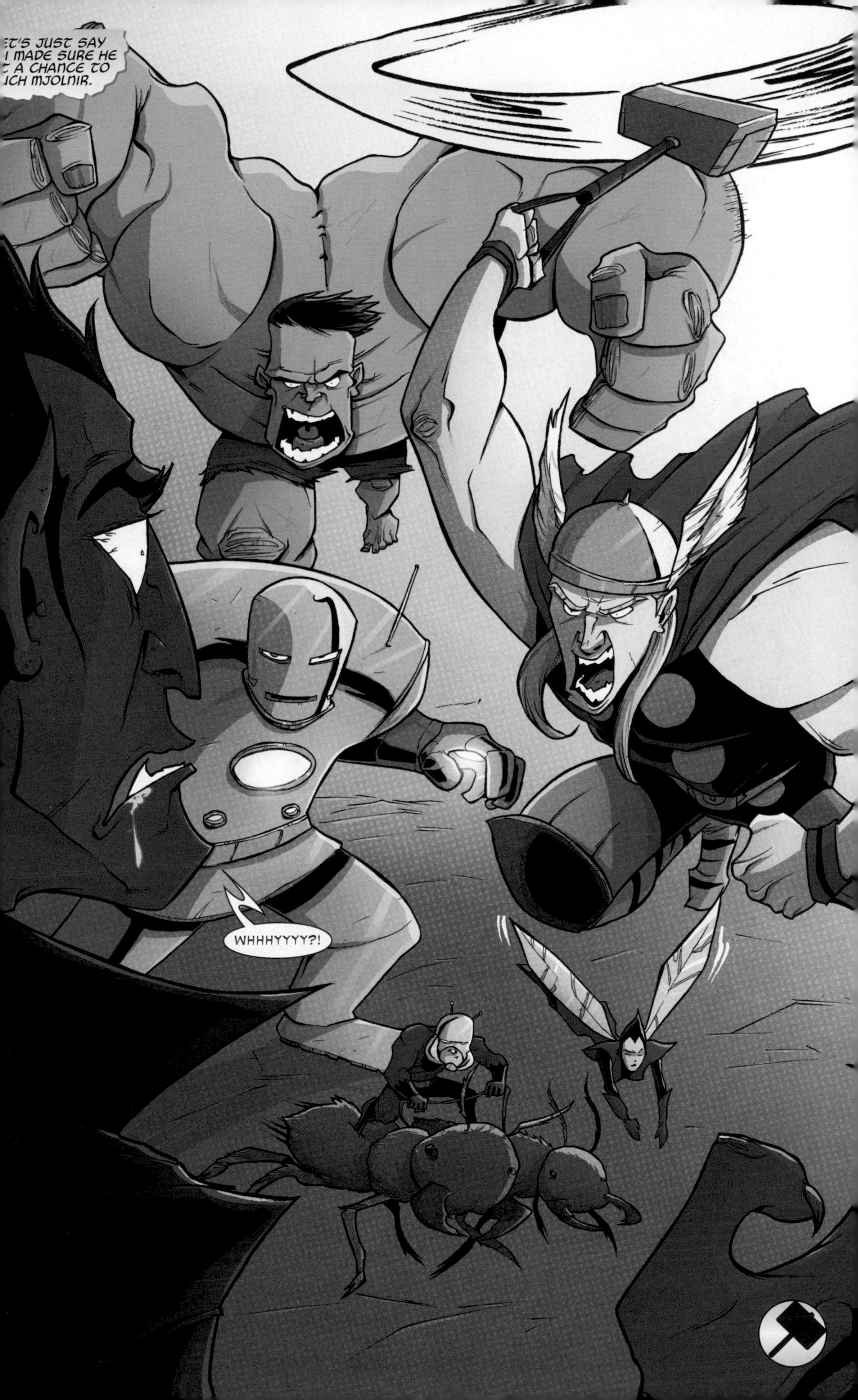
ET'S JUST SAY
I MADE SURE HE
T A CHANCE TO
ICH MJOLNIR.
WHHHYYYY?!

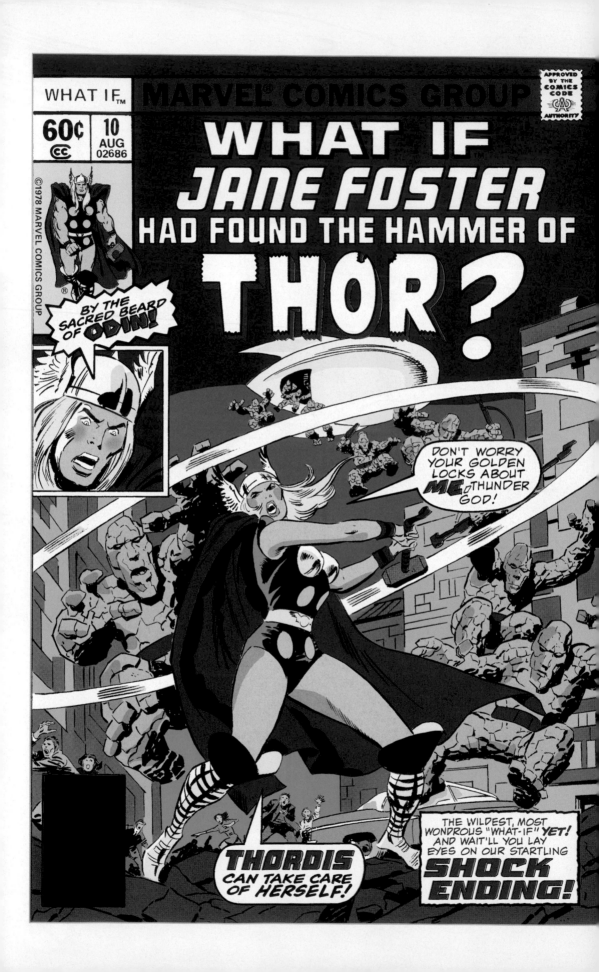

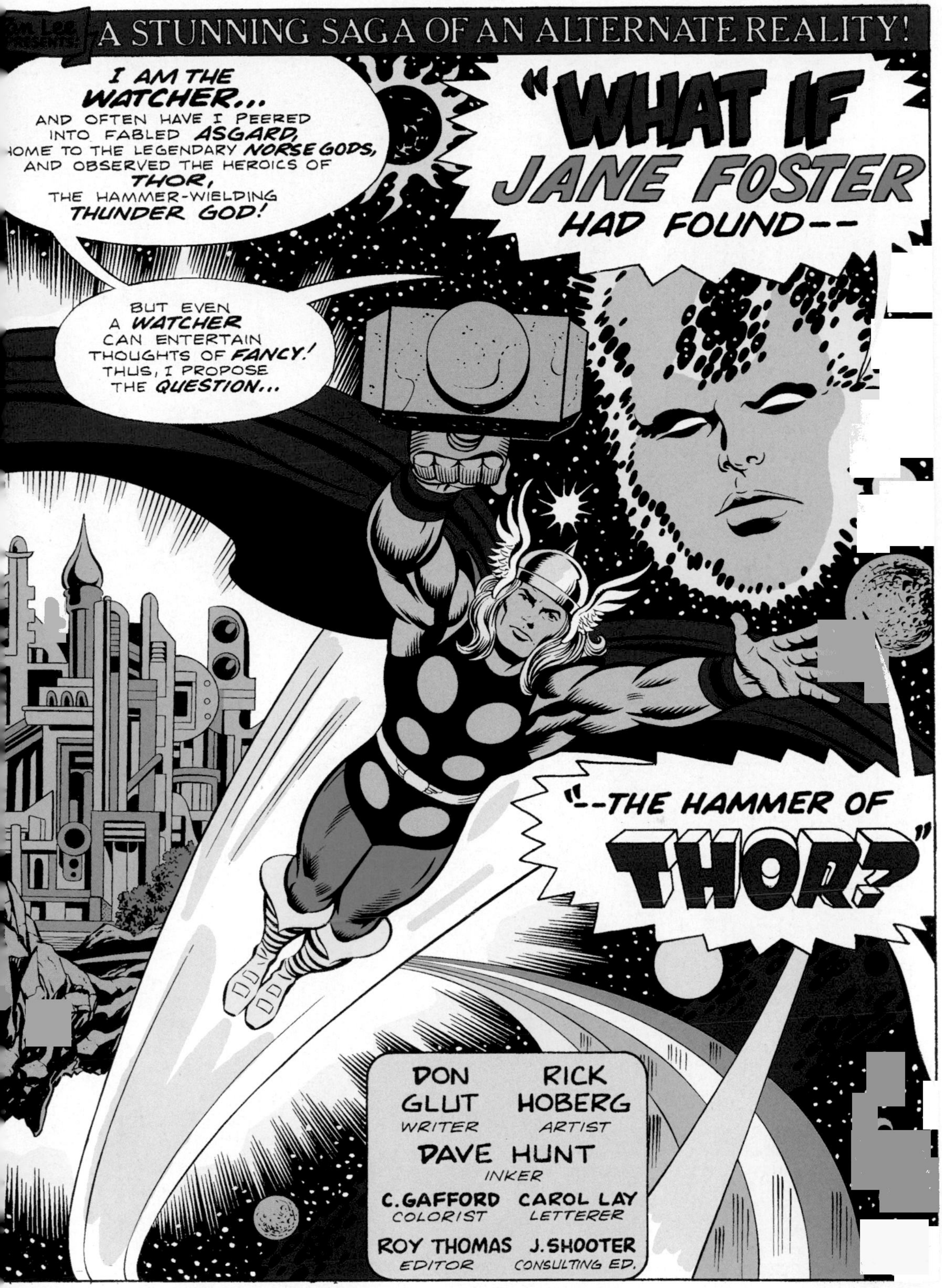
PRESENTS
A STUNNING SAGA OF AN ALTERNATE REALITY!
I AM THE WATCHER... AND OFTEN HAVE I PEERED INTO FABLED ASGARD, HOME TO THE LEGENDARY NORSE GODS, AND OBSERVED THE HEROICS OF THOR, THE HAMMER-WIELDING THUNDER GOD!
"WHAT IF JANE FOSTER HAD FOUND--
BUT EVEN A WATCHER CAN ENTERTAIN THOUGHTS OF FANCY! THUS, I PROPOSE THE QUESTION...
"--THE HAMMER OF THOR?"
DON GLUT WRITER
RICK HOBERG ARTIST
DAVE HUNT INKER
C. GAFFORD COLORIST
CAROL LAY LETTERER
ROY THOMAS EDITOR
J. SHOOTER CONSULTING ED.

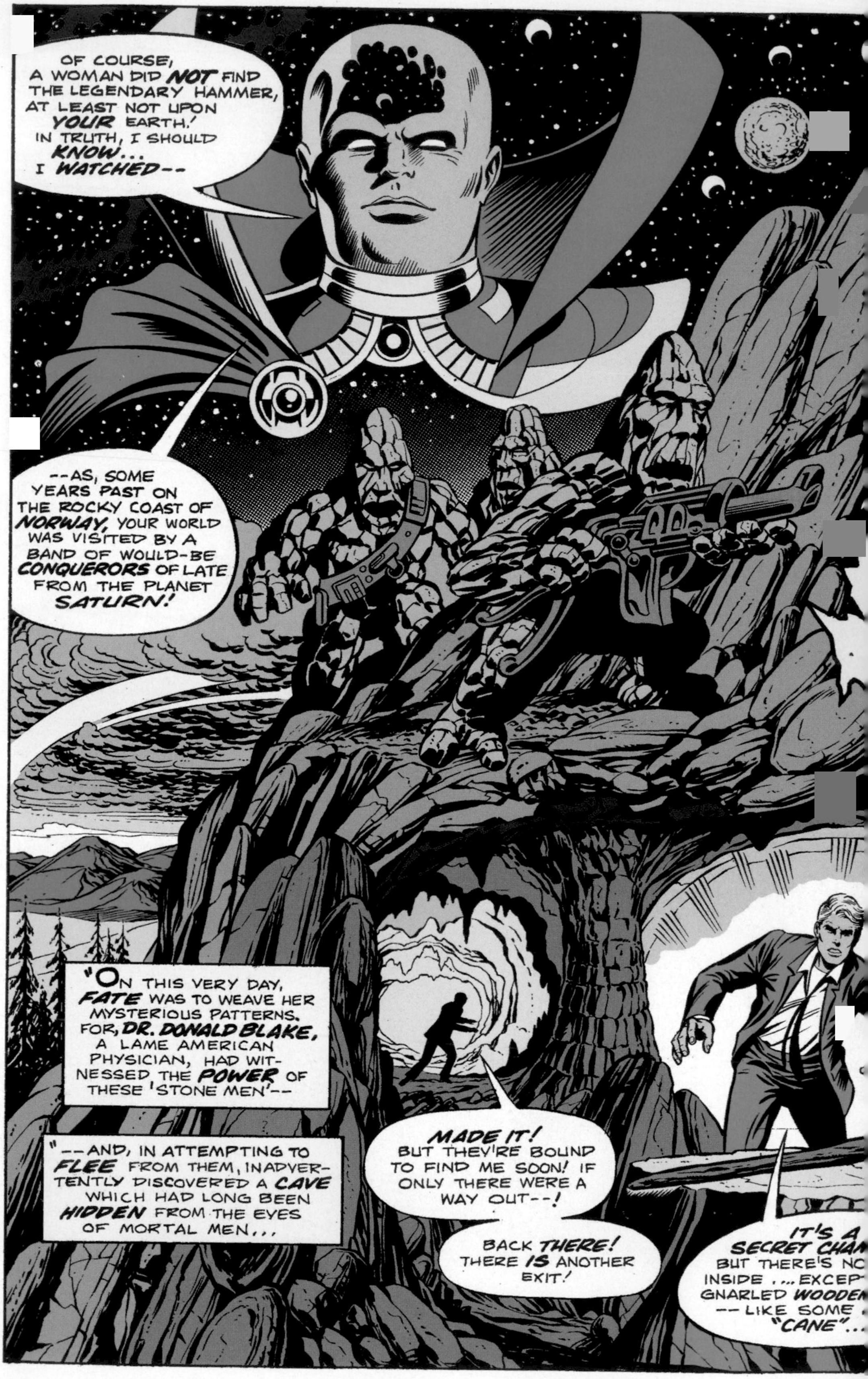

OF COURSE, A WOMAN DID NOT FIND THE LEGENDARY HAMMER, AT LEAST NOT UPON YOUR EARTH! IN TRUTH, I SHOULD KNOW... I WATCHED--
--AS, SOME YEARS PAST ON THE ROCKY COAST OF NORWAY, YOUR WORLD WAS VISITED BY A BAND OF WOULD-BE CONQUERORS OF LATE FROM THE PLANET SATURN!
"ON THIS VERY DAY, FATE WAS TO WEAVE HER MYSTERIOUS PATTERNS. FOR, DR. DONALD BLAKE, A LAME AMERICAN PHYSICIAN, HAD WITNESSED THE POWER OF THESE 'STONE MEN'--
"--AND, IN ATTEMPTING TO FLEE FROM THEM, INADVERTENTLY DISCOVERED A CAVE WHICH HAD LONG BEEN HIDDEN FROM THE EYES OF MORTAL MEN...
MADE IT! BUT THEY'RE BOUND TO FIND ME SOON! IF ONLY THERE WERE A WAY OUT--!
BACK THERE! THERE IS ANOTHER EXIT!

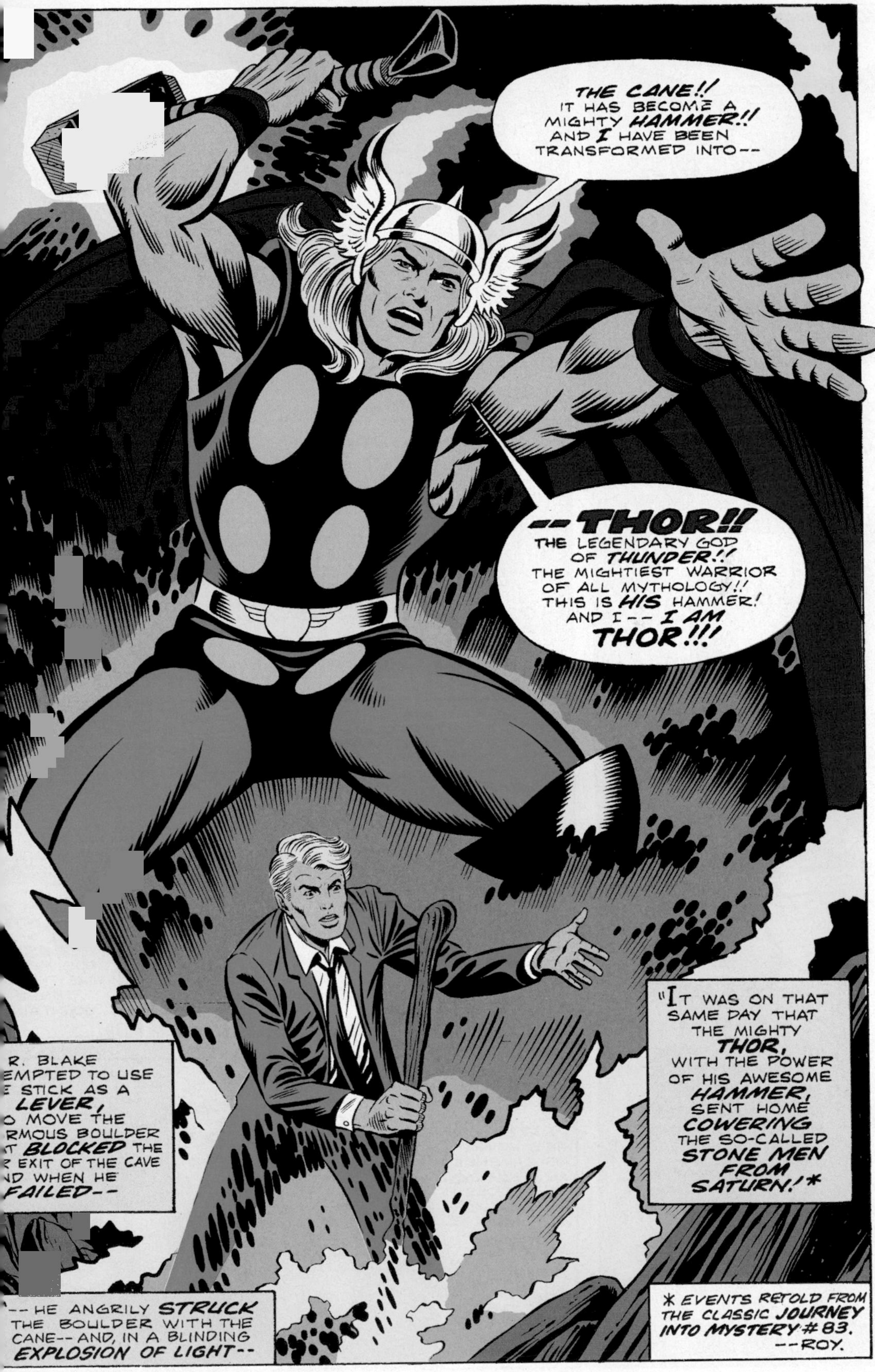
THE CANE!! IT HAS BECOME A MIGHTY HAMMER!! AND I HAVE BEEN TRANSFORMED INTO--
--THOR!! THE LEGENDARY GOD OF THUNDER!! THE MIGHTIEST WARRIOR OF ALL MYTHOLOGY!! THIS IS HIS HAMMER! AND I-- I AM THOR!!!
R. BLAKE EMPTED TO USE E STICK AS A LEVER, O MOVE THE RMOUS BOULDER AT BLOCKED THE R EXIT OF THE CAVE ND WHEN HE FAILED--
--HE ANGRILY STRUCK THE BOULDER WITH THE CANE-- AND, IN A BLINDING EXPLOSION OF LIGHT--
"IT WAS ON THAT SAME DAY THAT THE MIGHTY THOR, WITH THE POWER OF HIS AWESOME HAMMER, SENT HOME COWERING THE SO-CALLED STONE MEN FROM SATURN!*
* EVENTS RETOLD FROM THE CLASSIC JOURNEY INTO MYSTERY #83. --ROY.

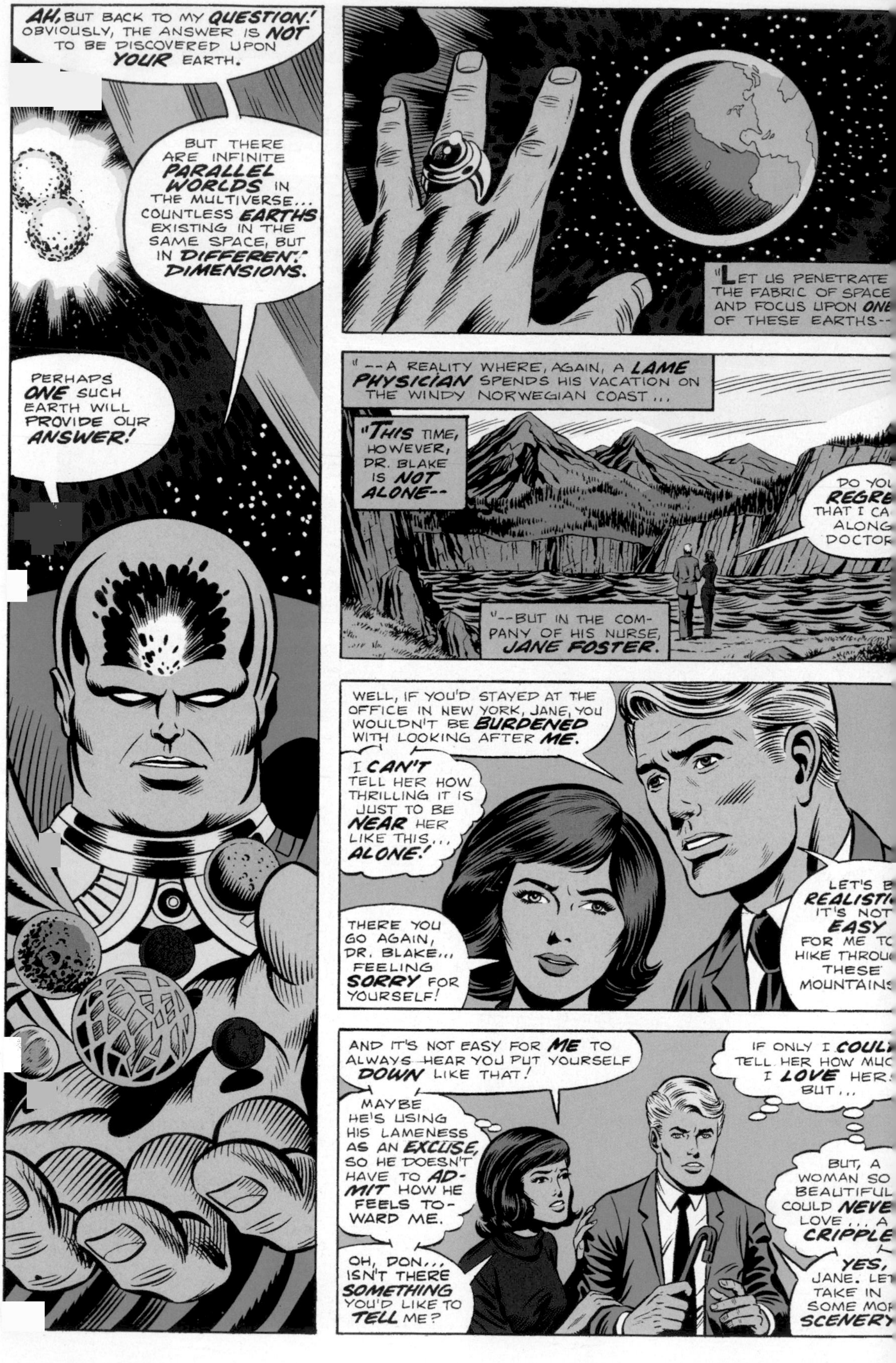
AH, BUT BACK TO MY QUESTION! OBVIOUSLY, THE ANSWER IS NOT TO BE DISCOVERED UPON YOUR EARTH.
BUT THERE ARE INFINITE PARALLEL WORLDS IN THE MULTIVERSE... COUNTLESS EARTHS EXISTING IN THE SAME SPACE, BUT IN DIFFERENT DIMENSIONS.
PERHAPS ONE SUCH EARTH WILL PROVIDE OUR ANSWER!
"LET US PENETRATE THE FABRIC OF SPACE AND FOCUS UPON ONE OF THESE EARTHS--
"--A REALITY WHERE, AGAIN, A LAME PHYSICIAN SPENDS HIS VACATION ON THE WINDY NORWEGIAN COAST...
"THIS TIME, HOWEVER, DR. BLAKE IS NOT ALONE--
"--BUT IN THE COMPANY OF HIS NURSE, JANE FOSTER.
DO YOU REGRE THAT I CA ALONG DOCTOR
WELL, IF YOU'D STAYED AT THE OFFICE IN NEW YORK, JANE, YOU WOULDN'T BE BURDENED WITH LOOKING AFTER ME.
I CAN'T TELL HER HOW THRILLING IT IS JUST TO BE NEAR HER LIKE THIS... ALONE!
THERE YOU GO AGAIN, DR. BLAKE... FEELING SORRY FOR YOURSELF!
LET'S B REALISTI IT'S NOT EASY FOR ME TO HIKE THROU THESE MOUNTAINS
AND IT'S NOT EASY FOR ME TO ALWAYS HEAR YOU PUT YOURSELF DOWN LIKE THAT!
IF ONLY I COUL TELL HER HOW MUC I LOVE HER BUT...
MAYBE HE'S USING HIS LAMENESS AS AN EXCUSE, SO HE DOESN'T HAVE TO ADMIT HOW HE FEELS TOWARD ME.
BUT, A WOMAN SO BEAUTIFUL COULD NEVE LOVE... A CRIPPLE
OH, DON... ISN'T THERE SOMETHING YOU'D LIKE TO TELL ME?
YES, JANE. LET TAKE IN SOME MOR SCENERY

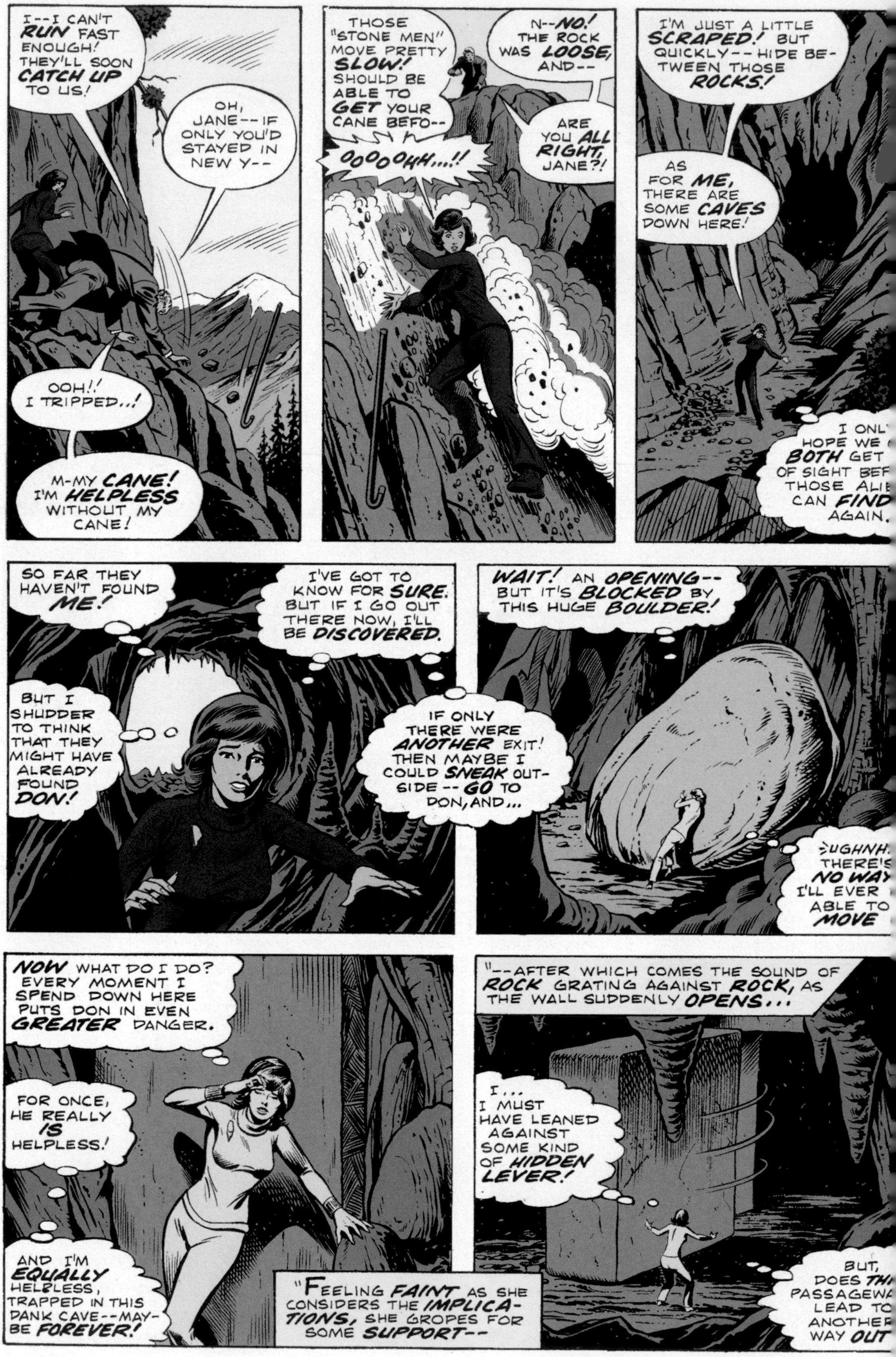
I--I CAN'T RUN FAST ENOUGH! THEY'LL SOON CATCH UP TO US!
OH, JANE--IF ONLY YOU'D STAYED IN NEW Y--
OOH!! I TRIPPED..!
M-MY CANE! I'M HELPLESS WITHOUT MY CANE!
THOSE "STONE MEN" MOVE PRETTY SLOW! SHOULD BE ABLE TO GET YOUR CANE BEFO--
OOOOOHH...!!
N--NO! THE ROCK WAS LOOSE, AND--
ARE YOU ALL RIGHT, JANE?!
I'M JUST A LITTLE SCRAPED! BUT QUICKLY--HIDE BETWEEN THOSE ROCKS!
AS FOR ME, THERE ARE SOME CAVES DOWN HERE!
SO FAR THEY HAVEN'T FOUND ME!
I'VE GOT TO KNOW FOR SURE. BUT IF I GO OUT THERE NOW, I'LL BE DISCOVERED.
BUT I SHUDDER TO THINK THAT THEY MIGHT HAVE ALREADY FOUND DON!
IF ONLY THERE WERE ANOTHER EXIT! THEN MAYBE I COULD SNEAK OUTSIDE--GO TO DON, AND...
WAIT! AN OPENING--BUT IT'S BLOCKED BY THIS HUGE BOULDER!
NOW WHAT DO I DO? EVERY MOMENT I SPEND DOWN HERE PUTS DON IN EVEN GREATER DANGER.
FOR ONCE, HE REALLY IS HELPLESS!
AND I'M EQUALLY HELPLESS, TRAPPED IN THIS DANK CAVE--MAYBE FOREVER!
"FEELING FAINT AS SHE CONSIDERS THE IMPLICATIONS, SHE GROPES FOR SOME SUPPORT--
"--AFTER WHICH COMES THE SOUND OF ROCK GRATING AGAINST ROCK, AS THE WALL SUDDENLY OPENS...
I... I MUST HAVE LEANED AGAINST SOME KIND OF HIDDEN LEVER!

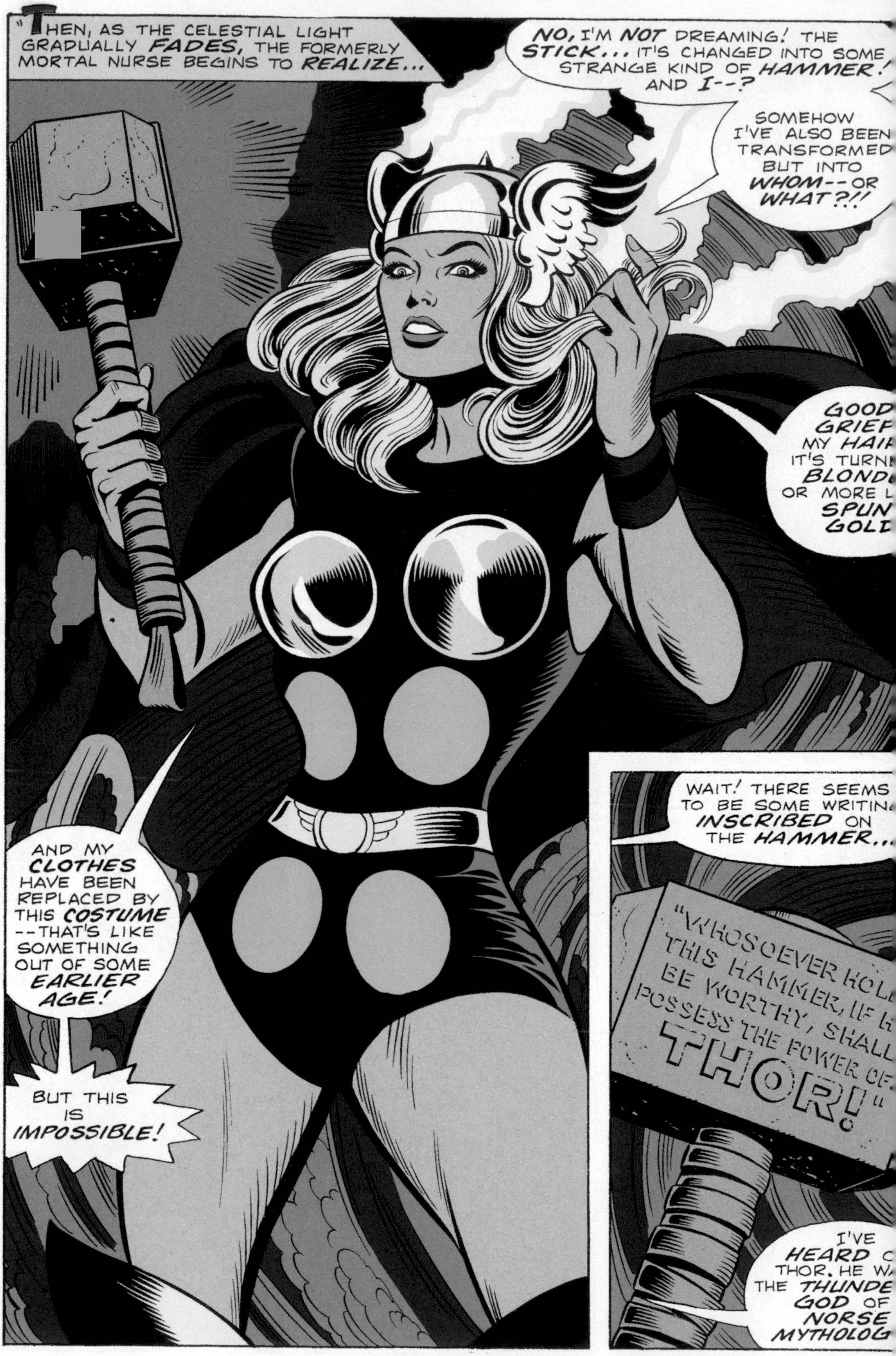
"THEN, AS THE CELESTIAL LIGHT GRADUALLY FADES, THE FORMERLY MORTAL NURSE BEGINS TO REALIZE...
NO, I'M NOT DREAMING! THE STICK... IT'S CHANGED INTO SOME STRANGE KIND OF HAMMER! AND I--?
SOMEHOW I'VE ALSO BEEN TRANSFORMED BUT INTO WHOM--OR WHAT?!!
GOOD GRIEF MY HAI IT'S TURN BLOND OR MORE L SPUN GOLD
AND MY CLOTHES HAVE BEEN REPLACED BY THIS COSTUME --THAT'S LIKE SOMETHING OUT OF SOME EARLIER AGE!
BUT THIS IS IMPOSSIBLE!
WAIT! THERE SEEMS TO BE SOME WRITIN INSCRIBED ON THE HAMMER...
"WHOSOEVER HOL THIS HAMMER, IF H BE WORTHY, SHALL POSSESS THE POWER OF THOR!"
I'VE HEARD THOR. HE W THE THUNDE GOD OF NORSE MYTHOLOG

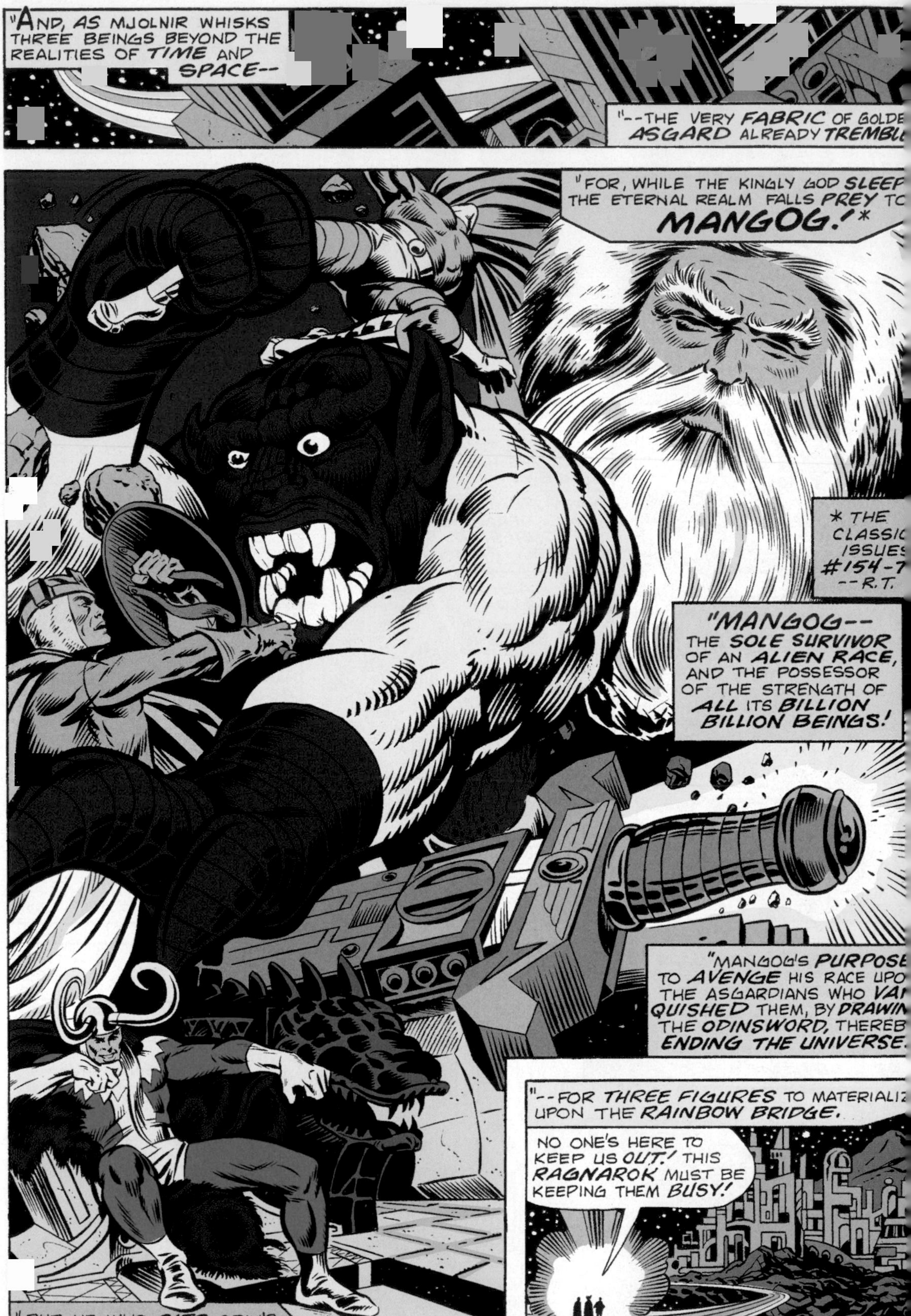
"AND, AS MJOLNIR WHISKS THREE BEINGS BEYOND THE REALITIES OF TIME AND SPACE--
"--THE VERY FABRIC OF GOLDE ASGARD ALREADY TREMBL
"FOR, WHILE THE KINGLY GOD SLEEP THE ETERNAL REALM FALLS PREY TO MANGOG!*
* THE CLASSIC ISSUES #154-7 --R.T.
"MANGOG-- THE SOLE SURVIVOR OF AN ALIEN RACE, AND THE POSSESSOR OF THE STRENGTH OF ALL ITS BILLION BILLION BEINGS!
"MANGOG'S PURPOSE TO AVENGE HIS RACE UPO THE ASGARDIANS WHO VA QUISHED THEM, BY DRAWIN THE ODINSWORD, THEREB ENDING THE UNIVERSE.
"BUT, HE WHO SITS ODIN'S THRONE MERELY WAITS--
"--FOR THREE FIGURES TO MATERIALIZ UPON THE RAINBOW BRIDGE.
NO ONE'S HERE TO KEEP US OUT! THIS RAGNAROK MUST BE KEEPING THEM BUSY!

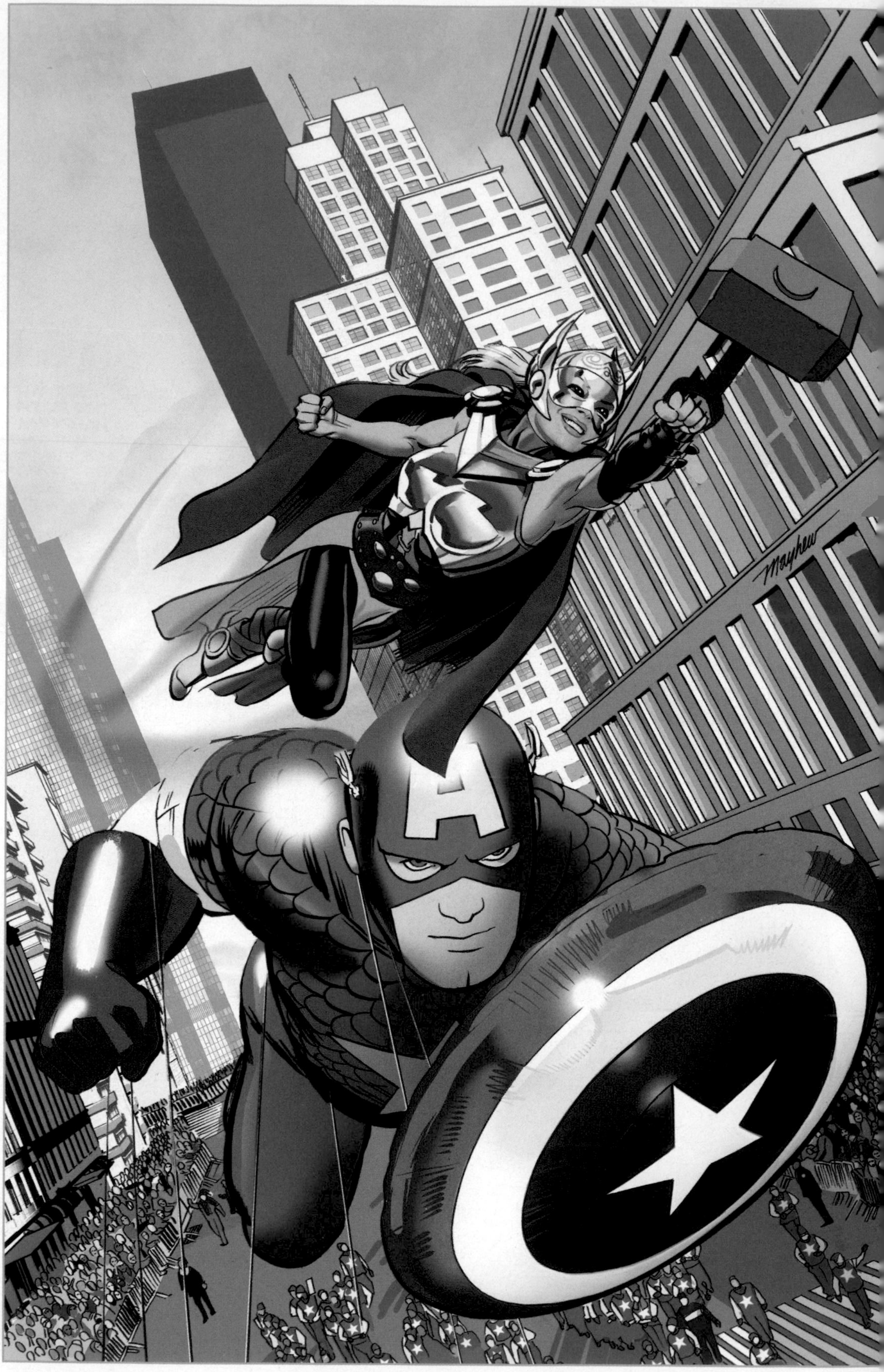
Mayhew

THOR # 8 NYC VARIANT
BY **MIKE MAYHEW**

THOR ANNUAL # I VARIANT
BY **MARGUERITE SAUVAGE**

THOR ANNUAL # I VARIANT
BY **ROB GUILLORY**

MARVEL AUGMENTED REALITY (AR) ENHANCES AND CHANGES THE WAY YOU EXPERIENCE COMICS!

TO ACCESS THE FREE MARVEL AR CONTENT IN THIS BOOK*:

1. Locate the **AR** logo within the comic.
2. Go to Marvel.com/AR in your web browser.
3. Search by series title to find the corresponding AR.
4. Enjoy Marvel AR!

*All AR content that appears in this book has been archived and will be available only at Marvel.com/AR – no longer in the Marvel AR App. Content subject to change and availability.

THOR AR INDEX

Issue #6
Heimdall and the Rainbow Bridge .... Page 6, Panel 1

Issue #7
Who's who on the page .... Page 20, Panel 1

Issue #8
Writer Jason Aaron .... Page 20, Panel 1

TO REDEEM YOUR CODE FOR A FREE DIGITAL COPY:

1. GO TO MARVEL.COM/REDEEM. OFFER EXPIRES ON 7/8/17.
2. FOLLOW THE ON-SCREEN INSTRUCTIONS TO REDEEM YOUR DIGITAL COPY.
3. LAUNCH THE MARVEL COMICS APP TO READ YOUR COMIC NOW!
4. YOUR DIGITAL COPY WILL BE FOUND UNDER THE *MY COMICS* TAB.
5. READ & ENJOY!

YOUR FREE DIGITAL COPY WILL BE AVAILABL

| MARVEL COMICS APP FOR APPLE® iOS DEVICES | MARVEL COMICS AP FOR ANDROID™ DEVIC |